SAINTLY SEX

SAINT JOHN PAUL II, SEX, GENDER, AND THE CATHOLIC CHURCH

Anthony M. Alioto
Columbia College

John P. McHale, S.F.O
Illinois State University

Front cover image:
Christa
Edwina Sandys, 1975
(Bronze on a Lucite Cross, 4' x 5')
Photo credit: Adam Reich

Background and back cover images © Shutterstock, Inc.

www.kendallhunt.com
Send all inquiries to:
4050 Westmark Drive
Dubuque, IA 52004-1840

Copyright © 2014 by Anthony M. Alioto and John P. McHale

ISBN 978-1-4652-4442-0

Kendall Hunt Publishing Company has the exclusive rights to reproduce this work, to prepare derivative works from this work, to publicly distribute this work, to publicly perform this work and to publicly display this work.

All rights reserved. No part of this publication may be reproduced, stored in a retrieval system, or transmitted, in any form or by any means, electronic, mechanical, photocopying, recording, or otherwise, without the prior written permission of the copyright owner.

Printed in the United States of America
10 9 8 7 6 5 4 3 2 1

In loving memory of
Arianna Alioto:
May spirited young women like Arianna
always know they are appreciated, valued,
and blessed in their femininity

Contents

Preface   vii

PART I	The Golden Legend of the Saint
Chapter 1	The Third Millennium 1
Chapter 2	The Heisenberg Uncertainty Principle of Biblical Hermeneutics or the End of Theological Determinism 13
Chapter 3	Portrait of the Saint as a Young Philosopher 19
Chapter 4	The Apology: A Handmaiden's Tale 29

PART II	In Persona Christi: Misogyny
Chapter 5	Defective Men 39
Chapter 6	"Blessings of the Breast and Womb" (Genesis 49:25): Women in Western Religion 47
Chapter 7	Was Jesus a Feminist? 57
Chapter 8	Women Priests in the Early Church: From *Was* to *Should Be* 67
Chapter 9	Did Jesus Have a Wife? 77
Chapter 10	Married Priests, Bishops, and Popes in The First Thousand Years of the Catholic Church 85
Chapter 11	Witchy Women 93
Chapter 12	Big Brothers, Little Sisters 101
Chapter 13	Father Knows Best 109

PART III	Sex and Sex Scandals
Chapter 14	Sex in Heaven 119
Chapter 15	Clerical Sex 127
Chapter 16	Suffer the Children: John Paul II's Response to Child Abuse 137
Chapter 17	A Thoroughly Incomplete History of Sex in Religion 143
Chapter 18	The Archaeology of Theological Prehistory 155
Chapter 19	Once Again, Celibacy 161
Chapter 20	A Fable: The Mother Who Died 169

PART IV   Preaching the Kingdom
Chapter 21   Ecclesia in Europa   175
Chapter 22   Apology without Reform   183
Chapter 23   Analysis of Image Restoration Strategies   189
Chapter 24   The Kingdom of God   193
Chapter 25   An Interpretation of a Dream   205

Bibliography 215
About the Authors 229

Preface

The cover of the February 15, 2014 edition of *Rolling Stone* magazine featured a photo of Pope Francis with a caption featuring the title of Bob Dylan's song *The Times They Are A Changin*. Bob Dylan was a featured performer at Pope John Paul's 1997 World Eucharistic Congress in Bologna, Italy. There is indeed a fresh breeze blowing through the Vatican under Pope Francis. Where that wind blows the Catholic Church remains to be seen. But the faithful, wishing and praying for needed reform, have reason to remain hopeful.

One of the authors of this book, Dr. John P. McHale, is a productive scholar, an active Catholic, and a member of the Secular Franciscan Order. When leaving a memorial Mass for John Paul II, his five-year-old daughter asked McHale if she could be pope. McHale answered no, to which McHale's daughter retorted, "But I can be president, right?" McHale said yes, but regretted his inability to explain the paradox. The opportunity to publish the book, *Saintly Sex: Pope John Paul II, Sex, Gender, and The Catholic Church*, with Dr. Anthony Alioto is McHale's delayed response to his daughter's question. Especially pertinent to this book, McHale stopped going to that particular Catholic Church when he learned from a local newspaper that the parish had used contributions to pay off a settlement related to accusations that a clergy member at that church had inappropriate sexual contact with a child.

The central thesis of this book is the Catholic Church can enact effective corrective action to prevent sexual abuse of children and subsequent efforts to hide these crimes through inclusion of more diverse clergy. First, the Catholic Church should once again accept female clergy, as was the case the first three hundred years of the Church. Second, married clergy should be ordained, as was accepted in the first thousand years of Church history. Third, these two reforms would alleviate an atmosphere that is conducive to sexual abuse of children by clergy members and the conspiratorial efforts to hide these heinous crimes.

Pope John Paul II is celebrated for his ecumenism, his tolerance, and his pro-democratic views. It is time to highlight his accomplishments, but also time to scrutinize his legacy. Anthony Alioto and I challenge readers to recognize a dilemma: The Catholic Church patriarchal authoritarian hierarchy desires to appear moderate (even liberal) while maintaining conservative attitudes of misogyny and opposition to clerical marriage. Our book explores this paradox in the context of discrimination against women, marriage in the priesthood, sexual repression, and the atrocious scandals of sexual abuse within the Catholic Church.

Sex is hardly ever equated with saintliness. Many saints, male and female, but mostly male, have wrestled mightily with this greatest of foes. The fall of humanity in Eden, St Augustine taught—and he had intimate knowledge of the details—twisted what was the divine procreative act into self-serving lust. Once subject to the powers of reason as God intended, after the Fall sex subjugates humanity with the power of unreason. And all this because of a woman. If Christianity has a female trinity, the persons would be Eve, Mary of Magdala, and Mary the Virgin Mother of Christ. As models of female identity, the first two are sinners, the third is uncorrupted by sex.[1]

Clement of Rome, or rather pseudonymous works of the fourth century bearing the name of the first century church father, thought the example of King David instructive. Here was David, God's favorite, "a man after His own heart," "anointed of the Lord" (*mashiah*), a righteous man—poor, saintly David was caught like a fish on a hook when he spied Bathsheba—naked. What wickedness came from the mere sight of an unclothed woman. Yes, but so did the great King Solomon.

David's example appears to instruct the faithful that women are uncanny creatures. Physically, in their bodies, they possess in some mysterious way the power of life. Morally, however, they are a danger to the spirit. They seem to embody spiritual death. They threaten purity as well. Every month they leak blood, causing ritual pollution. Yet they are able to transform the male's seed into a living being, hopefully another man, ideally a priest.

They corrupt themselves, says another Church Father, Cyprian of the third century. They adorn their bodies with silks, bracelets, pearls, and other ornaments. And so, "having put on silk and purple, they cannot put on Christ." When they pierce their ears—listen closely, fashionistas—they are arrogantly trying to remake what God has crafted. Beware, you painted women. When the resurrection comes your Maker may not recognize you and may turn you away.

This is but a tiny representative sampling of the Church Fathers. They appear to be a misogynistic lot. They are Catholic tradition. Followers of that tradition are informed that the Holy Spirit, the "Spirit of Truth" speaks through tradition as it does through scripture, forming "one sacred deposit of the word of God" (*Dei verbum—Dogmatic Constitution on Divine Revelation* from the Second Vatican Council, 1962-1965; also the Council of Trent, Section IV, 1545). To be fair, *Dei verbum* also explains that there is a growth in understanding of the words and realities which have been handed down. This may be so and it may sound reasonable in hopeful ears. But what happens if contemporary understanding comes to conclusions that *contradict* former "deposits"?

Therefore, it is important to ask: What does scripture say?

The Bible speaks in a cacophony of discordant voices, in different languages, from enormous spans of time, from enormous varieties of cultures, no matter what so-called testament. Theologians, like those who contributed to *Dei verbum*, would almost certainly protest such an assertion, but most can generally agree, with maybe a few exceptions, that *the voices are all male*. The writers make a tiny male elite, hardly representative of

---

[1] Karen L. King, *The Gospel of Mary of Magdala: Jesus and the First Woman Apostle*, (Salem. Oregon, 2003), p. 149.

the majority folk religion, which is largely invisible in the form of literary deposits (more on this later).

A vast number of readings is possible, not all are probable. Some Christians would like to think that misogyny belongs to the Hebrew Bible, the *Tanakh*, which they call the Old Testament. In this reading, Jesus represents a proto-feminist correction to the old law. But this is surely Christian triumphalism and, given Paul, apocryphal Acts of the Apostles, the Church Fathers, and a library of male theologians, certainly a modern reconstruction. On the other hand, there *are* some disturbing stories in the Hebrew scriptures.

One is Judges 19:15-30, similar in some ways to the story of Lot in Sodom when a mob demands "to know" strangers hiding in the town. In Judges, a Levite accompanied by his *nameless* concubine from Bethlehem stops in the town of Gibeah of Benjamin for the night. An old man takes them into his house while outside a mob gathers. They too want "to know" the stranger. Instead of this "outrage," the man pushes his concubine out the door. The mob rapes and abuses her all night. In the morning the woman comes back and collapses on the doorstep. The Levite picks her up, puts her on his donkey, and heads for home. When he arrives at his destination, he takes a knife and cuts her up into twelve parts.

Well, yes, it could be argued that we're dealing with symbols and images pointing to other realities, "the metaphorical imagination." But symbols do give rise to thoughts, and thoughts into action. Thoughts become habits of thinking that also indicate realities.[2]

In the sacred Book of Judges these barbaric acts—barbaric to our modern sensibilities, again with some exceptions—are followed by an assault upon the tribe of Benjamin. After two days of setbacks (the Israelites lose 22,000 and 18,000 respectively), they take Gibeah, and put the whole town to the sword.

And it gets better. Since the tribe of Benjamin faces extinction, the Israelites massacre the men, women, and children from another town, sparing only the virgins, which they then give to the remnants of Benjamin. Unfortunately, there are not enough virgins to go around. To solve this dilemma they instruct the men of Benjamin to seize the girls from Shiloh who happen to be dancing at the annual feast of YHWH.

Gang rape, murder, mutilation, massacre, abduction—women are the primary victims. And they are *our own people*, that is, Hebrew women. Some may wish to argue that, well, people are sinful and fail to live up to God's commandments. But if women are perceived as property, *which they are,* the Levite seems to be acting within the Law. Rather, it appears as if all morality, indeed humanity itself, has drained away from the hearts of men. There is a moral of the story, and that moral lesson seems to be that all this violence occurred because there was not a king in Israel.

One might conclude that despite the Law given to Moses on Sinai, people are not themselves moral until forced to be so by some greater power *on earth*, otherwise, as

---

[2] Elizabeth A. Johnson, *She Who Is: The Mystery of God in Feminist Discourse* (Crossroad Publishing Company, 1992, 2002), p. 6. Johnson quotes Phyllis Trible who claims that the unknown woman of Judges 19 is the "least" of all the characters in scripture.

Thomas Hobbes once said, the life of man is "solitary, poor, nasty, brutish, and short." *And it is worse for women.*

Women are understood as property to be dealt with as men see fit. As God sees fit, since one can easily imagine that God is speaking from a script prepared by male writers. The title of the script is *Patriarchy*.

The last of the Ten Commandments says that you shall not covet your neighbor's house; you shall not covet your neighbor's wife, nor his male or female slave, or his ox, his ass, anything that belongs to your neighbor—in short, his property. A man's property therefore includes his estate, his livestock, his means of transportation, *his wife*. Women are property in the Bible. As in other ancient societies, adultery is theft, sexual misconduct is the *violation of property*.

If as many believe the moral basis of our civilization is God's Law, then there can be no such thing as equal rights for women. Men who do not own them must not covet the women of those men who do own them. Of course, a man is free to do with his property as he pleases, so the Levite who slaughtered and mutilated his concubine (technically not covered by the commandment) is not acting against the Law of God.

This is a literal reading. "Deeper theological thinking" has a great deal of work to do in order to make such obvious misogyny palatable to modern tastes. There can be little doubt, however, that such stories, be they fiction or no, illustrate ancient patriarchal values.

One should not jump to the conclusion that the male God condones rape, at least not within our tribe (or nation, or whatever select group happens to claim God's most favored nation status). Deuteronomy 20:23-26 reports that if a man should rape a virgin *in a town*, and she's engaged to another man, they shall both be stoned to death. The man suffers capital punishment because he violated another man's property, and the maiden because *in the town she did not cry for help.* Apparently, her crime, for which she suffers the death penalty, is that she did not *scream loud enough*. In an ancient town someone is bound to hear and come to her rescue. If the rape occurs in the country, out of earshot, the girl is to be spared because there is no one around to hear her.

One could multiply such examples. But let us jump forward to the Middle Ages.

Circumstances do not improve much for women in the Christian centuries. In some ways they get worse.

Women are property. They are also predatory. Their desires spring from what they lack: strength, reason, self-discipline, reticence—a penis. A popular text of the Latin Middle Ages was the Greek philosopher Secundus (the Silent) from the first or second century. Translated into Latin around 1167, Secundus, having taken a vow of silence, answers questions quite succinctly. "What is a Woman?" the Emperor asks him:

> Man's undoing; an insatiable animal; perpetual trouble and non-stop combat; man's daily
>
> ruin; a storm in the home; an impediment to peace of mind; the wreck of a weak-willed

man; instrument of adultery; expensive war; the very worst creature and heaviest burden;

fatal snake; human property.[3]

Here at least Christians were in agreement with pagans. Much later, two learned Dominicans will instruct on why it is that women are more superstitious than men: they are more credulous, impressionable, with slippery tongues and feebleness in mind and body. Intellectually they are like children because they are formed from the rib of man (not his head like Athena), and she is more carnal because the rib is bent in the contrary direction (!)—"when a woman weeps she labors to deceive a man."[4]

For these and other reasons, women succumbed to the devil, became witches, and paid for their evil in Christian flames. Pope Gregory the Great actually praised the woman who immolated herself in order to burn away her desires.

Sex with women is not for saints, and, thus, not for priests. Poor St. Jerome bore witness to this fact. Alone in the wilderness, starving—saintly fasting—exposed to the elements, his skin like old leather, scorpions and other wild beasts his only companions, he found himself surrounded by visions of dancing girls. *Women are not for saints.*

Until Pope John Paul II.

At the dawn of the new millennium, the Catholic Church staged a ceremony that caught the world by surprise. In March of the Great Jubilee Year 2000, Pope John Paul II led the Church in a public act of purification by apologizing and seeking penance for sins committed by the Church's erring children. On Sunday, March 12, 2000, members of the clergy implored forgiveness for specific past and present sins of the Mother Church's sons and daughters. Seven articles of confession followed. Misogyny (sins against women) came in number six.

The seventh article was hardly a confession of *Catholic* sins, rather it was a confession in relation to the fundamental rights of the person, which included the "unborn killed in their mother's womb," and those exploited by the (false) promises of technology. Such promises, said the *apology*, distort the aims of science. Even while asking for forgiveness (from God), the Church took a well-aimed blow at what theologians call "scientism." It took a stand against abused children (killed in the womb). There is more to say about this bit of disingenuous sleight of hand later.

Former Jubilees—the first was celebrated under Pope Boniface VIII in 1300—were occasions for penance and reconciliation. Public reconciliation of sins, called "canonical

---

[3]Secundus, "What is Woman?" trans. by Alcuin Blamires from Ben E. Perry (ed.), *Secundus the Silent Philosopher*, (Ithaca, 1964), p. 96, quoted in Alcuin Blamires, ed., *Woman Defamed and Woman Defended: An Anthology of Medieval Texts*, (Oxford, 1992), p. 100.
[4]Heinrich Kramer and James Sprenger, *The Malleus Maleficarum*, 1486, trans. Montague Summers, (New York, 1971), pp. 43-44.

penance," goes back to the fourth century and was formalized by a number of Church councils in their canons (rules).

Of course, there can be no real change in the Catholic Church, but a deeper understanding of *Truth* deposited by Christ in His Church. According to the document *Memory and Reconciliation: The Church and Faults of the Past* (December, 1999), which prepared the ground for the 2000 Apology, such a confession of sins reaches back to Leviticus 25, the Hebrew Fifty Year Jubilee. For example, it made good sense in a tribal society to forgive debt rather than allow a strangling of the majority by the tiny fortunate rich. Naturally, God is the final arbitrator, and He did not bring the Hebrews out of slavery in Egypt only to see them become slaves of the wealthy.

Beyond this, there still seems to be very little precedence for such a sweeping acknowledgement of past wrongs committed by the Church. But then there was hardly a pope like John Paul II.

Adopting the modern instruments of mass media and image restoration—what John Paul II liked to refer to as the "Areopagus of the modern world"—the Church enacted the apology as purification of memory in order to enter the new millennium renewed and prepared to complete the task of preaching the gospel to all nations. As the self-appointed focal point of moral goodness on earth, the Church required a major make-over of its public image in order not to appear hypocritical if not plain ridiculous. The old image of the Church, an image of the Inquisition, of crusades and anti-Semitism, of sexual predators and misogynists, had to go.

It is hardly a remarkable fact that any institution should contain weak and erring members within its ranks. One might argue that some of the so-called "sins," using the Church's language, are social. It takes quite a few more than one or two sinners to go on a crusade, to manage inquisitions, to burn witches and heretics. Yes, true, says *Memory and Reconciliation,* but such sins are always the "accumulation" or "concentration" of personal sins.

If this is so, one may wonder how exactly such an "accumulation" actually appears on the earth? Does it not manifest as an institution?

The Catholic Church is not just any institution. It is the self-professed guardian of "truth" in this world, an institution that claims infallibility when its head, the Pope, pronounces *ex cathedra* on faith and morals. Today it claims to be the defender of life against the "culture of death," as John Paul himself characterized the secular world. It defends the helpless, the weak, victims of a world that denies the dignity of human beings by reducing them to objects.

What if Christianity's own sacred texts reduce women to property? What if the Church's male clergy prey upon the helpless and the weak?

If the Church is the moral institution, it claims to be, and if sincere apologies require that the guilty reform behavior, has the Church taken firm steps to insure that her children, weak though they may be, undertake real attempts to identify and treat the illnesses that drove them to sin? Might it be necessary to reform, maybe even delete dogmas and teachings that may have tempted the children to commit crimes against their fellow human beings? Or, have the statues been washed and the frescoes cleaned, yet the harmful stories the art illustrates still allowed to breed the infections of violence, persecution, intolerance, misogyny, and the most terrible of all, abuse of children?

Can the modern Church so easily dismiss past "authoritative interpretations" of scripture? Do such ancient interpretations (and not so ancient ones) magically transform into benign first approximations after convenient "deeper theological thinking" in the wake of historical atrocities?

Catholic officials insist the Church as the spiritual Bride of Christ is without sin. Pure and immaculate in the supernatural realm, "she" is also the visible community of the baptized led by her clergy and extending through history. *Lumen Gentium,* the *Dogmatic Constitution of the Church,* which came from the Second Vatican Council and was promulgated by Pope Paul VI on November 21, 1964, admits that the Church is a visible assembly and a spiritual community, a hierarchal structure and a Mystical Body. But it quickly warns that these are not to be confused as two distinct realities, rather they form a single complex whole, combining the divine and human element, like the unique person of Jesus as described by the Council of Chalcedon (451 C.E.). And like Jesus, exactly how they are related remains a mystery.

Mysteries tend to possess a great deal of flexibility. The apology asks the audience to make a distinction between the visible entity whose members, both clergy and laity, are weak and prone to sin and *the Church*, Spouse, Mother, sacramental *mediatrix* of grace, scripture, tradition, dogma, that is, a living entity spanning the centuries. This Mother does not, indeed cannot, sin. As one can see, because all sin is individual, the corporate entity is blameless.

What, then, is this strange ghostly entity that rises above its embodiment in flesh and blood human beings and yet is not a separate reality? It seems to float above or beyond living persons who have names, who write dogmas and doctrines, who preach sermons—sermons that are sometimes vicious and violent diatribes against other persons (like Jews and women)—and who make infallible pronouncements. Does not this pure Church that spans the centuries exist somewhere in some ancient platonic world of the forms? Does it not reside across the border of our world, outside the grubby cave inhabited by those poor sinful children whose concentrated individual sins are somehow able to wound the metaphysical entity itself?

How can the actions of embodied natural beings, even touch this metaphysical monster? Perhaps such actions only serve as spectacles in the passive sense, say as amusement? Yet, spectacles of human suffering, as Epicurus had it, would be beneath the dignity of the divine. Naturally, this is a jest. But one can wonder why this realm of spirits defends the "pure" Church but does not come to the aid of real human suffering? After all, at this writing, priests still abuse children, and women and married men are still banned from positions of authority. And it is a grave sin to ordain a female priest or a married man.

This ideal Church may be (or may not be) a holy society "without wrinkle." It is, alas, a holy institution frequently run by unholy *men* (the use of the male gender is no accident). Again, Catholics are admonished to believe that its history transcends mere *history* since it includes the conveniently pliant spiritual dimension, which is the activity of God. Therefore, one cannot judge *the Church* based upon one-dimensional historical criticism. And of course, as if to send one to the back of the class, one's own reconstruction of the past, as the Church sternly warns, includes one's own biased interpretations.

Defenders say that it is far too easy to judge people of the past by the moral conscience of the present (but is there a whiff here of historical relativism?) History is more than simple facts, as if such things existed like exhibits in a museum. History includes existential meaning, what the past means to people and to their existence as human beings. In religious terms, one does hear the Word of God in the recitation of mere historical facts, but in submitting oneself to the authority of the text and its witnesses through the centuries. Only then is one able to interpret the Bible is as authoritative. Interpretation bestows meaning. Traditionally, the Church's interpretation was not up for discussion.

Innocent of her children's sins, the Church resembles the person of Christ: truly God and truly man, each nature preserved without confusion or separation (The Council of Chalcedon, 451). *She bears the burden of her children's sins and yet remains innocent of them.* In fact, the Church suffers along with the victims of Catholic misogyny and priestly abuse. Some individuals in this world have fallen away from their lofty state. Their willful actions have perverted an inherently good nature, as St. Augustine taught. But there is no spiritual form of evil. It is like a tear in a seamless robe, a lack, an absence. It is a deficient cause. The Mother Church suffers, but cannot be its source. And the Mother is defined by those male theologians to whom she gives birth.

The time is long past when such absurdities counted for apologies. The continued suffering of the innocent bears witness to this fact.

Pope John Paul II and the Magisterium manipulated the distinction between the spiritual and the historical, the supernatural and the natural, the Mother and her children, for their own benefit. This manipulation in the end makes for a certain blindness and denial of responsibility (it could equally be that they saw all too clearly). They appeared to welcome critical historical research and analysis, but when it seemed to challenge their assumptions they quickly retreated to a safe haven beyond history. They claimed time and time again that critical history was not enough. The *truth* required an account of the spiritual. The natural requires the supernatural if it is to be understood correctly. And—surprise—in every case examined, *this spiritually reconstructed past* turns out to illustrate if not prove the Church's doctrines and beliefs—and its innocence.

The disastrous consequences of such a strategy are most clearly seen in the Church's continued denial of the legitimate aspirations of women and married men, its primitive teachings on sex, and most especially the continuing scandals that disfigure the Church's self-awarded image of moral leadership in the realm of human dignity. It can only be viewed as a great irony, if not an obscene joke, when John Paul II's sycophants declared him a new feminist.

John Paul II and his scholarly minions, most notably Cardinal Ratzinger (later Pope Benedict XVI) built a bridge of interpretation between the City of Man and the City of God. Theirs was a neo-Augustinian view that perceives the secular world as fatally infused by evil with the Church as a bastion of grace and goodness. It could be said that such an outlook is part of the continuing debate over the legacy of Vatican II.[5] They awarded themselves the exclusive right to cross back and forth freely. When in peril, they fled over the bridge and into their spiritually reconstructed world like political refugees seeking asylum. Drawing up their bridge, they stood safely behind their enchanted walls and fired back complaints and condemnations of modern society, of critical history, and contemporary thought in general. The protecting walls were built from the brick and mortar of their own privileged interpretations of history and what they decided is sacred scripture. So too their power.

By such means, the apology becomes a case of image restoration designed to manipulate world opinion in order to save the Church from shrinking into a vestigial organ irrelevant in the lives of modern people, even some Catholics.

The so-called open windows of the Second Vatican Council are closing. A kind of rigormortis paralyzes the Church, a deadening rigidity has set in that is the opposite of life. Image restoration may not be enough to save the organism. Ironically, John Paul condemned the so-called culture of death outside Church walls, but he did nothing to save the Church from perhaps succumbing to its own fatal culture of denial.

---

[5] See Maasimo Faggioli, *Vatican II: The Battle for Meaning*, (New York, 2012), p. 69. Faggioli says that for Ratzinger, the *City of God* was an antidote to the ethical and political totalitarianism of Nazi Germany, p. 72. Today it serves the same purpose in the modern world. Therefore it cannot be simply reduced to another institution among others in secular culture. Any outside judgment of the Church must arise in a thoroughly wicked context, and therefore criticism from beyond its walls is illegitimate. It is not hard to see a siege mentality in such views.

We make no claims for naturalism (the assertion that nature is all there is and causation is closed).[6] Nor need one make assertions against it—nature may be all that is the case.[7]

It must be noted, however, that the very idea—hopeful idea—of some other world, some supernatural realm, Mother Church, state of grace, or whatever one calls it, is by implication a denunciation of the material world in which we live. Even if God saw that the natural world was good, and instructed people to be fruitful (have sex), our world remains impoverished. A supernatural world highlights the imperfections of this one. Sensuality is corruption. Love becomes lust, sex becomes pollution, and celibacy declares war on reproduction. The very existence of a supernatural world is a value judgment. We will argue that the priestly sexual abuse of a single child is not worth the preservation of fictive other-worldly innocence.

Despite all this, one can simply take the Pope at his word: Look, says John Paul II, here are some historical instances in which children of the Church seemed to behave badly. Catholics, especially the Magisterium, must critically examine these instances. If the Magisterium discovers that Catholic bad behavior has occurred the Magisterium must apologize and reform the things that gave rise to such acts.

Does a change of behavior require a change of dogma, of doctrine, maybe even of scriptural interpretation? If so, the Church faces a dilemma. Any change of dogma is impossible for *the Bride of Christ* possessed of the absolute truth, which is Christ, as John Paul II never tired of repeating. What actually happens is that while much is made of the so-called recognition of Catholic sins, supernatural agents suddenly appear as if out of nothing. These strange beings preserve the so-called purity of the "Church," which exists above any sort of possible guilt, and therefore criticism. Humanity must wait for the end of the world, the Church proclaims, before truth is revealed in all its fullness—even as believers are assured that the present Church possesses this truth *now.*

The supernatural is usually inferred through the experience of believers, or through the abstract manipulation of logical categories. In themselves, bodiless agents are completely empty of content until they are abstractly defined as such. What actually happens is that they are filled with any sort of fantastical being the Church wishes to conjure at the moment, be that being Christ, the Virgin Mother, the Spouse of Christ…but why not Zeus, Krishna or the Force? In response, definitions of our specific sort of supernatural being

---

[6]Ontological naturalism denies the existence of a spiritual world; methodological naturalism seeks natural causes and closes the causal chain. But naturalism is far more complex. The old version identified the natural world with the physical. A material body was more or less spatially defined, endowed with mass, subject to transformations by means of energy, and open to third person observation. However, after relativity and quantum theory, many of these assumptions must be amended: space and time are no longer absolute; fields and masses can only understood within the framework of observer dependency, not spatial invariants and an absolute now. The experimenter's frame of reference and the system under scrutiny form an inseparable whole (entanglement), and physical matter on the subatomic level (and maybe higher) "exists" as abstract probability distributions prior to observation. A more sophisticated version of naturalism includes information states, consciousness, spacetime, abstract fields and more. See B Alan Wallace, *Hidden Dimensions: The Unification of Physics and Consciousness*, (New York, 2007), Chapter 2.

[7]We tend to agree with Leszek Kolakowski when he writes: "Therefore our knowledge, vast as it may become, remains forever within the brackets of our contingent position in the world, of our fundamental inability to acquire a non-relative vantage point (in the physical, biological, historical sense) for observing the World." *Religion If There Is No God…On God, the Devil, Sin and Other Worries of the so-called Philosophy of Religion*, (South Bend, Indiana, 2001), p. 61.

must be constantly refined and honed in order to meet such objections, and meanwhile the original inference (most often some *historical* sacred text) has disappeared long ago over the horizon.

For example, the argument is often formulated in certain ways coming down to the basic idea that Zeus is not, say, creator ex nihilo while the God of Genesis is. (But which god? Genesis 1, Elohim, or 2:4, YHWH? And the Hebrew text reads *tohu wabohu,* "welter and waste", not *nihil*).[8] Or, Zeus is identified with some natural phenomenon as the lightning bolt (so is Indra) while YHWH Elohim is transcendent (yet he is living on a mountain). Such assertions are purely arbitrary and dependent upon special readings of sacred texts like Genesis. Any inference is permitted and can be made plausible with creative interpretations of obscure ancient texts (but which ones?) and the creative application of logical categories *that ignore historical context.*

It is important to keep in mind that a living religion is not necessarily concerned with historical facts but with the successive experiences of its leaders. Institutions, however, and formal dogmas that claim universal validity are. History yields reasonable probabilities, hardly the absolutes the Church so desperately requires. Furthermore, the documents themselves are uncertain. Scholars possess copies of copies, of copies... How could one even recognize the original from among them? And if one could, how would one be able to say that it was the author's final draft and therefore definitive? How could one ever know what the author intended to write, to add, to delete? How much so-called *revealed* scripture belongs to the category of the unwritten?[9]

There is no such single and static entity labeled the Bible.

Spiritual entities once again come to the rescue. The Holy Spirit speaks through traditional readings and blesses them with validity. But this leads to trouble.

As an example, take the problem (it is a problem) of the extermination of the Canaanite peoples by the Hebrew tribes under Joshua and the Judges. Such crimes would count as congealed sins of the people Israel, according to *Memory and Reconciliation,* committed against other human beings. These "sins of the Fathers" (mothers are apparently blameless) are confessed to God. Why not ask forgiveness from the aggrieved parties? Well, mostly they are not around.

A literal reading of the texts clearly records what can only be called genocide. The faithful are not told if any their descendants remain in any significant numbers. Are these not, then, crimes against humanity? *Memory and Reconciliation* takes a different escape route. It informs readers that the Hebrew bible is "theocentric," and such horrendous acts are understood to be following God's orders, which exclude any possible request for forgiveness. It is also possible that Israel suffered at the hands of these peoples (paragraphs 8-9).

---

[8] According to Robert Alter, the second term looks like one coined to rhyme with the first. *Tohu* means emptiness or futility, associated with the trackless vacancy of the desert. Robert Alter, *The Five Books of Moses,* (New York, 2004), p. 17.
[9] See George Steiner, *Grammars of Creation,* (New Haven, 2001). Maybe even God was distracted when he was in the process of creating the universe, and simply let it fall away unfinished, pp. 37-38.

Catholic officials were only following orders...? The onus then rests upon God? If this is so, one must fall back upon the old tired excuse that what appears evil in our world ultimately serves some good, which is only known to God in His infinite wisdom, to be revealed later (truth in its fullness at the end of the world?). In the words of David Tracy, this is a perfect example of the "careless mystification of our blood-drenched history as a civilization."[10]

What if such orders to exterminate came to real flesh and blood men (again reading literally) in some sort of numinous experience they identified with YHWH, "a Man of War?" Conveniently, such divine instructions legitimized the Hebrew conquest (fortunately—in moral terms—archaeology has not unearthed evidence for the mass destruction of Canaanite cities). The whole thing seems to be fiction, a national myth. Fictional excuses (the Canaanites harmed Hebrews) and mysterious supernatural agents (God ordered the genocide for reasons known only to His divine self) justify fictional atrocities.

Surely, someone will protest at this point, you two silly fellows do not expect the Church *not* to appeal to the supernatural?

Well, sure, the Church cannot *not* speak of the spiritual just as human beings cannot *not* sin according to St. Augustine. *How* does the Church wield the spiritual in our world? If the supernatural dimension is ultimately a great mystery in its details (God cannot be just another being among beings), how can one know that any single interpretation of that mystery *as experienced by embodied human beings* is privileged over any other? This issue is the other side of the problem of textual readings. Many readings may be possible, but surely not all are probable. However, in the metaphysical realm where all colors are gray, any interpretation is possible as long as it serves the interest of the corporate body.

Metaphysical interpretations are like multiple universes in modern physics. The Church naturally favors the universe that contains the conditions for its existence—and its power. Outside this universe are no others. Repression is sure to follow and apologies become hand waving blessings to the adoring crowd.

The papal office is a creature of space and time, said Pope John Paul II, but its holiness is eternal. Finally, the critic becomes the criticized. The disasters of the modern age, far worse than any Church sins, arise from an "anthropological error," neglecting the spiritual dimension that gives humans their basic dignity. Criticisms of the Church derive also from the same "anthropological error" (basically, the Enlightenment concept of human autonomy). Implicitly—slyly—the critic is identified with the modern purveyors of genocide, fascists, communists, evolutionists, atheists all.[11]

---

[10]David Tracy, *The Analogical Imagination: Christian Theology and the Culture of Pluralism*, (New York, 1981), p. 50.
[11]Bruce Lincoln charges al Qaeda with atavistic thinking: "Most broadly, however, it challenges the Enlightenment restructuring of culture and its preferred model of the nation state, which entails a secular state, pluralistic nation, and minimalist religion." Bruce Lincoln, *Holy Terrors: Thinking about Religion after September 11*, (Chicago, 2003), p. 76.

Constructive criticism is necessary. There is the opportunity to enact image restoring corrective action, and historically, philosophically, and theologically acceptable steps for positive reform within the Catholic Church. These steps could revitalize an aging and depleted Catholic clergy and bring new ideas and consideration of the Creator to a stagnant Catholic Church. The Catholic Church can throw off the yoke of misogyny, elevate the value of families, and protect children from abuse by returning to the traditions of the earliest Christian (Catholic) communities if such traditions can be historically established with a reasonable probability.

The holy office of the inquisition burned people at the stake in the name of that spiritual dimension, a fantastic dimension drawn straight from favored interpretations of uncertain texts. Teachings remain unchanged while methods are declared barbarous. The Church no longer burns witches (and sometimes their children) at the stake, no longer persecutes Jews, or preaches genocide—whether or not it is following divine orders. But modern violence is blamed upon erroneous teachings (anthropological error). Catholic violence, however, comes from other sources, the "spirit of the times," for example, or its "over-zealous" erring children.

Violence and intolerance, specifically in the case of women, married clergy, and abused children, arises not simply from the "spirit of the times" but from the spirit of some of the teachings.

One need not subscribe to naturalism to see the dishonesty behind such a method. It is like a novelist who writes his characters into an inescapable situation and then bestows upon them supernatural powers that allow them to emerge victorious (*Deus ex machina*). The plot tension was nothing more than an illusion and in the end the reader finds that there was no reason for reading the book. The purpose of such a book is to simply sell books. The purpose of an apology that is really no apology is to sell the Church. Selling the Church is another term for evangelizing. Reform needs to include acceptance of female and married clergy. This reform would improve the current environment in which is sometime conducive to sexual abuse of minors and efforts to cover-up those crimes.

Pope John Paul II loudly extolled the virtues of truth and of human dignity. One can take him at his word and apply these principles to his own writings and especially his apology.

What one discovers—and this report is preliminary—is not encouraging.

One must wonder if something is *true* when it is declared absolute and unchangeable *truth* by a body of human persons, all unmarried males, who grant themselves the exclusive right to pronounce this "truth?" Can this self-granted right be based upon a self-granted (or traditionally granted) interpretation of a multiply redacted collection of ancient texts that modern archaeology, history, language analysis and other disciplines now read in a multitude of alternative ways? Again, there is no single Bible. This misconception arose after the codification of the current canon after the Council of Nicaea in 325. Before the time of Christ, and even after, the so- called Old Testament was a fluid library as various books fell into or out of favor. The unresolved discordance of multiple voices within a text that itself contains no clue as to its overall interpretation, not to mention its overall form. Is it legitimate to make intricate arguments (called deeper theological reflection, or fresh appropriation of the sources of faith) based upon such uncertain texts that may not and probably do not record the original words of the principle players? We will never hear their voices. Does it serve the cause of peace and understanding to wield these arguments against modern culture, specifically against the human rights and aspirations of women?

One need not argue for the vapid proposition that all readings are equal. Rather, as George Orwell might have said, some readings are more equal than others. Some readings occur without historical context, without attention to ancient literary genres or literate culture. These readings come as if from outer space. Others are obviously selective, contentious, or simply flat-out mistaken. Does the Holy Spirit guide the Church's favored interpretations? Once again, dear friends, into the fog of the supernatural. Who decides for the Holy Spirit? The Holy Spirit's inspired interpretation is simply a term—like tradition—for the authority of Catholic interpretation which awards the Church the exclusive right of interpretation. This, too, is on trial before the modern (and post-modern) court.

When John Paul II offered apologies for the condemnation of Galileo, for example, he readily admitted, as do many theologians, that in some things like the physical universe holy scripture is historically conditioned. Why not women? Why not sex? Scripture does not teach about the heavens, as the saying went in Galileo's day, but how to get to heaven. Scripture invites readers to share a religious vision of creation. This vision grasps the reader. Obsessive claims for literal interpretations actually blind believers to the possibilities for spiritual experiences that scripture offers. Such experiences may not be found on the historical surface, in the shifting sands of the historically conditioned. Such visions exist far beyond the reach of the most powerful telescope.

Very well. But what if there are some of our fellow human beings who after a friendly reading find that the Bible does not speak to them? Even after sincere and patient study, Scripture does not grasp them. Perhaps they turn to the *Qur'an* or the *Bhavagad Gita*. Eschewing literalism as they were instructed to with the Bible, they find that these texts grip them and they experience a religious vision. What can the Pope say to such people? Having accepted the Bible as "historically conditioned", it would seem that the Magisterium has no grounds to insist that its version of the religious vision, its *truth*, is superior to any other—*for all people*.

Very well. But this is precisely what the Church does when it declares that Christ is truth, or that Christianity possesses the fullness of the truth (but a humanity will have to wait for the end of the world).[12] To make such claims, there must be at least a few literal

---

[12] The Gospel of John personifies the Holy Spirit as the other advocate (*parakletos*), a comforter or counsellor who proceeds from the Father to all believers. Geza Vermes says: "The constant procession from Father to Son culminates in the Holy Spirit...and foreshadows the idea that the whole revelation was not handed down by Jesus during his life...Here lies the seeds of the idea of doctrinal development that the authoritarian church, suspicious of change, has always found difficult to accommodate." *Christian Beginnings: From Nazareth to Nicaea*, (New Haven, 2012), p. 126.

facts, or clearly stated truths, in the Bible that *are not historically conditioned*, that are recognized by everyone, and that are not found in other texts. Some things in the Bible must transcend history. The problem of critical history and authority reaches back to the days of Spinoza and the 17th century, and even earlier. Above all else, critical history questions the reliability of its sources. Historical analysis since Spinoza seeks to understand the scriptures within their historical context.

The challenge of history to biblical authority is like a festering wound in any body of theology, Catholic or Protestant. The problem is far from solved. In terms of sheer quantity alone, scholars possess more information about the 1st century than ever. And more interpretations.

When popes and councils venture out of their comfortable theological generalizations and enter the fractured landscape of historical particulars, they risk appearing naïve and foolish beneath the lens of modern scholarship. On the other hand, if the Bible is historically contingent, then its ultimate truth can only be subjective in the personal experience of those who share its religious vision. Others may find divine truth elsewhere—for the same reasons. Or none at all.

Does the fact that humans seem to possess reason and free will prove humans are created in the image of God as John Paul II claimed? Does not such an assertion derive ultimately—after hundreds of hymns sung to reason—from an ancient text (the Priestly Source, maybe 6th century B. C. E.)? Does it not derive from an *interpretation* of the P-Source? Some modern studies of the *Tanakh* suggest that traditional interpretations may not reflect the historical context of understanding. Theology, then, must mine the text for deeper theological insights. How many of these so-called insights are phantoms of theological imagination? The results of conditioned habits of thought? Can such insights be restrictive? Are Catholic women to stop questioning and thinking when they arrive at the clerically erected barrier labeled "thinking with the Church?"

Of course, there is nothing absolute about modern pronouncements. Theology tends to make the best of this perceived but misunderstood—or perhaps they understand it all too well—weakness. For example, John Paul II claimed that biology could never grasp the whole human person since its own method banishes it from the spiritual. The Church claims a monopoly on the spiritual, even deciding upon its definition.

Where knowledge is incomplete—in a certain sense *all* scientific knowledge is incomplete—a gap opens and the Church wiggles in. But science has a way of expanding its methods and of honing more precise instruments. There will always be gaps. Good theories create them. Further, the distinction between the natural and the supernatural is historically contingent. It is like a fading boundary line on an ancient map. The spiritual may turn out to be an occasion for deeper insights into nature and human history. A spiritual truth is always in danger of being slain by an archaeological discovery or a more compelling reading of an ancient text. When such events do occur, be they authentic discoveries or publicity-seeking hoaxes, the Church turns abruptly critical. It is always at the forefront of the debunking assault when the new discoveries seem to contradict long-held Catholic teachings.

Illustrations of the workings of this Kafka-like method in the case of misogyny and the sexual abuse of children are illuminating. It is why the apology ultimately fails.

These questions concern all people, Catholic and non-Catholic. Since it is apparent in these times that religion is not going away (in some countries), and religious beliefs motivate many people to behave in certain ways (in all countries), it is one's duty to bring such findings before the public.

Therefore, this book is for many types of readers. For those who are quickly wearied by convoluted or esoteric arguments, the book takes a break and engages in a bit of rhetoric, comic exaggeration, and asides. Some tall tales are included for those who prefer a good yarn. Perhaps there is something in our book that will jar your thinking and challenge your beliefs. Nothing of this sort can do any real harm and maybe a lot of good as long as the reader keeps it in mind that nothing here is asserted absolutely. Nothing here is carved in stone. We, more than anyone reading this, are happily aware that every single pronouncement and suggestion is far, *far*, from infallible.

Our argument forms a triangle. Certain aspects of John Paul II's intellectual development are significant. Everything does not change when one becomes pope. This is the first arm. The second arm is the apology itself, whether or not it is a mere image restoration empty of substance. Included on this arm is an attempt to probe the very foundations of Christianity and its attitudes toward women and sex. Finally, the third arm contains analysis of misogyny and sexual misconduct in the Church.

No doubt some critics will immediately hang the charge of "anti-Catholicism" on this book. The label itself is ridiculous given the historical complexity of Catholicism. Is one anti-Catholic if one opposes the oppression of women, if one protests the burning of women for unverifiable supernatural crimes such as intercourse with a devil? Is one somehow prejudiced if one criticizes the Church for protecting some rather sick predatory criminals? The charge is also unfair. The Church reserves the right to criticize the secular world and does so with much relish. On the other hand, the newly polished face of the Church smiles sweetly and preaches moral sermons about respecting the dignity of those persons who follow a different path. To square this circle the Pope must separate beliefs and doctrines from the persons who hold them and act as if these exist in different worlds.

Compare this procedure to what was said earlier about the sinless Mother Church. The Mother Church is sacraments, history, Scriptures, doctrine, tradition, councils, and, significantly, real human beings who breathe and make love and suffer and sin. These living human beings include popes and cardinals and bishops and priests and scholars, yesterday and today. They are the tradition in the flesh. They are living incarnations of Church dogma, the physical appearance of belief in history. The Pope would have it that the children are guilty and deserving of censure while the *Holy Mother Church* is not. But when it comes to secularism and naturalism the Pope feels free to blame bad behavior on so-called prejudices (scientific biology does not include the spiritual dimension, modern philosophy commits an anthropological error), and whatever else he deems worthy of abuse. Individuals, however, are to be respected.

Might the bad behavior of Christian children be due to the instruction they received at the feet of Mother Church? This book will explore that.

Labels assume knowledge that the person wielding them simply does not possess. One of us (Anthony Alioto) taught an extended studies course for adults on the modern quest for the historical Jesus. A member of the class, apparently offended by what sounded in that person's ears like blasphemy and atheism (the Jesus Seminar) decided that the instructor was an "angry Catholic." Are the teachers of the Jesus Seminar "angry Catholics" (whatever this means—after all, the crusaders were fairly angry Catholics)? The assumption seems to be that ideas are confessions. One might easily argue that the quest for the historical Jesus is a huge test of faith. Victorian divines when confronted by fossil evidence in support of Darwin claimed that God placed the bones in the earth to test the faithful. Perhaps the course was a way of alerting believers to anti-Catholic conspiracies. Like old cold war fears of communists infiltrating the entertainment industry in order to disseminate covert propaganda, the course on the historical Jesus might be a means of awakening good Christians to the threat of atheistic historians corrupting higher education by disseminating anti-Christian ideas under the guise of religious studies.

The Catholic Church presumes to make moral and normative pronouncements on people's lives. The monopoly of the *truth* supposedly grants this right. Despite lip service to historically conditioned sources, these truth-claims are still founded upon a supposedly inspired ancient text and supposedly inspired interpretation of that text. Such inspiration must be ultimately supernatural as it descends from the Holy Spirit that dwells in the Church, which is the guardian of the text. Again, this makes the huge assumption that there is a *text* that is the fulcrum of interpretation. Readers, be they popes, saints, or even wicked scholars, help to create the text through their reading, just as God created the world according to the text.

Even if one grants supernatural inspiration in the case of the biblical writers, thinking individuals must question, and in some cases seriously doubt, the legitimacy of the assumption that grants the Church such power over the very writers from whom it draws its legitimacy. Interpreted in such and such a way, the text awards the interpreter the right to interpret and from the results make sweeping judgments of how people wish to conduct their lives. Is it not monumental conceit to assume that you have the solutions and rules for people whose lives you do not share? Is it not arrogant and a sort of intellectual imperialism to claim that other religions contain bits of "truth" only insofar as such bits (seeds) approach the "fullness of truth" in Christianity?

It is perfectly fine for theologians to mine scripture and tradition for "deeper theological insights." Theirs is a harmless game that keeps them well occupied even if, as Nietzsche observed long ago, they play with loaded dice. But it is less harmless and not much of a game when they insist that their winnings award them the right to demand that other people live life by certain rules and prohibitions (mostly prohibitions). Removed from the concerns and suffering of everyday life, the Church elite decide whether and what to allow or forbid just an ancient scholarly *all male* elite wrote sacred scripture itself.

Not having endured the modern wilderness of theological apprenticeship, not having been indoctrinated into certain habits of thought, the "people of God," taking the term from *Lumen Gentium*, must not question the great encyclicals and bulls that presume to judge their personal experiences and problems. Thus, they become obedient pupils and docile children. They never grow up. But it does not end here. The modern inquisitors presume to decide for *all humanity*. They base their rules upon truths that the children in and outside the Church have never examined.

This book is an invitation to critically examine some of these truths, specifically in the case of women and sex. If they are really the *truth*, such an examination by the faithful will only serve to make them more robust and vivid. Even with the best arguments and the greatest numbers of authorities, many obvious truths grown hoary with the ages have turned out to be illusions of perspective, wishes, and even sinister dreams. All too often, belief, faith, and truth stand in the way of seeing things and people clearly, as they are for themselves. All too often observers see what they believe. One discovers in the sacred text what one has been taught to find. If anything robs people of their dignity it is this.

Our book critiques the root causes of misogyny and sexual abuse and offers solutions to these problems. In "Part I: The Golden Legend of the Saint," we establish the framework in which we scrutinize the legacy of Pope John Paul II. We begin in Chapter 1, "The Third Millennium," in which we explain the Catholic Church desired to enter the 3rd Millennium with a clean conscience. Pope John Paul II's Apology of March, 2000 was meant to accomplish this task, especially on the abuse of children and misogyny. We argue that the apology was an attempt to deflect criticism and play the victim.

We continue this critique in Chapter 2, "The Heisenberg Uncertainty Principle of Biblical Hermeneutics." We highlight Church claims it has a monopoly on the "truth" based upon its interpretation of scripture. Their favored interpretation forbids the priesthood of women and married priests. We challenge this claim with a discussion of the uncertainty of any interpretation.

In Chapter 3, "Portrait of the Saint As A Young Philosopher," we move from this critique of Catholic dogma to highlight the views of John Paul II and Pope Benedict, in particular, who held the view that the modern secular world was close to a moral abyss (the Culture of Death) and opposed liberal interpretations of Vatican II. Their views on women and sex arise from these assumptions. We trace these origins to John Paul's studies and teachings in philosophy.

We conclude this section with Chapter 4, "The Apology: A Handmaiden's Tale." Pope John Paul II and Pope Benedict argued the Church is humanity's last stand against the moral disaster of dehumanization. As such, it must defend at all costs the institution and hierarchy, which excludes women and married priests.

In "Part II: In Persona Christi: Misogyny" we explore the dogma that causes discrimination against women through exclusion of female and married clerics. We begin this section with Chapter 5, "Defective Men," in which we explore ancient and medieval biological understanding of women, which led Catholic Church patriarchs in the Middle Ages to label women as defective men (Aquinas). We show how such biological determinism lingered in the thought of the so-called "feminist" John Paul II and his successor Pope Benedict.

In Chapter 6, "Blessings of the Breast and Womb," we identify that the biblical basis of misogyny is undeniable, yet we show that ancient Hebrew folk religion did worship a goddess who does makes appearances in the Bible. We also identify that God, as portrayed in the Old Testament, had female characteristics.

We continue our exploration of the institutionalization of misogyny in Chapter 7, "Was Jesus a Feminist?" We offer a female-friendly reading of the New Testament Gospels. We critique the Church's interpretation of the views of Jesus on women presented in the canonical Gospels. In Chapter 8, "When Women Were Priests," we explore the post-Gospel epistles from the New Testament, non-canonical Gnostic writings, and archeological findings that indicate women clergy served the Catholic Church in its first three centuries, and longer in some cases.

We continue alternate exploration of the views of Jesus on the issue of married clergy in Chapter 9, "Did Jesus Have a Wife?" We examine versions of Christianity the Church declared heresy. The celibate Jesus is an interpretation of the Gospels that favors a certain patriarchal outlook. We argue that the historical Jesus may have been quite different.

The wide acceptance of married priests and bishops is clearly established in Chapter 10, "When Priests Were Married." Virtually all sources agree that married clergy were accepted through the first thousand years of the Catholic Church.

In Chapter 11, "Witchy Women," we explore how women as they are defined by the Church, past and present, are at the same time creatures of weak wills and insatiable lust. Therefore, they are subject to demonic possession and witchcraft. We show how John Paul's views and Pope Benedict's views must logically result in a lower regard for women or men who are married to women.

We examine John Paul's obsession with the Virgin Mary in Chapter 12, "Brothers, Little Sisters." We also examine and critique the tendency of the Church to leave people in "spiritual infantilism." We critique John Paul's claim that he was a feminist in Chapter 13, "Father Knows Best."

In "Part III: Sex and Sex Scandals," we outline the causes of sexual abuse in the Catholic Church, explore the pervasiveness of the problem and shed light on the systematic, institutional conspiracy to cover-up these heinous crimes. In Chapter 14, "Sex in Heaven," we explore how John Paul's admirers claimed that he possessed unique insights into the psychology and theology of human sexuality. We find that his so-called insights, along with the Church's teachings on sex, create a climate conductive to sexual abuse.

We postulate the idea that clerical abuse of children follows naturally from such attitudes in Chapter 15, "Clerical Sex." Since the institution (the Holy Mother Church) stands above individual members, and since the institution is the last defense against moral disaster, it must be defended at all costs. Apologies become attacks on critics. In Chapter 16, "Suffer the Children," we examine the sexual abuse of children by some members of the clergy and the Church's response.

In Chapter 17, "A Thoroughly Incomplete History of Sex in Religion," we identify conceptions of human sexuality change over time. Abuse will continue as long as the Church sees sex as a moral problem. We analyze the Church's doctrine of original sin by returning to the original sources in the original languages in Chapter 18, "The Archaeology of Theological Prehistory." We offer an alternative view that could solve the problems outlined above.

We once again examine clerical celibacy in Chapter 19, "Once Again, Celibacy." The Faith does not require it. The Catholic Church's demand for clerical celibacy can be destructive and may result in abuse. We also examine homosexuality and find the Church's teachings (that homosexuality is in itself not sinful as long as homosexuals remain celibate) absurd. In Chapter 20, "A Fable: The Mother Who Died," we explore the John Paul's personal biography, which we contend cannot be so easily dismissed as many of his admirers tend to do.

"Part IV: Preaching the Kingdom" is a summary of our argument that the apology was a self-serving form of evangelizing, especially in Europe where the Church is losing ground. We begin this section in Chapter 21, "Ecclesia in Europa," by examining the selling of spirituality in the market place and claim that while John Paul cleverly used the media, the media transformed him (and his Church) into an empty spectacle.

In order to end misogyny and abuse, which themselves have become negative spectacles, it is evident the Church must critically examine (as we have) its doctrines and truth-claims, which we posit in Chapter 22, "Apology Without Reform." The Catholic patriarchy claims to have done so but we found this claim empty, mere theatre. In Chapter 23, we again offer Benoit's "A Typology of Image Restoration Strategies," an analytic lens through which we critically examine Pope John Paul's *apologia*. The promise of corrective action in John Paul's *apologia* must result in actual dogmatic and theological reform to be effective. This, as yet, has been lacking.

We argue that the Church still does have a unique role to play in the modern world in Chapter 24, "The Kingdom of God." In Chapter 25, "An Interpretation of a Dream," we contend, at its best, the Church must bear witness to the dignity of all people: women, children, and men. Only then may its members claim to be true disciples of the Jew named Yeshua.

In sum, the central thesis of this book is the Catholic Church can enact effective corrective action to prevent sexual abuse of children and subsequent efforts to hide these crimes through inclusion of more diverse clergy. First, the Catholic Church should once again accept female clergy. This would also constitute authentic corrective action as promised by Pope John Paul II in response to charges of Catholic misogyny. Second, married clergy should be ordained again. Third, these two reforms, or return to early Catholic Church tradition would alleviate an atmosphere that is conducive to sexual abuse of children by clergy members and the conspiratorial efforts to hide these heinous crimes. The efforts by the Catholic Church to mortify (apologize) for past mistakes by members of the clergy and Church leadership and promise corrective action in the areas of misogyny and sexual abuse rings hollow when the root cause for the problems, dogma and policy, are left unchanged.

PART I
The Golden Legend of the Saint

"Benedict stressed the need for Catholics ... embrace the whole ... faith."

Vatican City, Jul 6, 2005; Obtained online at
http://www.catholicnewsagency.com/new.php?n=4314

Chapter 1
The Third Millennium

In this chapter, we explain the Catholic Church desired to enter the third Millennium with a clean conscience. Pope John Paul II's Apology of March, 2000 was meant to accomplish this task, especially in regard to the abuse of children and misogyny. We argue that the apology was an attempt to deflect criticism and play the victim. In the apology, John Paul also promised corrective action. These promises have yet to be fulfilled.

Seen from the windows of the Vatican, the dawn of the new millennium did not reveal an encouraging picture. Illuminating those lands formerly known as "Christendom," the sunrise of the third Christian millennium revealed a Europe in which religion was no longer a major factor in people's lives. Some statistics indicate that nearly half of the population *never* goes to church, and less than a fourth feels that religion is important in their lives. In Catholic Poland, the homeland of Karol Wojtyla, the man who would become Pope John Paul II, the percentage is a bit higher, one-third feel religion is significant. In Germany, the homeland of Pope Benedict XVI (now retired), formerly Joseph Cardinal Ratzinger, the percentage is about 21% and drops even lower in other European states.[1] Such statistics apply to religion in general, not just Catholicism. Having weathered philosophical deconstruction, revolution, the higher historical criticism, communism and Nazism, the Catholic Church is faced with perhaps its most implacable foe yet, indifference. The third millennium could become the age long

---

[1] See J. Rifkin, *The European Dream: How Europe's Vision of the Future in Quietly Eclipsing the American Dream*, (New York, 2004), p. 20. Also see *The Pew Forum on Religion and Public Life*, December 19, 2011. However, the percentages are higher of those who say they believe there is a god, 80% in Poland, 74% in Italy, 47% in Germany, 38% in the UK, and 34% in France. Excommunicated Bishop Marcel Lefebvre says this: "...many Catholics and even priests no longer have a very clear idea of the Catholic religion in civil society. Secularism is everywhere." *An Open Letter to Confused Catholics*, (1998), p. 15.

3

anticipated by thinkers of the Enlightenment in which the Church becomes irrelevant. Ironically, perhaps only in Christendom.

Pope John Paul II led the Catholic Church into this third "Christian" millennium. The third longest reigning pope in Catholic history, John Paul traveled more than any other pope (129 countries) to address the hundreds of millions of Catholic believers, nonbelievers, and non-Christians. Since his election in October of 1978, the relatively young and athletic Pope was a highly visible and vocal presence in the global village for over two decades. He quickly became a media favorite, "John Paul Superstar." As one of the few respected world leaders only marginally associated with a nation-state, he was an active participant in the discussion of the momentous issues with leaders from around the world. For example, in the 1980s the apartheid government in South Africa prohibited travelers from visiting ethnic African 'homelands.' In 1984 John Paul "the untouchable" traveled only to these prohibited areas while preaching the intrinsic evil nature of racial discrimination. This is an indicative example of John Paul II's ability to communicate not only with words but also with dramatic action. The former actor knew the value of symbolic gestures.

The Soviet dictator Joseph Stalin once asked with his yellow-eyed sarcasm: How many divisions did the Pope command? Stalin implied that without brute material force the Church was no longer a major player in the great game of *weltpolitik*. History was his witness. Despite all the anathemas hurled by the pope on the new Italian state in 1870, Pope Pius IX's spiritual legions were helpless against Italian cannon. Pope Pius IX, who had condemned the modern world became its prisoner, "the prisoner of the Vatican." He died in 1878, the same year as the first King of united Italy, Vittorio Emanuele.

But things changed in the 20th century. Pope John Paul II, commanding an army of moral authority, played a significant role in the dismantling of Soviet-imposed communism in Poland. According to his admirers, he was an important catalytic agent in the fall of the Berlin Wall if not the eventual demise of communism itself. In the early 1990s, one would see posters about Rome celebrating his triumph. Expropriating an image from the Sistine Chapel, that of the punishing angel expelling Adam and Eve from Eden, the posters pictured John Paul in the angel's role as he banished Marx and Lenin from the garden of human history.

Even as the communist governments of Eastern Europe collapsed, the Catholic Pope demanded that these nations newly freed from Stalinism should not replace the cult of communism with a cult of consumerism, a problem he thought significant in the U.S. and other western developed nations.

Pope John Paul II, "the people's pope," victor over communism, the liberator, the new feminist, had surely secured his place among the saints of the Church. Admirers already call him "John Paul the Great."

So goes the golden legend. As with all legends, its hero rises from obscurity, is severely tested, slays the dragon (in this case a bear), and dies in glory and approbation.

But was he able to reverse the creeping indifference to religion? Was he able to restore the Catholic Church as a major cultural force in the modern and post-modern worlds? Will the third millennium become what he hoped for, the flowering of the Catholic Church and its Christian mission? Or will it be the age that finally ushers in the denouement hoped for by many of the Eighteenth Century *philosophies*, the withering away of Christianity in Christendom?

A significant aspect of Catholic restoration following the Second Vatican Council was John Paul II's unprecedented *mea culpa* (from the Latin for by "my fault; I am to blame") for a variety of sins committed by members, clergy, and leadership of the Catholic Church. John Paul's March 12, 2000 millennial *mea culpa* was a cleansing of the conscience, an act of penance and purification. The self-proclaimed sins for which John Paul offered image restoration discourse included anti-Semitism, persecution of other religions, persecution of women, the sexual abuse scandals among the clergy, and the persecution of Galileo for heretical teaching of scientific truth.

In one sense, there can be nothing truly "unprecedented" in the Catholic Church. Everything rests upon tradition which is the gradual unfolding of Truth bestowed by Christ and preserved in His Church. As noted in the Preface, the *apologia* arises from the sacrament of penance. Therefore, it is directed to God. It is the Church asking for *God's pardon* for past sins committed by inherently sinful children. Rather than an admission of wrongs directed to the injured parties in *this world*, the Pope's apology is a confession to a metaphysical entity of questionable existence, that is, *qualitatively and quantitatively* unverifiable except by methods blessed by the Church (faith in search of understanding). It is a solemn act of repentance meant ultimately to return to the good graces of that entity. As such, says George Weigel in his hagiography of John Paul II, *Witness to Hope* (first published in 1999, Perennial edition in 2005 after John Paul's death on April 2, 2005), it is more serious than a mere apology. It does not pander to interest groups like secular politicians (p. 877). It can hardly be called an apology at all in the usual sense of the word. This assertion will be tested.

Viewed from a different perspective, one less ethereal and more critical, the *apologia* is unprecedented. Such a sweeping papal *mea culpa* has never been seen or heard by so many in so many lands and in so many tongues. And it may even turn out to be an act of desperation.

If as Pope John Paul and his successors believe, the Church is in possession of the Truth, which is Christ—modern philosophy cripples itself, John Paul wrote in his encyclical *Fides et ratio* (1998), by refusing the Truth of divine revelation (paragraph 75)—then if follows that the Church must also be committed to promoting and sharing its truth in this world. The modern age, John Paul protested, makes the *search* for truth its ultimate goal instead of the truth itself, which it declares to be inaccessible to men.

Besides its refusal to consider revelation, he criticized modern thought for making the quest alone an end in itself (paragraph 46). This is because modern philosophy had given up faith in the possibility of discovering *the Truth*. In doing so, philosophy had brought on the crisis of the modern age in doubt, fear, genocide, moral decay, selfish hedonism—in short, everything the Pope opposes. The list is so long one might wonder why it doesn't include the fashion industry (which is not as factious as it sounds: some theologians of the Fourteenth Century blamed the plague on the change in women's fashions).

Modern philosophers have become self-absorbed, the Pope complains, more interested in *how* they know than the truth of what they know, and the *telos*, the end to which their knowledge points. Absorbed with subjectivism and refusing absolutes, philosophy, and possibly even science, have surrendered to relativism, and, finally, nihilism. Whether or not this criticism can be justified (it is doubtful many scientists would agree), investigators could simply ask John Paul: What if your quest for deeper Truth discovers truths that make Catholic dogma unbelievable? What if Church dogmas and doctrines—your so-called Truth—share responsibility for sins of the past? What if, having unearthed the causes of past crimes, the Church discovers that those causes are the natural outgrowths of doctrines that can no longer be maintained?

Since the Second Vatican Council, the Church hierarchy realized that it could no longer violently or otherwise crush freedom of conscience, freedom of inquiry (as in the case of Galileo) or persecute other faiths (as with the Jews or Muslims) while promoting its mission to preach the gospel to all the nations. Therefore, it had to reform its image by erasing those stains of violent intolerance, repression, and persecution. *The Catechism of the Catholic Church* (1995) is quite clear on the purpose of the apology:

> On her pilgrimage, the Church has also experienced the "discrepancy existing between the message she proclaims and the human weakness of those to whom the Gospel has been entrusted." Only by taking the "way of penance and renewal," the "narrow way of the cross," can the People of God extend Christ's reign. For "just as Christ carried out the work of redemption in poverty and oppression, so the Church is called to follow the same path if she is to communicate the fruits of salvation to men." (p. 853).

If this is an act of penance having nothing to do with pandering to interest groups as Weigel says (one of his examples is Clinton's apology for slavery), the fact remains that the Church went to great lengths to publicize it. Why not pray to God in private, unlike those hypocrites who make a big show of their supposed piety, as Jesus once admonished his followers? The world stage replaced the quiet theatre of a private room for prayer. This fact alone, combined with the *Catechism's* statement, ought to arouse our suspicion. The Pope was indeed pandering. He was pandering to the largest interest group of all, to world opinion in the name of the Catholic mission. Given the dismal scene in Europe at the third millennium's dawn, the Church finds itself in the ironic position of having to re-evangelize Christendom.

Why did the sons and daughters of the Church, Christians who knew the Sermon on the Mount, commit these sins in the name of a rabbi who supposedly taught nonviolence?[2]

Authored by the International Theological Commission and released by the Vatican in December 1999, the document *Memory and Reconciliation: The Church and the Faults of the Past* sets out the strategy if not the theology of the *apologia*. The Holy Mother Church, believers are told, is pure, without sin, unstained by the sins of her children (p. 12). This Church is that invisible transcendent body of Christ, the bearer of divine light. Of course, as one can know from *Lumen Gentium*, it forms a unity with the earthly Church even though exactly how this happens is a mystery like the trinity. Shortly, this work shall trace the origin of this idea to St. Augustine. For now, the *apologia* confesses that here on earth the visible Church is inhabited by both saints and sinners. Holy and perfect though it is, at the same time it is ever in need of purification. Like Christ, the Holy Mother Church takes on the sins of her members (p. 15). Guiltless like Christ, she is wounded by them for she bears the cross created by every transgression. According to this logic, the Church is innocent. Her erring children are guilty. Apologies are like confessions, an aspect of penance.

What about these poor fallen children? Are the sinful children of the Roman Catholic Church inherently sinful? Are they sinful because of their temporal culture? Are they constitutionally weak creatures who find themselves simply unable to resist the temptations of that Dark Spirit in the wilderness? Or—dare one say it—are they sinful because of what Mother Church taught them?

Anticipating what follows, the Church hierarchy past and present—and there is no reason to doubt future—plays a game it cannot fail to win. *Memory and Reconciliation* begs the faithful to distinguish between Christian believers and the society of the times in which these believers lived (p. 7). What one today might label barbaric, sinful, or brutal acts and prejudices must be understood and evaluated within their temporal context. Scholars and believers require a more sophisticated hermeneutics, the authors of *Memory and Reconciliation* argue, one that uncovers deeper meanings in history, doctrine and even biblical narratives. In such a manner are contradictions resolved.

But watch closely what happens: deeper meanings begin to exhibit ever more tenuous connections to contingent historical events[3] This is similar to the old excuse theologians used to trot out when some statement in scripture contradicts established scientific laws and observations. God has "accommodated" his revelation to the

---

[2]Jesus' nonviolence may be more in the minds of hopeful readers than the pages of the New Testament. For example, Jesus does preach hate in Luke 14:25–27: one must hate father and mother, wife and children, etc., to be his follower. But what about the Commandment to honor your parents? Does Jesus oppose the Torah? See Hector Avalos, *Fighting Words: The Origin of Religious Violence*, (Amherst, NY, 2005), Chapters 8 and 9.

[3]See Hans Frei on how this happens to biblical narratives. Hans W. Frei, *The Eclipse of Biblical Narrative: A Study in Eighteenth and Nineteenth Century Hermeneutics*, (New Haven, 1974), p. 130.

cosmology of the times. The supposedly unscientific statements in scripture about the physical universe must be understood—explained away—as God speaks in the language, concepts, and world-views of the historical epochs in which He makes His voice heard. Or else the offending passage must be re-interpreted, to the point of retranslating ancient Hebrew or Greek, even adding words that are not in the original text (we'll give examples of this sleight of hand later).

These days apologists like to pick and choose from modern scientific theories that seem to agree with or support certain readings of the Bible. The most notorious was in 1951 when Pope Pius XII declared that because the Big Bang demonstrated that space and time had a beginning, here was scientific evidence for a creator. Therefore the creator god of Genesis (but which one?) is supported by scientific evidence. Since then, many apologists like to use the fine tuning argument. Taken together, many of nature's constants like the cosmological constant (1.38×10^{-123} in Planck units), the ratio of the number protons to electrons, the ratio of the electromagnetic force to gravity, the expansion rate of the universe and the mass density of the universe are so precisely tuned, to thousands of decimal points, that a tiny change of a single place would not support life (life as *humans* know it, which brings up the selection problem). Randomness, the new guise of Satan, is laughingly banished as an explanation, and henceforth only God (one of them) remains.

Such people tend to argue for God as the most plausible logical inference given the existence of a universe containing the conditions for life as determined by such constants. It may well be plausible too, that they grit their teeth and pray that physics does not come up with any unifying theory that explains these parameters *naturally*; that is, how they follow necessarily from some universal principle, much as the equality of inertial and gravitational mass in Newton's day, seemingly a case of fine tuning, actually followed from General Relativity.[4] Einstein summarized the issue when he wondered if God, the Old One, had a choice when he created the universe? (If He did, then how could a necessary being make a choice? If not and there's something necessary about the universe, why have Him?)

Or, natural theologians might argue from the old default position of how can something come from nothing. But again, watch what happens when science does develop its own *plausible* responses. Perhaps mathematical models and experimental evidence will force scholars to redefine more precisely the concept of the vacuum.[5] The lowest energy state is a vacuum; a false vacuum is the original state of the universe with the forces unified into a single force. Apologists howl. Your nothing is not our "real" nothing if it is filled with potential (see the Preface of *A Universe From Nothing*, by Lawrence Krauss).

---

[4] Paul C. W. Davies writes: "The ultimate hope is that this meta-unification will stem from a deep physical principle akin to Einstein's principle of general covariance, and we will find that all the fundamental properties of the physical universe flow from a single, simple reality statement." "John Archibald Wheeler and the Clash of Ideas," in *Science and Ultimate Reality: Quantum Theory, Cosmology and Complexity*, eds. Paul C. W. Davies, John D. Barrow, and Charles L. Harper, Jr., (Cambridge, UK, 2004), p. 17.

[5] Lawrence M. Krauss, *A Universe From Nothing: Why There is Something Rather Than Nothing*, (New York, 2012).

There are many more sophisticated probability arguments, and many conclude that *our* God is a more plausible explanation. In fact, meaningful patterns that do not appear random can indeed happen by pure chance over time.[6] Plausibility is at heart subjective, especially when it inhabits some other realm of existence, say the spiritual world of wish-fulfillment.[7]

In the middle of all this plausibility one wonders whatever happened to scripture given that most of the fine-tuners are Christians. Abruptly, the faithful begin to hear about morality, the so-called "objective" good. Was not the Levite who mutilated his nameless concubine acting upon his perception of objective good? The faithful hear sermons on love, on the historicity of Jesus, or forlorn attempts to somehow prove the resurrection. One ultimately returns to history, a rather untrustworthy ally.

The commission that generated *Memory and Reconciliation* demanded a historical hermeneutics be applied in the name of simple fairness. For example, one cannot judge people of the past by modern sensibilities. A violent medieval society that glorified militarism in the image of the knight cannot be held to modern standards for giving birth to the crusading mentality.

How the game is played begins to become apparent. Responsibility for such horrific acts as the burning of women and the abuse of children, just as, say, the sack of Jerusalem in 1099 or the destruction of Orthodox Constantinople in the thirteen century is subtly deflected from the Church and transferred to historical contingency. There it is joined to such human failings as greed, hatred, lust and so forth—as if any "historical hermeneutics," even a "holy hermeneutics," is able to disclose people's inner motives, even when they state them openly—that is, psychoanalyze the dead. Is it not rather that deeply held beliefs lead people to act in habitual ways? Saints commit crimes for some perceived good. Even so, this principle must be tested somehow in each individual case.

Not only is the Church innocent as *the Church*, but in some way so are its "sinful children." Religious tolerance towards Muslims (and Jews) as well as other Christians exists beyond their historical and therefore mental, even ethical, horizon. But how can this be true for modern women?

If it is unfair to judge the past by the standards of the present, or by any standards that exist outside the historical dimension in which real people live and act, the Church seems to admit a degree of relativism (its impeccable foe) into the discussion. On the other hand, one may not impose meanings that ultimately ignore the context of

---

[6] Leonard Mlodinow, *The Drunkard's Walk: How Randomness Rules Our Lives*, (New York, 2008), p. 181.
[7] "Fundamental religious beliefs only *look like* propositions insofar as they may take a subject-predicate form...from the vantage point of deductive logic it makes no sense to try to verify or falsify utterances about the supernatural because they are 'category violations'...an emotional but bodiless deity...Such an utterance allows contradictory inferences...and therefore permits any inference to follow and so precludes no inference in principle." Scott Atran, *In Gods We Trust: The Evolutionary Landscape of Religion*, (New York, 2002), p. 290.

historical events as it generally accepted today. Contingent history does have religious significance. But watch out, there could be some more scrolls buried in the desert just as there may be other universes. And so, one way or the other, one stares down into the black chasm of historical relativism.

In order to meet this terrible dilemma, *Memory and Reconciliation* insists upon the bond between past and present (and future), a permanent principle which is based upon the unifying action of the Spirit of God found in Revelation. Transcendence guards against relativism (p. 18). Revelation—Christ—is the Truth, the universal norm. The mystical body of Christ preserves the Truth. Intoxicated by the "spirit of the times," some of its weaker children fail to abide by those norms. The critic, however, refuses to accept the transcendent and therefore cannot see the Truth.

Suddenly it seems the discussion is now on a new field playing a new game governed by different rules. In response to the charge of historical relativism (which in its weak form simply warns that historical truths are tentative, open to revision on further evidence), defenders of the Church escape into spiritual realms where the final score is posted before the game is played. The new rules (declaring the winner before the competition starts) go under a number of names: deeper theological thinking, hermeneutics, or the mining of the inexhaustible Truth of the Spirit.

For example, in a valiant attempt to escape the historical, archaeological, and literary difficulties of the quaint little garden fairy tale in Genesis, John Paul in *The Theology of the Body* introduces the idea of a "theological prehistory" in which literal history is rooted (p. 53). Using this alternative dimension, he is then able to preserve in our dimension of history the dogma of original sin and spin out a hermeneutical spider web of complexities entitled: "reformed anthropology." And—surprise!—he discovers that traditional Church teachings on sex, contraception, marriage and love are that *Truth* deposited by Christ in his Church and only there.

The rules of critical historical analysis give way to faith (trust) in the veracity of our revelation.

In sum, defenders excuse Catholic sins of the past by what is at heart a relativist argument. At the same time, the Church in possession of the Truth granted to it by Christ condemns relativism. Spiritual hermeneutics dissolves the apparent contradiction. The Spirit of God discovered in Revelation unites the Church past, present and future and thus transcends mere history. But, as Hans Frei warns, the actual *content* of this revelation *is itself historical.*[8] So too any interpretation that introduces into the argument the so-called Spirit of God. Why is the revelation of Christ *true* and, say, the revelation of Krishna not? Because Jesus *really existed in history, really rose from the dead, and the apostles really founded the Church* (including Christ "really" awarding the keys of the kingdom to St. Peter).

In short, Catholics still rest their belief on historical evidence as well as the Church's authoritative *interpretation* of that evidence, which compels them to reject or argue away

---

[8]Hans Frei, *The Eclipse of Biblical Narrative*, p. 127.

the case for Krishna or any other non-Christian revelation. Today, however, scholars are busy cross-examining such evidence in numerous fields.

Critical scholarship generally agrees that the gospels themselves are already interpretations of Jesus and serve the specific interests of historical communities.[9] There is no such thing as an early monolithic Christianity. There are multiple interpretations of oral traditions which are themselves interpretations that intersect on many levels, split off and diverge. Orthodoxy and heresy do not exist.

Further, where is the line drawn that separates explanations? When do believers rely on the Spirit of the Times and when do the faithful call upon the Spirit of God? The most obvious question is: Who decides? The Church? But the Church is a party to the dispute.

In this chapter, we explained that the Catholic Church desired to enter the third Millennium with a clean conscience. Pope John Paul II's Apology of March, 2000 was meant to accomplish this task, especially in regard to the abuse of children and misogyny. We argue that the apology was an attempt to deflect criticism and play the victim. In the apology, John Paul also promised corrective action. These promises have yet to be fulfilled.

---

[9] The old master story of Christian origins is now being challenged and rewritten, says Karen L. King, *The Gospel of Mary of Magdala: Jesus and the First Woman Apostle* (Salem, OR, 2003), p. 39.

Chapter 2

The Heisenberg Uncertainty Principle of Biblical Hermeneutics or the End of Theological Determinism

In this chapter, we highlight that the Church claims to have a monopoly on the "truth" based upon its interpretation of scripture. Therefore, it forbids the priesthood of women and married priests. We challenge this claim with a discussion of the uncertainty of any interpretation.

Christianity like its parent Judaism and its younger sibling Islam is preeminently a religion of the book.[1] Many believers will say that that their Scripture has a divine origin, written by human beings guided by the Holy Spirit (or some angel), in the case of Catholicism given for safe keeping to the Church. The Church, however, is not the ultimate author. Belief, it is said, did not create Scripture. The Bible, therefore, is the ultimate truth-text if one assumes, as does the Church, that "God is Truth."

In the first place, the argument is obviously circular. Authoritative interpretations of the Bible are granted by biblical authority that is established by authoritative interpretations. Secondly, the statement is already an interpretation (it is, after all, the *human writer* who makes the claim for inspiration). Interpretation, St. Augustine argued, must keep interpreting until it discovers what scholars already know to be true, an implication

---

[1] See F. E. Peters, *The Voice, The Word, The Books, The Sacred Scripture of the Jews, Christians, and Muslims*, (Princeton, NJ: Princeton University Press, 2007).

of the famous "faith in search of understanding." One must use reason—it is true—but reason informed by faith. Like weighted dice, the whole enterprise is crooked from the start.

Modernity challenged Christianity's truth claims. John Paul's apology, if not his entire pontificate, only makes sense in the wake of this challenge. Beginning with Benedict Spinoza (1632–1677), and evolving into the present with its so-called Third Quest for the Historical Jesus, scripture has been dissected, dug up, disenchanted, demythologized and denuded down to its historical skeleton, and possibly into a fine dust of fantasy.

Following Spinoza's lead, but with far more sophisticated tools, scholars have excavated the remains of the ancient world. Linguists have analyzed the ancient Hebrew, Aramaic, and Greek of the authors. Historical context is richer and more detailed. What is the meaning of the text according to its times? What are the authors saying in their language, in contrast to the theologically assumed "truth" of their words? Ironically, it seems that the more one knows about these details, and many others, the more opaque it all becomes. The more possible meanings there are.

Gregory Dawes tells the long story of this challenge in his book: *The Historical Jesus Question: The Challenge of History to Religious Authority*. His account focuses on the ingenious theological answers to the problem. In many cases, the solution was to separate so-called theological meaning from critical historical analysis and its eternal *suspicion* of the sources (which is an artifact of modernity). This meaning now becomes the ideal reference, everything is built on its foundation, not on the shifting ground of suspect historical facts and sources.

Religion must avoid ossification. It cannot be mummified. Yet in the end, if one is to remain Christian, if one talks about legitimizing historical tradition, there must be *something historical* that remains. Even if the meaning or theological truths are no longer the prisoners of historical fact claims, some form of history must still be their basis. Dawes' conclusion (he calls it inescapable) is not encouraging:

> There *is* no way of reconciling Christian claims to religious authority with the knowledge and methods of the discipline of history. The historical viewpoint of our age undermines claims to biblical authority, while the Jesus of history is not a figure who can be re-appropriated for our own time (pp. 368–369).

This dilemma can be called: *The Heisenberg Uncertainty Principle of Biblical Hermeneutics*. If one insists upon the religious meaning of the texts—say theological claims such as original sin—the historical position (p) becomes indistinct if not invisible. If one insists upon fixing the text's historical position (p)—say the contextual and possible linguistic meanings—one must surrender the momentum of theological certainty (q). Religious claims become free-floating, like the wind they blow where they will. The mathematics of Heisenberg's uncertainty relation in quantum theory did not obey the commutative law of simple algebra: multiplying position (p) by momentum (q) *does not equal* multiplying q by p (in matrix calculus). If one begins with religious meanings and follows up with the history one gets as different answer than if one begins with the history and follows with theology. Spinoza clearly saw the principle when he observed in his *Tractatus Theologico-Politicus*: "We see, I say, that the chief concern of theologians on the whole has been to extort from Holy Scripture their own arbitrarily invented ideas, for which they claim divine authority."

Defenders of the Church admonish opponents to see things through the eyes of faith otherwise they will never understand how it is that the invisible manifests in the visible. But it is certainly fair to ask for the historical "p": who exactly are these visible, sinful children of the invisible Body of Christ? Have popes sinned? Councils? Various Church institutions? Have declarations that supposedly embody "the Truth" made grievous errors that caused persecution? And what if the historical society that partially bears the blame is Christendom itself? The fact remains that for the majority of its history the visible Church flourished in a society, it had a significant hand in designing. The values, goals, philosophy, science, art, literature—even leisure time—were Christian, for roughly fifteen hundred years.

This does not imply that Christianity itself was some static monolith. It was interdependent with constantly changing social and cultural conditions, not to mention the variations within the religion itself. Christianity of the literate elites, the male elites, mixed in complex ways with folk religion. Or sometimes not at all.[2] A precise historical definition of a Christian is arbitrary, as it is today.

If people acted badly due to the "Spirit of the Times," then apologists must also concede that this Spirit of the Times was Christianity itself in one of its many incarnations, shaping the times and shaped by the times. How is it possible to blame society without implicating the Church's collusion?[3]

Popes, cardinals, bishops, councils, the Church Fathers, and all their dogmatic pronouncements, the New Testament itself, comprise this earthly Church. At the same time, these fallible men define the "Truth" which is the mystical body of Christ. Like the marble of St. Peter's statuary, they chisel the invisible form visible. Do they not also bear the burden of Catholic misconduct? Is it possible that saints, popes and doctors of the Church, maybe even the New Testament, created habits of thought that found expression in bad behavior? And still do?

Once the evidence is in, it is ultimately up to the reader to decide. But if this is the case, it is a case that John Paul II cannot admit. For by acknowledging what may be a significant source of Catholic intolerance, violence, and persecution, John Paul would be in effect setting himself up as judge and jury (and perhaps executioner) over the *historical Catholic Church*. He would be usurping God.

Defenders might argue—as will be highlighted later—that such sins were due to mistaken or unjust interpretations of Scripture or of the Church Fathers. But what if those "unjust interpretations," which is itself yet another interpretation, turn out to be Church dogma? What if certain popes, including some up for sainthood, turn out to be

---

[2] A shepherd in 14th century England when asked if he knew who the Father, Son, and Holy Spirit were, answered: "The father and the son I know well for I tend their sheep, but I know not the third fellow; there is none of that name in our village." Quoted in Keith Thomas, *Religion and the Decline of Magic*, (New York, 1971), p. 165.
[3] To come.

guilty? And, how can one be certain that the gospel interpretations themselves do justice to the "real" teachings of the first century rabbi named Yeshua?

So-called progressive interpretation of scripture tends to progressively separate one from historical context, which itself is interpretation due to change with new discoveries and new minds. Finally the theologian need no longer worry about imposing modern sensibilities upon ancient people. Ancient Aramaic speaking Jews and their Greek speaking propagandists begin sounding like—well, the Congregation for the Doctrine of the Faith.

The *apologia* is mostly short on names and specifics. If sin is individual, then without specific names, responsibility for crimes—hence corrective action—is impossible. The papal court forbids cross-examination.

The apologetic Pope has faced yet another dilemma. It is no longer heresy to teach a heliocentric theory as did Galileo. The Orthodox Church is one of two lungs comprising the body of Christ and no longer stands condemned as in 1054. Martin Luther is a son of the Church and no longer the wild boar raging through the vineyard of Christ as Pope Leo X declared in 1520—not if one wishes, as John Paul II did, to reunite the body of Christ, "that they be one," or claim that scientific truth does not contradict Catholic truth, because "truth cannot contradict truth." So how does John Paul maintain that Catholic Truth is absolute and eternal while for practical purposes conceding that some truths, *at one time declared absolute by former popes speaking with the voice of St. Peter,* have been determined partial or simply false? One way out is to claim that popes as popes had not condemned Galileo (or even Luther). Popes as men had. This would surely have been news to many past popes. It also raises the question: how do we know when contemporary popes are speaking for the Church? Perhaps they're all fit to be ignored?

Pilate's question still haunts the Church. John Paul claimed in the encyclical *Fides et ratio* (1998), that the pilgrim Church (code for the visible Church) shares with humanity the struggle to arrive at the truth (2). Every truth attained is a step towards the fullness of Truth, which will appear with God's final revelation (2). *God's final revelation*! Meanwhile, the Church explains away contradictions by waving the magic wand of deeper theological meanings. Revelation is an inexhaustible source of Truth and the theological enterprise mines this treasure—and, lo, contradictions dissolve in the wash of deeper theological thinking. Larger diamonds dug from deeper shafts are distinct from smaller diamonds uncovered centuries ago, yet they are all diamonds.

Not only does this method come perilously close to the old condemned medieval doctrine of the "double truth," that the natural science of Aristotle, though it seemed to contradict the theological truth was true in its own realm, but it commits the fallacy of calling upon further discovery as proof of a present argument. At the end of the world (final revelation), all paradoxes will be resolved in the "fullness" of the Truth. Practically speaking, then, the Church can never be wrong. Papal Bulls, condemnations, official declarations, infallible statements on faith and morals are never mistaken interpretations or unjust, or simply erroneous. Rather, they are markers on the long journey of the pilgrim Church's struggle for the Truth. The Truth is just beyond the horizon, realized in some imagined transcendental future. Even if plain reading creates contradictions when compared to modern truths, the Church assures one that all its truths will cohere in the "fullness" of Truth—only the faithful need to be patient, until the end of the world.

Some victims of Church abuse may not wish to wait that long, *especially because the abuse continues. Especially children. Especially women.*

This sort of casuistry spreads through the *apologia* like a cancer. It weakens, perhaps fatally, all possibilities of corrective action. When it is convenient, the Church trots out empty abstractions and fills them in with whatever "deeper theological insights" are necessary to explain away dogmatic statements that seem to contradict the sparkling clean image the Church wishes to project. The plain meaning of the Bulls, encyclicals, the pronouncements of councils, even New Testament passages, is tortured into its opposite or whatever suits the Church's mission.

Such a method leads to the very abuse for which the Church seeks pardon. That is why *Memory and Reconciliation* sternly lectures that sin is always personal, and social sin is the accumulation and concentration of individual sins (6). Pope John Paul II and his cohorts fiercely attacked "wicked" ideologies and beliefs, implying that such things are impersonal (although some individuals, like Karl Marx, are almost limitless fuel for a continuous *auto-da-fe, ad majorem gloriam Dei*). At the same time, they claimed to respect the human dignity of those individuals who held them. Therefore, John Paul supposedly never attacked people. He respected human dignity—which, ironically, arises from a Christian assertion that humans are made in the image of God, which rests upon interpretation of the Eden myth. Interpretation arises from human minds, images of God, albeit sinful images of God. John Paul seriously questioned using our image-of-God brains, which *must be personal*—and *naturally* come in two sexes, male and female—to critique Christian truth. Yet, he felt free to assail ideas, even though they must arise from dignified human minds. The problem is that such minds, dignified though they may be, are not thinking with the Church. And so closes the circle of his Kafkaesque world.

Of course it is true that *ad hominem* attacks do not count as arguments. It is also true that if doctrines or ideologies cause people to torture and kill then it is our duty to criticize them. Naturally, this must apply to our own ideas as well. Ideas, good, bad, or neutral flow from real human minds and are concretely expressed in people's lives, in their behavior and relationships with their fellow human beings. But here thinkers need to proceed with caution. For many people, religion is more than logical argument, ideas, or beliefs. In some cases it is none of these things, even though rituals and such may point that way. Religion for many in this world is a way of life that defines them as individuals and members of a community.

Religion is self-realization, ritual, habit—their very being—that may rest upon some belief system or historical events of which they may not be aware. Our duty to criticize harmful doctrines—open to criticism when judged by the suffering they cause—becomes educational; such doctrines result in violent behavior, and offer alternative readings of sacred documents, give people a choice they may not have previously had. *The goal is to educate people, not to abuse or mock their beliefs.* Gandhi observed that you can't change a man's mind by cutting off his head. Without making these subtle but necessary distinctions, an attack on someone's religious beliefs will surely wound the dignity of the "another."

During its centuries of political, intellectual, cultural, and social power, the Church has shown itself all too ready to cross the line between abstract critiques of ideas and physical violence: the slaughter of Muslims, the persecution and burning of heretics, Jews, witches, and other non-European peoples. Christ said to love one's neighbor and love your enemy. Medieval theologians, as if they had read those sections in *Memory and Reconciliation* about sin, claimed that love of neighbor was an individual thing; the love of your enemy was of an individual, personal enemy. *But did not apply to the social enemy.* And so are Christians released from the nearly impossible task of "loving our enemy." Followers of Christ are free to hate the social enemy, to go on crusade, slaughter Muslims (and Jews), execute heretics as was recommended by St. Thomas Aquinas, and burn women, without worrying that they violated the teachings of Christ, *if the Jew Yeshua really did teach nonviolence.*

Like Christ, the Church bears the sins of its children. Like Christ, its children's sins are wounds to its holy body. *But it does not bear responsibility.* Let one hunt for this creature here on earth. Let one fix the "p." It can be none other than the concrete authoritarian leadership (patriarchy) of the Church comprised of real flesh and blood popes, cardinals, and bishops, past and present. Thus do they absolve themselves of responsibility. They absolve themselves and their predecessors of responsibility as well. They absolve their own "wicked" dogmas with the ploy of "deeper theological reflection." Yet it is from such "truths," later discussed in this book, they derived the right, in fact the duty, to condemn, to persecute, to burn, to slaughter.

And they still abuse children. *It is the burden of the Church to explain why, even after the apology, women still feel estranged and suppressed, and the male clergy continues to commit sex crimes.*

In this chapter, we highlighted that the Church claims to have a monopoly on the "truth" based upon its interpretation of scripture. Therefore, it forbids the priesthood of women and married priests. We challenge this claim with a discussion of the uncertainty of any interpretation.

Chapter 3

Portrait of the Saint as a Young Philosopher

John Paul II (and Cardinal Ratzinger) held the view that the modern secular world was close to a moral abyss (the Culture of Death) and opposed liberal interpretations of Vatican II. In this chapter, we identify their views on women and sex arise from these assumptions. We trace these origins to John Paul's studies and teachings in philosophy.

Before he became pope, Karol Wojtyla was a philosopher and professor of philosophy at the Catholic University of Lublin from 1954 to 1958. His supporters take great pains to caution that once he became pope, the philosopher in him gave way to the Pope, who thinks and speaks in the medium of the Magesterium of the Church in its historical development.[1]

Nevertheless, his philosophy does influence his thinking in the Church (how could it not?), especially in this area for which he is most famous: ethics and the emphasis upon human dignity, his critique of modernity and its so-called culture of death, and most important for what follows here, his assertion of the Truth which is Christ. Without the Truth of Christ, he maintained, there can be no freedom, no personhood, and no human dignity—which is the so-called anthropological error of modernity that lead to all the disasters of the twentieth century and today's culture of death.

Dualism haunted his philosophical world view. The Church is a moral society divinely inspired, the only one. Opposing it is the evil secular world poised precariously

---

[1] Rocco Buttiglione, *Karol Wojtyla: The Thought of the Man Who Became Pope John Paul II*, trans. Paolo Guietti and Francesca Murphy, (Grand Rapids, 1997), p. 306.

on the edge of a moral chasm. It could be said that this moral dualism is "the dominant message of John Paul's pontificate."[2] The Church must be defended at all costs.

When the Second Vatican Council opened its windows to the modern world, the fresh winds of change brought in dangers as well as possibilities of renewal. According to conservatives, indifferentism masquerading as tolerance, relativism as freedom, utility as ethics invaded the Church like airborne germs. For conservatives, *aggiornamento* (up-dating) was a fifth column in the service of secularism.

Karol Wojtyla's philosophical project had been to take modern philosophical methods, especially the phenomenological method of Edmund Husserl (that studied how intentional objects were meaningfully constituted by consciousness), and combine them with pre-modern traditions, especially the recovery of ontology, the science of Being, as taught by St. Thomas Aquinas. The goal was to reintroduce the vertical dimension into the definition of the human person—in short and somewhat crudely, resurrect metaphysics after its crucifixion at the hands of Hume, Kant, Feuerbach, Marx, Darwin, Nietzsche, and their twentieth century heirs, the so-called New Atheists (who react more gleefully to God's demise than the old).

The future Pope claimed that modern subjectivism takes consciousness as absolute and it is therefore no longer an aspect of the larger category, the "person." In his major work, *The Acting Person* (Polish edition 1969), he wrote that in such circumstances values lose their status of being and cease to be anything real, remaining moments of consciousness (p. 58). Later, in audiences given as Pope from September of 1979 to November of 1984 (*The Theology of the Body*), John Paul described what he believed to be the sexual consequences of ignoring the "person" as created in the image of God. The two, real persons and real values, go together. It is the vertical dimension that like Jacob's ladder restores the reality of values as well as the being of the person. The source of human dignity is that people are created in the image of God.

Karol Wojtyla's philosophical stairway to heaven becomes John Paul's ladder of dialogue. Sincere dialogue respects the other as a person, a "someone," rather than a "something" (*The Acting Person*, p. 74). Only under these conditions may the Church propose rather than impose Christ. Past attempts to "impose" Christ are what led to the apology of 2000. The seeds of the Pope's apology are there in the philosopher's "person."

The John Paul history of Western philosophy goes something like this: Modern philosophy has been nothing less than a disaster for human beings. The scientific revolution of the sixteenth and seventeenth centuries had overthrown the physical universe of Aristotle and Aquinas, but it also narrowed the scope of reality, reducing the real to what could be measured, observed, and established through repeatable experiments. At last, science no longer spoke the language of final causes, essences, and Being. Left out in the cold, philosophy turned to subjectivity as its proper subject.

Descartes played the villain in this modern drama. Descartes, according to Karol Wojtyla, replaced the old scholastic category of Being by the subject—*cogito ergo sum*—as

---

[2] Quoted in Matthew Fox, *The Pope's War: Why Ratzinger's Secret Crusade Has Imperiled the Church and How It Can Be Saved.* (New York, 2011), p. 136.

the ground of truth. Even the clear and distinct ideas of mathematics, by which so-called objectivity is constructed, are found in the mind. At least that is where Descartes found them. But he required God to guarantee their truth. However, he also discovered a bonus. With the concept of infinity, Descartes found he could prove the existence of God, in a sense resurrecting the old ontological proof of St. Anselm.

But his own method betrayed him. As science matured, providing natural explanations for what was once supernatural, God became superfluous, a hypothesis, no longer needed to explain physical nature and, perhaps someday, the nature of human beings. Thus, modern philosophy became subjectivism, which, according to John Paul in *Fides et ratio,* rejects any truth that transcends human subjectivity (paragraph 5). Modern philosophy's concentration on human knowing abandons questions of the soul, Being, and God.[3]

Disaster followed. Obsessed with subjectivity or inwardness, a widespread skepticism seized power in the republic of philosophy. Both philosopher and pope (ironically by making this distinction, his followers introduce a personal dualism into their hero. Or perhaps it is two natures?) agreed that truth as subjectivism results in the rule of a relativism that hides beneath the sheep's clothing of tolerance. All positions are equally valid when one seeks truth in "subjective" issues such as of the meaning of life or personal existence, values or religious preference (*Fides et ratio,* paragraph 5). Truth becomes partial and provisional.

What remains, John Paul lamented, is the primacy of power, from which follows totalitarianism. But how does totalitarianism flow from relativistic epistemology? One would think it would be the opposite. Totalitarianism knows the Truth absolutely, even if that truth is absolute power.

Meanwhile, scientific truths are reductive; measurement has conquered the physical world including humans themselves. For, when reduced to an object *of* some subject, the "other" becomes an object *for* that subject, in short, a means to that subject's end.

The audiences that comprised *The Theology of the Body* explored the human relational results of such reduction, the relationship between man and woman. Intellect and free will define the image of God in human beings. Love, as God loves, is the sincere giving of self which requires an act of free will (subjectivity), meaning to rise above our physical, call it instinctual, nature, what is physically objective and therefore the proper subject of the science of biology. Adam and Eve, the Pope taught—and here one senses

---

[3] Making mathematics (and logic, and morality, and everything else) dependent upon God's arbitrary decrees is actually a step towards dropping God altogether (Kolakowski, *Religion If There Is No God,* p. 21). God is not the only game in town. Husserl began by attempting to "ground" logic, which led him to study the meaningful constitution of objects in consciousness. Philosophers through the ages have attempted to construct a rational morality that requires no divine origin or supervision. If the good (or logic) comes from some divine arbitrary whim, how do we know it is really (objectively) the good (or logic)? Einstein called scientific concepts "free creations of the human mind." To be fair, many mathematicians have felt divinely inspired. Some even believed that "the set of all sets" might be God Himself. See Loren Graham and Jean-Michel Kantor, *Naming Infinity: A True Story of Religious Mysticism and Mathematical Creativity,* (Cambridge, MA, 2009).

the philosopher whispering like a prompter off stage—possessed this grace and justice subsequently lost to original sin (p. 99).

Instead of self-donation, sex becomes the *use* of the other to gratify selfish desires or drives. The result is depersonalization in which the original person (God's image) becomes a mere object for the other. Sex is no longer a communion of persons, it is coercion of the body (like animals) and a loss of interior freedom (p. 127). All sorts of modern evils arise: abortion, birth control, homosexuality, in short, the whole culture of death.

Such is modernity. It is a moral abyss, the gravedigger of the sacred world.

Such assertions will be explored later in this book. But here it should be noted that beneath the philosopher's finely reasoned anthropology, like some ancient temple buried under layers of geological sediment, rests the creation stories in Genesis. And here too, the philosopher-pope is forced to call upon hermeneutics in order to pan out the theological "truths" from the historic mud. Yet somehow, speaking about the modern predicament, critical analyses must include the historical with the theological. The pope-philosopher ("...in two natures which undergo no confusion, no change, no division, no separation...") pronounces his magic words and like gold extracted from an alchemical furnace the faithful get:

> The state of sin is part of "historical man"...therefore, naturally, also of modern man. That state, however—the "historical" state—plunges its roots, in every man without exception, in his own theological "prehistory," which is the state of original innocence (p. 32).

But the Heisenberg Uncertainty Principle of Biblical Hermeneutics is not so easily ignored. What happens to all this finely constructed "theological prehistory" if the quaint garden myth is nothing more (or less) prosaic than a reflection of the transition of human beings from a life of hunters and gathers to the life of the agriculturalist? A new life of toil, of labor, the creation of a social hierarchy that begins with the family in which the female bows to the will of the male, what if all this and more turns out simply to be the "original sin" of civilization?

One of the joys of supernatural analytical philosophy is that it can ignore historical context and the flowing contingency of Heraclites' river. All it requires is a premise that does not move. Systematic theology is like this. It builds upon what it accepts to be a firm foundation. From here it can reach the heavens. Yet, the vertical dimension meant to free practical theological authority (in order to pronounce on such things as family and social relations), so laboriously built by philosophical hermeneutics, may collapse like the tower of Babel, in this case brought down by the earth's gravity after its foundations have been undermined by archaeology.

Seen from the dizzying heights of the vertical dimension, modern secular politics understands the human being as just another thing in the world, to be manipulated like any*thing* else and utilized for ends that are other than their own. Totalitarianism is a kind of social macro-subjectivity.[4] And once more, the historical complexity of the Nazis and Soviet Communists is forced—"rooted"—into a theological explanation. But this explanation for all its complex language, its purported depth and subtlety, comes back in the end of a rather simple Sunday school lesson: The poor sinful children have forgotten God... And the Church.

Wojtyla sensed in Husserl's Phenomenology a method of return to the objects themselves. The goal was, as Husserl had written in *Ideas* (1913), to give expression to distinctions directly given to one in intuition, exactly as they present themselves without presuppositions based upon hypotheses or interpretations (p. 72). Husserl was interested in the relation between thinking and the things thought about. He believed that the separate sciences were in trouble in that they lacked essential foundations, especially due to the fact that all use logic. But what grounds logic, Husserl asked? Could it be assumed that the science of psychology accounts for fundamental laws of reasoning?

Husserl decided that these laws cannot be grounded in psychology as Mill and others held, because psychology uses those very laws to analyze its proper investigations—the argument becomes circular (as he wrote earlier in *Logical Investigations*, 1901, p. 95). Psychology *describes* mental activity empirically, yet logic actually prescribes how one *ought* to think if one is going to think logically. Also, the effect of such reductionism has been to treat the entire human being as just another *thing* in nature, which is the theme that threads its way through the thought of both philosopher Wojtyla and Pope John Paul.

Therefore, Husserl decided to "bracket" (*epokhe* in Greek, abstention) all prejudices about the world and examine how things were constituted in consciousness, that is, what is given in pure intuition. In so doing, he could, he believed, uncover the essential structure of pure consciousness itself.

The plot of his novel goes like this. Consciousness is always consciousness of something, it is intentional. Examination of intentional objects revealed the nature of consciousness in its purity, which according to Husserl was *transcendental consciousness*. "Consciousness, considered in its 'purity,' must be reckoned as a *self-contained system of Being*, as a system of *Absolute Being*..." he wrote in *Ideas* (p. 139). Naturally, such a thing could be accused of reviving a new kind of super-Platonism, better Neoplatonism. But Husserl understood the transcendental a priori, like Kant, as the necessary preconditions for experience. For Husserl, it is a kind of intuition of the essence of a thing. Things manifest in different perspectives and different appearances in the flow of time, yet their

---

[4]Buttiglioni, p. 287. But is not a "macro-subjectivity" another term for a god? The state becomes god-on-earth, the New Idol in Nietzsche's language. As we say here, an absolute. The State incarnates a supernatural agent as does the Church. Supernatural agents establish laws and social solidarity far better than contingent and frail human "social contracts." See Scott Atran, *In Gods We Trust: The Evolutionary Landscape of Religion*, especially the Conclusion: Why Religion Seems Here to Stay.

identities are grasped by consciousness. However, this does not imply that transcendental consciousness exists in some other world. In fact, Husserl went beyond the old subject/object dualism. The world has no meaning apart from consciousness, but consciousness in its intentionality has no meaning apart from the world. They are one.

If one were looking for a religion that compliments Phenomenology, the best candidate would be Vedanta, such as in the Upanishads of ancient Hinduism. Absolute consciousness is Brahman who more or less dreams the world of forms (*maya*). Brahman manifests as the Self in human beings, the core of who human beings really are, *atman*, and not the shifting contingencies of the lived self, the *jivatman*. When human beings think, Brahman thinks, and the world manifests in its forms. Through a similar transcendental reduction, the guru shows the student that in reality the *atman is Brahman*. "You are that," says the guru, *tat tvam asi*. And yet the *atman* is not to identify with any object in the world. It is *neti, neti*, "not this, not that." The ethic, then, is to see and understand one's fellow human being as divine, as oneself, as the universe.

Wojtyla's fellow Polish philosopher, Roman Ingarden, said that Husserl's pure consciousness, after the Phenomenological reduction, began to assume a metaphysical character, which Husserl may not have intended because the relationship between consciousness and the world of objects is reciprocal.[5] According to Ingarden, however, with it "we find ourselves again at the gates of idealism."[6]

But in the eyes of Karol Wojtyla, such a thing could constitute another form of the reductionist subjectivism into which philosophy had fallen. So he would return to Aristotle and Aquinas.

Earlier, in 1901, sensing that he might be accused of returning to scholasticism (as if he somehow anticipated Wojtyla's move), Husserl warned in *Logical Investigations* that no one would accept returning to the defunct Aristotelian-Scholastic logic of the past (p. 214). But this is precisely what Wotjlya did. The essence of consciousness, he claimed, is not "intentionality" but it is characterized by action, to act—just as Aquinas traced the idea of Being back to the verb "to be," hence activity. For Aristotle and Aquinas, absolute actuality admitting of no potential would be absolute Being, which is God. The Christian could not follow the pagan Greek, however, in drawing the full consequences of such an idea: If thinking is an activity, and if the pure activity is the most perfect being, then God does not think of anything other than Himself.

Wojtyla held that in action the ego emerges and is revealed. In the language of Aristotle, the potential to do good, to be good, becomes actual in dynamic action. And, because consciousness is reflexive, the ego experiences itself as an ego, a "good person" through its emergence in action.

Karol Wojtyla was more interested in ethics. His early studies centered upon the phenomenologist Max Scheler who was opposed to the Kantian formal element of reason as the basis of ethics, that the will is free only when it lives for duty, which arises from the inner moral ought or categorical imperative and is practically realized in action.

---

[5] Roman Ingarden, *On the Motives which led Husserl to Transcendental Idealism*, (Der Haag, 1975), p. 19.
[6] Ingarden, p. 19.

Scheler, on the other hand, grounded ethics in experience. Values arise with the human response to experience, forming the content of intentional acts. Values are found in pure experience and nowhere else.

But, protested Wojtyla, the person in this way, becomes a mere subjective unity of these experiences, meaning that the entire dynamic being (Aquinas) is lost. The person remains a passive subject. But the person is an agent, an active being. Acts of such a being reveal that being's interior dimension (the spiritual) which eludes all external criteria of history. Once more true believers are able to escape history. For what can this agent be after the philosopher has gone beyond historical contingencies? The Christian soul, perhaps? Much later, the philosopher-Pope will add that the spiritual when it is manifest in the body becomes historical (*The Theology of the Body*, p. 124). The person cannot be reduced to "just another thing" in nature.

Phenomenology, then, ends up as yet another expression of subjectivism. Values and morals are reduced to social and historical relativism. But no, argued Wojtyla the Thomist, values are real features of the concrete person, actualized through ethical or unethical action. Realized in honest action, for example, the value of honesty creates an honest person.[7] Wojtyla perceived this as the essence of freedom. Thus he wrote in *The Acting Person*:

> Freedom thus manifest itself as connected with the will, with the concrete "I will," which includes, as noted, the experience of "I may but I need not." In the analysis of self-determination we reach right down to the very roots of the experience of "I will" as well as of "I may but I need not." The freedom appropriate to the human being, the person's freedom resulting from the will, exhibits itself as identical with self-determination, with the experiential, most complete, and fundamental organ of man's autonomous being (p. 115).

The reflexive expression of the good in action reveals the Truth about humans, *that there is an inherent potentiality toward the good*. With this principle in hand, bolstered by the Thomist assertion that the more complete the being of something the greater its goodness, Wojtyla returned to his critique of modernism. The good requires obedience to the Truth that human beings are persons, created in God's image (the Pope's theological prehistory), and not things to be manipulated like machinery. This is what of love neighbor means. But history as well as everyday experience shows that humans are inherently incapable of such love, not to mention other aspects of the good.

(Question: *where* outside "theological prehistory" or Paul's *interpretation* of the garden myth of Romans—that humans are fatally infused with the Hebrew *yester ha ra'*, an inclination to evil—is the *evidence* for such an *"inherent"* weakness? History? The primate brain of human evolution? And why *incapable*? Gandhi once said that the poor wretch who keeps calling herself or himself a sinner ends up becoming one. When challenged by the statement that most people cannot be Mahatmas, or saints—which would

---
[7]Kenneth L. Schmitz, *At the Center of the Human Drama: The Philosophical Anthropology of Karol Wojtyla/Pope John Paul II*, (Washington, D. C., 1993), p. 51.

probably be one Catholic response: the saints are few and their grace comes from God—Gandhi replied that such an objection was no more than spiritual laziness. Besides, prior to Augustine, the Fathers taught that individuals did possess moral agency, that autonomy and freedom were absolutely necessary if a person was to be held responsible for her or his behavior.[8]).

Human beings require help—which comes from heaven—which is grace.[9] And, of course, this grace is Christ (another interjection: Why Christ? Why not Krishna? Buddha? Muhammad? The answer must come back to historical evidence and faith in the truth of that evidence). Revealing Himself in Christ, said the Pope, God revealed at the same time the Truth about humans, that humans are flawed beings, weakened by sin, and that neither reason nor philosophy in able to embrace the totality of Truth (*Fides et ratio*, paragraph 51).

Yet the philosopher-pope for his talk about subjectivism still uses the phenomenological *epokhe*. And why is this? The answer is already known. By using (or misusing) the bracketing method, John Paul is able to banish historical contingencies, in addition to the *critical history* (bracket it), and concentrate on the so-called meaning-bestowing acts of (theological) consciousness. He is able to free "theological truths" from contingent historical facts. On the other hand, as he can claim that facts themselves are grounded in consciousness where they are already somehow meaningful, he can act as if the story in Genesis is "true" as any fact. But again, meanings change as new discoveries are made. No matter. He may well accept evolution as he will declare as Pope while exempting human beings. No primitive primate brains to blame for our faults!

There still must be some reference, no matter how tenuous, to critical history based upon such discoveries and new ways of thinking about the past. When such history serves his purpose, as this book explicates later, the Pope is quite prepared to adopt a modern historical analysis.

Secular morality is dominated by evil: abortion, contraception, feminists, homosexuality...sex, but not of the saintly kind. It is nothing new. Paul perceived the disorder of Roman sexuality as a sign of pagan's society's alienation from God.[10] In modern times the philosopher had discovered the source, the Pope would wage the war. First, he had to restore the image of the Church. Thus does our circuitous journey bring one back to the apology.

---

[8]Kyle Harper, *From Shame to Sin: The Christian Transformation of Sexual Morality in Late Antiquity*, (Cambridge, MA, 2013), p. 86.
[9]Buttiglione, pp. 363-364.
[10]Harper, *From Shame to Sin*, p. 94. Of course Paul also saw the corruption of society as a symbol of eschatology. The worse things get the closer we are to the end. Ratzinger saw the secular world posed on the edge of a moral abyss. So, what happens when we plunge into the chasm?

In this chapter, we identified John Paul II (and Cardinal Ratzinger) held the view that the modern secular world was close to a moral abyss (the Culture of Death) and opposed liberal interpretations of Vatican II. Their views on women and sex arise from these assumptions. We traced these origins to John Paul's studies and teachings in philosophy.

Chapter 4

The Apology: A Handmaiden's Tale

Philosophy is once again the handmaiden of theology. John Paul II reveals himself to be a philosophical reactionary dreaming of a return to the glory days of high Church scholasticism. What begins in the abstract realms of modern philosophy comes full circle to theological "truths" like original sin, the redemptive nature of Christ, the soul, and many more beliefs that John Paul *already accepts on faith*. Like any good scholastic, he returns by way of reason to "truths" he already knows.

In this chapter, we identify the Catholic Church patriarchs' belief that the Church is humanity's last stand against the moral disaster of dehumanization. As such, these patriarchs feel they must defend at all costs the *institution and hierarchy*, which excludes women and married priests.

Modern subjectivism may indeed be as flawed as John Paul maintained (or it may not). If we, for the sake of argument, accept his critique, the failure of the modern (or post-modernism) does not immediately lead to the truth of Christianity. Philosophy may be flawed, but not for refusing to accept the divine truth of revelation (*Fides et ratio*, paragraph 75). The totalitarian disaster that John Paul blames upon relativism and nihilism might, in fact, be due to the very opposite: it is not the content of faith but the problem of faith that attaches itself to some absolute dogma and thus refuses to consider new evidence that may contradict its "truth." Dogmas are often held in the face of all opposing evidence. Merely questioning them becomes a crime. Centuries ago, Edward Gibbon observed that knowledge was often the parent of heresy as of devotion (*Decline and Fall*, Vol. I, p. 441). The dogma that Christian revelation is definitive, leaves the Church vulnerable to new evidence. From this arises the constant need for reinterpretation as was noted earlier. But the Church cannot change. So, fairly simple ideas dissolve into a fog of deeper theological mystification. Historical context drops way like abandoned scaffolding. From the dust rises condemnations of secularism.

John Paul's critique assumes what needs to be shown.

Does relativism (whatever the word is tortured into meaning by the new scholastic-inquisitors) really come, *inevitably*, to barbarism and nihilism? Have not more people been persecuted, tortured, and killed in the name of some absolute truth? Do not unquestioned truths (to question means lack of faith), the dogmas of religion, enslave?[1] How can such truths "set you free" when they are imposed without critical examination? And if the "fullness of Truth" is only revealed at the end of time, how can one be sure that the truths one holds now will not turn out to be erroneous? Is not the statement itself absolute? Maybe the fullness of truth will ultimately show that "the fullness of Truth will be revealed at the end of time" is mistaken?

A good example is evolution. John Paul claimed to accept the theory. He cannot, of course, accept a theory of natural selection that excludes the human being as *imago Dei,* or casts doubt upon the original sin dogma. Scientific evidence may turn out to demonstrate the evolutionary or—oh, heresy!—historic contingent nature of many Church dogmas. Not a few, like the ban on women priests, may face extinction. John Paul, then, is forced to dismiss scientific objections to his faith by waving the magic wand of "scientism," asserting that scientific critiques of religious doctrines are metaphysical additions to science, not demanded by the evidence. There are realms of knowledge or existence, he protests, science is not equipped to handle. However, the history of science is more often than not a graveyard of such realms.

Absolute truth does exist, John Paul asserted. Knowing the truth binds one with a moral duty to live in the truth. Absolute truth is the revelation of God in Christ. What is asserted, however, needs to be demonstrated, and not by gaps in our present knowledge. If philosophy is coerced to accept this so-called Truth without further discussion, thinking comes to an end—that is to say; philosophy becomes theology, which is precisely what John Paul desired.

An analogous situation exists in the life sciences. If one accepts intelligent design, a great deal of research becomes superfluous. What does remain is to ask about the designer...which is God. Biology becomes theology. And science becomes mere description, cataloguing, and so forth, like some medieval bestiary. All scientific causality becomes secondary and only important as these causes point to final cause. *To admit supernatural causes is also to admit a hierarchy*. They are superior to natural causation by definition (*super*-nature). Therefore, the institution that embodies them is superior to secular institutions. In the end, it is all about power, telling people how to live their lives.

John Paul II was not a cheerleader for the modernist interpretation of Vatican II as is sometimes asserted. He was the implacable enemy of those modern winds that

---

[1] Hector Avalos says: "If there is anything "essential" about the Abrahamic religions, it is that they are still permeated by a slave mentality...God as the master of the universe.", *Fighting Words*, p. 371. There could also be a Master mentality at work within the slaves: rather than having to deal with the lack of purpose in the universe, one accepts guilt for perceived punishments that are simply random events. Implied is the idea that one has POWER over such events. We are Masters of the Universe. Thus is chance, as Nietzsche observed, robbed of its innocence.

brought fresh air into the Church. But he discovered that he could use them. Like a medieval monk with a cell phone, he adapted the cultural forms and technologies of modernity to wage war upon its intellectual foundations. The actor on the stage knows that the play is fiction, an instrument to convey ideas, emotions, or simply entertainment. The apology is one of those instruments.

Cardinal Ratzinger, our future Pope Benedict XVI, recognized the problem. Christianity's claim to truth, he wrote in 2003, (*Truth and Tolerance*, p. 226), is not of the same order as the standard of certainty posed by modern science. Its verification is quite different. Rather than mere experiment and observation to test or falsify hypotheses, Christian truth is demonstrated by pledging one's life—the saints guarantee the truth of Christianity.

Adopting this criterion of verification, one might be able to argue for the truth of Nazism or Marxism. Millions willingly gave their lives for Nazi Germany and the Soviet Union. War memorials pay tribute to the martyrs. People die for dictators too, just as crusaders died for Christ and his vicar on earth, the pope.

The desperation of Ratzinger's statement illustrates the problem faced by a Church that claims to possess unchanging and infallible truth. In a time when everything about Christianity is open to question—the historical Jesus, "lost Christianities," the existence of female apostles such as Mary of Magdala, the office of female priests, the contingent emergence of the Catholic Church itself, and so much more—the hierarchy responds by inventing new rules of evidence, which prove its modernity, and which it calls "historical hermeneutics." To these it adds metaphysical assertions such as the Spirit unites the Church past, present and future. Unconsciously (or perhaps quite knowingly), Ratzinger falls back upon the ultimately arbitrary distinction between divine speech and human speech, or between the Jesus of history and the Christ of faith. Thus does the rearguard of Catholic reaction join the vanguard of the Protestant revolutionaries, shoulder to shoulder with the likes of Protestant theologians like Rudolf Bultmann. But this takes one nowhere. Detached from historical evidence, all such assertions are in the end gratuitous. And borrowing an old warning issued by Father John P. Meier in his book *A Marginal Jew: Rethinking the Historical Jesus,* (Vol. I, 1991, p. 254); "what is gratuitously asserted may be gratuitously denied."

Yet such things are not simply asserted. They are enforced by a quite powerful institution whose leaders believe that the Church is the last stand of humanity against moral disaster. To paraphrase Luther, the Church is a mighty fortress. In war, discipline is everything. There can be no surrender of territory—to the poor of Liberation theology, to women of feminist theology, to homosexuals, to abortion, contraception. Abusing priests must be hidden, abused children ignored. Nothing may be allowed to compromise the moral authority of the Church.

The theological significance of Christ as the only means to redemption is therefore vitally important to John Paul's approach to the apology. In 2000, he referred to Jesus as God's sacrificial offering through which Christians could be forgiven for these past transgressions.

"*God so loved the world that he gave his only Son.*" Christ scourged, crowned with thorns, carrying the cross and, finally, crucified. Christ took upon himself the burden of the sins of all people.

The Mother Church, too, carries the cross. She too is tortured like Christ by the sins of her erring children. The Church cannot err, and the Pope is infallible in matters of faith (declared July 18, 1870 by the First Vatican Council). The spotless Mother Church bears the burden of sin, but the burden does not leave any stains. How is such a theory justified? St. Augustine, today called "Neo-Augustinianism," but really the same old story.

Within the public act of repentance that Sunday in March beats the heart of the North African Saint pumping Neoplatonic blood into the Church.

In his struggle against the Donatists who actually did hope for a visible Church of the pure elite, St Augustine enlisted arguments that ultimately arise from Platonic dualism. Plato taught that the world of the senses, changeable and contingent, is but a shadow world, filled with images of the true, perfect, and unchangeable forms. Forms or ideas (*eidos*) exist in a transcendental, spiritual world, like abstract mathematical formulas, but the flesh and blood mathematician can only imperfectly demonstrate them in the world of matter given to one through the senses. A chalk drawing of a right angled triangle illustrates the Pythagorean Theorem, but not the perfection the ideal theory demands. Drawn into a world where it can easily be erased, the Pythagorean triangle exists perfect and eternal as an abstraction in a world that no eraser can touch. Augustine saw this dualism in the very nature of the Church, its curia, and its sacraments.

There are two Cities, said the North African bishop, the City of Man and the City of God, or, one might say the Platonic duality of the sensate contingent world and the transcendent world of God. The visible, this-worldly Church, like the contingent chalk drawing of the Pythagorean triangle, is a reflection of the perfect invisible Church, which is the abstract theorem itself. The Church is on a pilgrimage in this *imperfect* world and has in *her* midst (Augustine uses the feminine pronoun signifying the Church as the Bride of Christ) some who, while participating in the sacraments in this world will not participate in "the eternal destiny of the saints." (*The City of God*, p.45).

The objective sacraments, however, are like mathematical equations; their operation and truth do not depend upon the moral character of the mathematician but upon the logical operation of the equation. Again, the Pythagorean Theorem holds for all right-angled triangles no matter how crudely they are constructed or who does the drawing, saints or devils. The theorem is a concrete instance of a mathematical idea the correctness of which is judged by the sheer objective operation of the rules of geometry. So too the sacraments. Their validity, their imparting of grace, is dependent solely upon their objective operation (*ex opere operato*), their performance alone, *not the moral character* of the priest. Ritual purity supersedes moral.

The Church in Rome contains both the fallen and the saved, good and evil. Imperfect itself, it is on pilgrimage in a corrupted world. It is bound to commit sins that require forgiveness. Yet, it is difficult, if not impossible, to separate the reprobate from the godly. As Augustine wrote: "many reprobates are mingled with the Church with the good…and in this world, as in a sea, both kinds swim without separation, enclosed in nets until the shore is reached." (*The City of God*, p. 831). This sort of metaphysical dualism justifies John Paul's assertion that all should not be blamed for the crimes of the few. The Mother Church is without stain.

There are no shortage of Neo-Augustinian defenders in the Church.[2] The writers of this book are not among them. The North African's inheritance has proved disastrous. He left the Church with an almost institutional absolutism. Grace descends from God and is embodied in the Church, in its sacraments, later in the institution itself. Adding Aristotle in the thirteenth century, the essence of grace, though still abstract, now exists *within* the physical manifestation, within popes, bishops and priests. As exposed later, abusing priests told children they were having sex with God.

The transcendent Church on High cannot err. Here the Will of God is intelligible and unchangeable Law says the Saint in *The City of God*, (p. 381). The visible, pilgrim Church, its pure waters mingled with earthly sludge, can and does commit sins. Acts of repentance conducted in the visible Church for the sins committed by a mixed population are to be expected. Going public with such acts, the fanfare and publicity connected with such apologia indicate a new consciousness of image, perhaps a more timely sensitivity to public relations on behalf of the Church.

But alas, many abuses derive not only from corrupt Catholic fish swimming in the same net. Intolerance derives from the essence of the Church itself, the Law on High. For even when supernatural agents speak through the mouths of *men*, be they popes, cardinals or saints, the words come out in translation. *Translator traitor*. Not only texts, but people reading the texts. And even if supernatural agents spoke for themselves in this world, humans could only communicate their understanding through evolved language. Who knows if there really are ears behind ears? The Church? What it has read confirms what its saints have heard, and what its saints have heard confirms what the Church has read. QED.

If Truth is founded in God who established the Catholic Church through Christ, power over all people is bestowed naturally. Believers are all slaves. The Pope as the Vicar of Christ may be called the sovereign of Truth, the KING OF REALITY. Such an assertion necessitates an authoritarian organizational structure, and absolute obedience.

Ironically, Pope John Paul II's image restoration rhetoric flows from modern methods, which derive from the morally corrupt world of public relations and advertising (turning everything including people into commodities) which he rejects. It cannot be ruled out that the method did not in the end betray him. The media, not God, created the saint. John Paul Superstar.

Benoit's (1995) theory of image restoration, a method we employ in our critical analysis, was developed through a synthesis of several previous theoretical discussions of restoration of one's image through communication. When a person is verbally attacked, that person can respond in a variety of ways. The theory of image restoration

---

[2]Faggioli, *Vatican II: The Battle for Meaning*, pp. 69–72.

assumes accused individuals have several possible response options: denial, evasion of responsibility, reducing the offensiveness of an act, corrective action, or mortification. Several of these general strategies can be enacted in a number of ways.[3]

Of particular interest to this critical analysis is previous criticism of religious apologia. It can be argued that Jesus himself, that is, the literary figure named Jesus, used certain image restoration strategies in response to a variety of attacks recorded in the Gospel according to John.[4] Jesus employed denial and transcendence as his two primary strategies in response to a number of attacks. In two instances Jesus attacked his accusers in response to charges he committed blasphemy. Particularly relevant to Pope John Paul II's image restoration is the apparent fact that Jesus' strategies could be deemed ineffective because he was crucified. However, it can also be argued that his discourse functioned primarily for a broader, historic audience, and that it succeeded in answering potential questions that could have left his ministry "stillborn."[5]

Jesus (as repeated this over and over in this book) was an ancient Jew, and his chroniclers may or may not have been. They wrote in *koine* Greek. In the sense of the ancient cosmos, the transcendent was a *natural experience*, that is, it was indeed exceptional and mysterious, perhaps even "the wholly other," but it was acceptable as an explanation. The world was still "enchanted," as in Charles Taylor's clever phrase. The self was still open to demons, spirits, magical forces—gods.[6]

Simple denial and attempts to reduce offensiveness of an act by employing transcendence or by attacking one's accusers could be considered quite effective for that time. In most ages, however, denial occurs when the accused simply denies that they have committed an undesirable action. Utilizing transcendence entails judging a deed in a different context, adopting a paradigm that assumes a differing set of criteria for evaluating the offensiveness of an act. The accused directs our attention to other, allegedly higher values, to justify the behavior in question. In a certain sense, the model for Christian image restoration already exists in scripture. It certainly seems logical that transcendence can be a powerful defense for an institution that must defend theological doctrines. But does it apply to our disenchanted world? In the ancient enchanted world, in which the self is not "buffered" against supernatural powers, such a strategy becomes almost a reflex action in religious discourse. It probably still is. But, again, does it really work today?

The third strategy is reducing the offensiveness of an act by attacking one's accusers. In this approach, the accused attacks the legitimacy of the source's accusations. This could probably be identified as a reflex action in any age. But is it what one would expect from the world's moral paragon?

---

[3] See W. L. Benoit, *Accounts, Excuses, and Apologies: A Theory of Image Restoration Discourse*, (Albany, N. Y., 1995).
[4] See J. R. Blaney and W. L. Benoit, "The Persuasive Defense of Jesus in the Gospel According to John, *Journal of Religion and Communication*, 20, pp. 25-30.
[5] Blaney and Benoit, p. 30.
[6] Charles Taylor, *A Secular Age*, (Cambridge, MA, 2007), p. 135. In Acts 14:12 The people of Lystra mistake Paul and Barnabas for Zeus and Hermes. The gods walked among men and did wondrous things. Also see Robin Lane Fox, *Pagans and Christians*, (New York, 1987).

Religious *apologia* concerns matters of God and the soul. In some cases it is fundamentally different from such rhetoric of celebrities, corporations, or political figures, upon whom much previous image restoration research has focused. Corrective action becomes problematic. Although the apology may have been an astute public relations effort, the pope's promises of corrective action ring hollow when the doctrines of the Catholic Church that justify these transgressions remain. There is a paradox that is evident in the pontiff's apology that is also a central obstacle faced by the Catholic Church at the dawn of the new millennium: The church seeks to appear socially tolerant and accepting while it remains theologically conservative and exclusivist: *extra eccelisiam nulla salus*. The tension between these goals is an important challenge for the future of the Catholic Church. There is growing difference between Roman Catholic beliefs proclaimed by the Vatican and the beliefs of Catholics.

During his inauguration mass in October of 1978, Pope John Paul II quoted the words of Christ to his disciples: *Be not afraid!*[7] The modern world, he said, was afraid of itself and its future. The outcome of the modernist project, which emphasized the autonomy of the human species, was in fact the opposite of its promise. Human autonomy led to loneliness, uncertainty, soulless hedonism, and doubt. The reduction of people to things, manipulated according to the calculations of power, enslaved human beings in totalitarian systems worse than the Pharaoh's Hebrew slaves in Egypt. Hunan dignity lost all meaning. The "culture of death" embodies the surrender of human freedom and the destruction of the inherent value of the human person.

Deep within the "modern soul," said John Paul that October, was the fear that besides lacking significance human life in general might be annihilated in the blazing light of a nuclear blast. (From Adam to Atom?) Fear of the future, the Pope proclaimed, was the price for rejecting Christ.

Is it so? He spoke these words in 1978. The Cold War would continue for roughly another decade. One might count it a miracle that the world in those years did not actually end in the searing light of nuclear sunset. The fact is that it did not. Even if the modern world today is characterized by fear, say the threat of nuclear terrorism—and the proposition has yet to established—does the source of such fear, in 1978 and at the dawn of the third millennium, reside in the lack of belief in Christ? Has fear really emerged, like the nightmare of reason, from a skeptical attitude, which might decide on the tentative nature of many truths, even if they belong to Scripture and Church dogma? And most especially when such truths are metaphysical?

If the Church responds with revelation, the voice of God heard from the apostles and their successors, the response could be the question posed by old garrulous Hans Luther to his son Martin, who said he heard the voice of God calling him into the monastery: How do you know the voice you heard was not that of the devil? Belief that throws

---

[7]Quoted by Weigel in *Witness to Hope*, p. 262.

contrary evidence out of court before it has the opportunity to give testimony breeds the very intolerance and oppression the Church wishes to purge.

And so women are still refused the priesthood; the very word "she" is not permitted at the high altar. Some very sick individuals are given shelter so as not to bring disdain upon the holy institution, although abused children commit suicide.

Perhaps, taking a cue from Husserl (and Buddha), one needs to bracket all beliefs before one can see the world—and our fellow human beings—clearly. Those who should be feared today are religious fanatics, claiming absolute "truth," armed with weapons provided them by a scientific outlook they reject.

In sum, in this chapter, we identified the Catholic Church patriarchs' belief that the Church is humanity's last stand against the moral disaster of dehumanization. As such, these patriarchs feel they must defend at all costs the *institution and hierarchy*, which excludes women and married priests.

PART II
In Persona Christi: Misogyny

Blessed art thou among women...

Luke 1:42

Chapter 5
Defective Men

In "Part II: In Persona Christi: Misogyny" we explore the dogma that causes discrimination against women through exclusion of female and married clerics. We begin this section with Chapter 5, "Defective Men," in which we explore ancient and medieval biological understanding of women, which led Catholic Church patriarchs in the Middle Ages to label women as defective men (Aquinas). We show how such biological determinism lingered in the thought of the so-called feminist John Paul II and his successor Pope Benedict.

Those persons who achieve notoriety in life, either fame or infamy, must have evidenced in their early years, some small predictive traits, meaningful only in hindsight. It appears offensive that the great should have come out of nothing, that such lovely flowers should have sprouted from common ground. Fate abhors a vacuum. Admirers are ever ready and willing to fill the void with legends, stories passed down through the ages that seem to exist without point of origin. The portrait of the hero as a young person cannot be faceless, nor can it be the portrait of Everyman.

Thomas Aquinas was born in 1226, the seventh son of Count Landulf of Aquino in the Apennines. Legend has it that this rather large, quiet boy showed early signs of theological inquiry: "What is God?" he once burst out. The Count, bowing to the inevitable, decided that Thomas should become the Abbot of the great Benedictine Abbey, Monte Cassino. But this was not to be.

Instead, Thomas joined the newly formed Begging Friars, the Dominicans. Combining poverty and missionary zeal against heretics, the Dominicans were a far cry from the wealth and honor of Monte Cassino, whose Abbot was really another feudal lord, keeping with the status of the Aquinas clan. Thomas, however, refused and proceeded to Paris.

Two of his brothers, the story goes, kidnapped him on the road—high comedy indeed, the abduction of a begging monk. They brought him home and locked him in a castle cell. Left alone in the isolation of a quiet room would appear to be more of a blessing than imprisonment, especially to our future theologian. Perhaps realizing their miscalculation and desperate to bring him back to his aristocratic senses, his brothers introduced a beautiful courtesan into his room. The idea, no doubt, was to tempt him back into the world by means of earthly pleasure. Admirers of Aquinas often refer to this episode as a "base temptation," by which they apparently wish to justify Thomas' next recorded outburst.[1]

A less-than-nimble Thomas sprang from his desk, seized a flaming brand from the fire, and threatened Mistress Temptation like a crusader brandishing a sword. The woman screamed and fled. He followed her to the door, like an avenging angel, flaming sword in hand, slammed the door shut and burned a huge cross into the wood. After this, he returned to his philosopher's saddle and spent the remaining years of his life battling other adversaries of the Church with the sharp sword of his intellect. What became of the woman legend does not say. Like the tragic woman of Bethlehem, her name is not even known.

And so it was for many women in the Catholic Church. Either they are virginal saints, clones of the Virgin Mary, or they are unnamed temptresses, which make up the majority by far, weak and dangerous at once, the true daughters of Eve. Again, the Hebrew scriptures reinforced such attitudes. In this case, the "old law" had it right.

Women have been barred from positions of authority, the doors of power closed firmly and sealed with the sign of the cross. They must pray with their heads covered, says Paul in I Corinthians 11:5, for a man in the image of God and reflecting that glory has no need to cover his head. A woman, made from man, reflects only the glory of man like second-hand clothes. Later we hear that in Church demons leap like stinging wasps from the nests of long female hair.

If there ever was a subject that lent itself to the apology's historical argument—the sinful children acted in the spirit of the times—it is misogyny. In fact, the Church's views on women were partially determined by the erroneous science of the day and how easily that science could be made to agree with scripture.

Our own Thomas Aquinas, now older and firmly set in his life's work, was perfectly prepared to accept the pagan philosopher Aristotle when it came to the female sex. In *On Generation,* Aristotle explained the mechanics of reproduction: the male, he wrote, is the active agent in the process, impressing the rational form of the human being on the unformed, material base which was the unformed matter provided by the female. The most perfect form of the human being is male. Coming from the father, semen is like the sculptor's instrument chiseling away at the passively resisting matter of the mother, with the goal (the *telos*) being the ideal form of the man. The male semen conveys the *spiritus,* the source of movement, the source of the reason, of the soul, of the divine. *The female, as female, is passive, and the male, as male, is active, and the principle of*

---

[1] G. K. Chesterton, *Saint Thomas Aquinas: "The Dumb Ox,"* (New York, 1956), pp. 60–65.

movement comes from him (Book I, 21). Activity is the nature of life, it is more real. The goal of every human embryo is to be male.

Women never reach that goal. A defect is the cause. Sometimes this defect is in the active principle, sometimes in the material receptor, or sometimes external. Therefore the female is a "misbegotten male" (Book II, 3 and quoted by Aquinas in *Summa Theologica*, Part I, Question 92, Article 1).[2]

Aristotle was giving "scientific" voice to an old idea. In Aeschylus' play *Eumenides* (458 B.C.) Apollo says:

> The male—who mounts—begets. The female, a stranger, Guards a stranger's child if no god bring it harm.[3]

The woman is therefore a passive receptacle, she receives and nurtures (guards) the male's seed. The image comes from agriculture. The sky god seeds mother earth as the human "sows" the crops. The word sowing is still a metaphor for sexual intercourse.

Yet women take heart. Things are not as bleak as that, at least for Aquinas. In reference to human nature in general, says one of the Church's greatest, if not *the* greatest, philosophers, women are not misbegotten but fulfill nature's intention (thus God's intention) in the work of reproduction. As God is the principle of the whole universe, man as the likeness of God is the principle of the whole human race (Article 2). But man required a "helper" in the task of generation, which is how Aquinas interprets Genesis 2:18: "I will make a fitting helper for him." The "helper" is meant to be for the sole purpose of reproduction (apparently Aquinas has intimate knowledge of God's intentions as reported by the J writer). But only reproduction? Of course, answers Aquinas, in all other things, man can be more efficiently helped by another man (Article 7). Other than a reproductive mechanism, a woman is practically useless.

From the perspective of saints she is an absolute hindrance. Poor St. Jerome, menaced by wicked dancing girls, already knew that women were insatiable creatures, filled with numberless wants. A woman will complain all night: the neighbor lady is better dressed than me! Why did you ogle her? Why were you talking to the maid? What did you

---

[2]In fact, one might say the opposite is the case. Asexual reproduction, requiring an all-female population, seems to make more evolutionary sense than sexual reproduction. Since *every* individual could produce offspring rather than half the population, a sexually reproducing population would be swamped by an asexual one. Besides, in terms of survival, sex consumes a great deal of energy (obviously) and is inefficient for many other reasons. Males are fundamentally useless if not a recipe for evolutionary disaster; the Y chromosome can be called a mutation, "a failed female." So why sex? One answer is a corollary of the Red Queen hypothesis: with the sexual shuffling of two sets of genes into billions of combinations—the sexually produced animal is not a clone of its mother but carries a combinations of genes from father and mother—the offspring have a better chance of fighting off parasites, diseases and predators. Otherwise in asexual reproduction, while hosts do experience evolutionary change (a mutation in the clone is passed on to her daughters thus creating different strains in a given population) a successful parasite decimates a given population of clones. But then without hosts, the parasite numbers plunge. Success is self-defeating. Another strain from the same population gets the evolutionary edge. Yet some parasites adapt to it and the race that goes nowhere continues. Like the Red Queen from *Through the Looking Glass*, it takes all the running you can do to stay in one place (see Carl Zimmer, *Evolution: The Triumph of An Idea*, 2001, Chapter Ten).
[3]Quoted in Sarah B. Pomeroy, *Goddesses, Whores, Wives, and Slaves: Women in Classical Antiquity*, (New York, 1975), p. 65.

bring for me today? Nagging wives and dancing girls tried the patience of the greatest of saints.[4]

Aquinas also knows why Eve was created from Adam's rib. Had she come from his head, like Athena from the head of Zeus, she might wish to be the socially dominant sex. Had she come from his feet, she would be subject to Adam like a contemptible slave. Therefore, she comes from his side. And Aquinas had discovered yet another bonus. The image carries a sacramental value, for from the side of Christ "sleeping on the Cross" flowed the sacraments, blood and water, on which the Church is founded (Article 3). And of course the angle of the rib, already shown, denotes female inferiority.

Aquinas was not alone in his opinion on the usefulness of women. Centuries earlier, Augustine had decided:

> Or if it was not for help in producing children that a wife was made for the man, then what other help was she made for? If it was to till the earth together with him, there was as yet no hard toil to need such assistance; and if there had been a need a male would have made a better help. The same can be said about companionship, should he grow tired of solitude. How much more agreeably, after all, for conviviality and conversation would two male friends live together on equal terms than man and wife? (*The Literal Meaning of Genesis*, Book IX, 5.9).

The patriarchal and patrilineal outlook that has dominated Western society is inseparable from Christianity. It is something of a given, an almost unconscious set of social values for navigating the world. The main value of the woman is reproduction, and even this value is acknowledged grudgingly. They are failed men, lacking the same fullness of humanity, hence actuality, as the male. Like Pandora, they introduce the potential for disorder and chaos into the world. According to Aristotle's disciple, Theophrastus, the more education they receive, the more they become lazy, talkative busybodies.[5] Because of their weakness, they invite catastrophe, as does Eve when she succumbs to the temptation of the Evil One who is ultimate chaos.

Recall *The Malleus* Maleficarum. Weak and passive, they are susceptible to demonic penetration; they become witches who physically engage in demonic sex and other acts of lewdness and debauchery. Witches are the cause of impotence, illness, accidents, bad luck, even failed financial deals, in short, any disaster which cannot be explained—except by chance, but randomness in Aristotle's world is no explanation. A good Christian man suddenly discovers he is unable to copulate with his wife. A witch must be the cause. Why?

> And the reason for this is that God allows them more power over this act, by which the first sin was disseminated, than over other human actions. (*Malleus Maleficarum*, p. 118)

Women are walking sacks of pollution. Death entered the world through Eve, but life through Mary, a *virgin*. Sex, therefore, is first and foremost a moral problem of cosmic

---

[4]St. Jerome quoted in *Woman Defamed and Woman Defended*, ed. Alcuin Blamires, p. 70.
[5]Quoted in Pomeroy, p. 131.

significance. Scripture reinforces such values; these assumptions support Scripture. Science and religion are in agreement.

In the case of the female sex, truth does not contradict truth. One gets the feeling that should Intelligent Design someday come to rule education, departments of science would teach similar ideas. Say, instead of fertility treatments, a "Design Certified" physician might prescribe the use of an Egyptian slave-girl. This could be labeled "the Hagar Infertility Cure," similar to Margaret Atwood's *The Handmaiden's Tale*. Misogyny might become a prescription drug.

Pope John Paul II recognized, one senses grudgingly, the fact that members and officials of the Catholic Church have been guilty of misogynistic attitudes and actions against women. On this particular subject, the dignity of women, John Paul considered himself something of an expert. He claimed to be a new feminist, uniquely equipped from his pastoral work with the youth of Poland to speak on love, the body, sex and marriage. He was certainly prepared to admit that women's dignity had been denied in the past, but he refused to perceive the problem as having its roots in Catholic culture. Rather, he adamantly proclaimed, the problem is sin.

He agreed with Aquinas that men *and* women were created in the image of the God (the P Source). But the women's liberation movement should not be against their own *"distinctive vocation as women"*[6]. True, equality is a good thing, but not the kind of equality that denies a woman her own feminine characteristics, which were a part of the original unity that God intended (the question of how theologians and popes know God's original intentions becomes, at last, tiring. Mostly they rely on the P Source in which God pronounces everything "good." But this hardly seems adequate).

John Paul's soothing words are certainly a welcome change from the misogynistic and absurd statements one finds in Aquinas. Yet, are they a real change in deeply held presuppositions? Liberation, according to John Paul, does not mean the female appropriation of male characteristics in place of the feminine genius. It is not androgyny. What, then, is this new feminism?

First, it requires an apology to women. The image of the Church as a misogynist, male-dominated tyranny that banishes women (except as servants) and slams the door in their faces, requires repair. If, however, one exchanges the background for the apologetic foreground, and make the vague sketches of hills and towns and mountains become distinct, it will be easier to answer the new feminism question and give content to such abstractions as female and male characteristics, the distinctive vocation of women, the feminine genius—maybe the significance of the Virgin Mary herself. Do male-only characteristics include the dignity and power of the priesthood? Does feminine dignity include freedom of the female body? Do feminine characteristics include

---

[6] Quoted in Weigel, p. 579. Notice how easy it is to slip from biology to some kind of specific vocation, as if biology determines job status. At last, feminine characteristics become God's original intention. Flesh and blood women become abstract essentialist entities determined by vacuous supernatural agents ultimately traceable to ancient mythologies. But it is not to be understood as biological determinism. Oh no. In our eyes, it is a kind of supernatural determinism in biological dress. Real dresses too. In the early days of the Olympic games, American women, when they even allowed to compete, were required to wear dresses.

self-determination? Leadership? Holiness? Brought into exacting focus, such questions begin to cloud the bright, beneficent images the Church wishes to project.

George Weigel, despite his usual John-Paul-knows-best approach, recognized that in the areas of love, sex and women's rights, there were opinions, even among Catholics (!), quite different from the Pope's. Naturally, he left these opinions unstated, and he quickly followed this reluctant admission with fawning praise for the Pope's ideas. He then certified these ideas with a privileged, pope-club membership card that reads, "for those open to the possibility".[7] Such membership privileges need to be examined in order to judge the effectiveness of the apology.

In the March 2000 *apologia*, John Paul II led officials of the church as they recognized that sins have been committed by those within the church "against the dignity of women and the unity of the human race." As Cardinal Francis Arinze explained during the mass in which the image restoration attempts were enacted:

> Let us pray for all those who have suffered offenses against their human dignity and whose rights have been trampled; let us pray for women, who are all too often humiliated and emarginated, and let us acknowledge the forms of acquiescence in these sins of which Christians too have been guilty (*Confession of Sins Against the Dignity of Women and the Unity of the Human Race,* No. VI, March, 2000).

In this instance, the highest level of the Catholic Church recognized that members of the Church have humiliated and marginalized women. Admission of sin is evidence that such abuses exist. But is this how the Church hierarchy understands it? Yes, they admit, children of the Church sinned. Yet, exactly who are these sinful children? Did the teachings of the Mother Church contribute to their bad behavior? Are they found among the sacred legends, among the saints and fathers?

This recognition of sins against women was similar to an image restoration statement issued in the spring of 1995 by the Jesuit order. The Thirty-fourth General Congregation approved a document on women. The Jesuits admitted that their order had sometimes contributed to the persecution of women:

> To answer for that responsibility, we Jesuits first of all ask of God the grace of conversion. We have taken part in a civil and ecclesiastical tradition that has given offence to women. Like many men, we find in ourselves the tendency to tell ourselves that there is no problem. Even without wanting to do so, we have been partners in a form of clericalism which has reinforced male domination, giving it the stamp of divine approval. Recognizing this, we want to react as individuals and as a community and we intend to do everything possible to change this unacceptable situation. (Decree of

---

[7]Weigel, p. 581. A truly momentous discovery. But Cardinal Ratzinger, Pope Benedict XVI, referred to the feminist movement as "radical feminists and lesbian movement" (quoted in Fox, *The Pope's War*, p. 11). Opus Dei, of which John Paul was huge fan and supporter, claimed that freedom of conscience leads to loss of faith, freedom of speech to demagoguery, mental confusion, and *pornography*. What the Pope gives with one hand, his storm troopers take back with thousands.

the General Congregation: "The Jesuits and the status of woman in the Church and in civil society," 1995).[8]

This statement acknowledges that the Jesuit order has offended women, although such an admission is immediately diluted by the rather bland excuse that there exists a general human tendency to deny the existence of a problem. The human propensity for denial ought to be news to no one. Notice, however, how it tends to deflect specific responsibility from the Jesuits and, by implication, the Church. What about confession? Like Alcoholics Anonymous, confession requires that those desiring growth resist the denial tendency and accept their problem. Also, "do everything possible," which appears to promise corrective action is vague. Are female Jesuits "possible?"

There have been many accusations of mistreatment of women by members of the Catholic Church, clergy, and the institution of the Church. Church leaders need to go beyond mere restatements of the accusations and unearth the religious roots of the problem. Naturally, Weigel and his ilk deny the existence of any such thing; there is nothing inherently misogynist in Christianity, they declare.[9]

And, naturally, this begs the historical issue—and it also requires an updating of the blatantly misogynistic notions in Augustine and Aquinas, if not scripture itself. But one must not forget that all interpretations of scripture are narratives superimposed upon ancient writers who probably lack the modern concept of the person and construct their characters, historical or fictional, in terms of *types*.[10] Even if one claims that the ancient authors are speaking for themselves—which is itself a modern construct and literally debatable—one still hears them, as one would hear supernatural voices, through contemporary ears. However, like the pigs of *Animal Farm*, some interpretations are more equal than others. Those that strive for context, understanding without manipulation, informed by the realization of the past's nearly infinite complexities are more equal pigs, though they remain, as contemporary language games, noisy grunts in the ears of the skeptics.

An adequate discussion of the many historical occasions when members of the Catholic Church treated women with disrespect, persecution, and discrimination could generate a multi-volume treatise. It must be emphasized that not all Catholics are or have been misogynistic. Most have not. There may well exist a disconnect between the official theology of the Catholic Church and Catholic laity. This is a recurring theme. It is important to recognize the difference between the rigid dogma of the patriarchy and the personal beliefs of Catholics.

In this chapter, we explored ancient and medieval biological understanding of women, which led Catholic Church patriarchs in the Middle Ages to label women as defective men (Aquinas). We showed how such biological determinism lingered in the thought of the so-called feminist John Paul II and his successor Pope Benedict.

---

[8] Quoted in L. Accattoli, *When a Pope Asks Forgiveness: The Mea Culpa of John Paul II*, Trans. J. Autmann, (Boston, 1998), pp. 109–110.
[9] Weigel, pp. 579–580.
[10] Karen L. King, *The Gospel of Mary of Magdala*, p. 135.

Chapter 6

"Blessings of the Breast and Womb" (Genesis 49:25): Women in Western Religion

The biblical basis of misogyny is undeniable, yet we show that ancient Hebrew folk religion did worship a goddess who does makes appearances in the Bible. We also identify that God, as portrayed in the Old Testament, had female characteristics.

It is hardly a revelation that the history of civilization in the West has been dominated by patriarchal and patrilineal values and culture. Catholic history is not unique. A brief review of the history of women in Western culture seems to be in order in the name of fairness. This does not make Catholic misogyny any less repugnant, nor, to repeat, may it be used in defense and denial—they acted in the spirit of the times. Many religions are based upon patriarchal assumptions. How did this happen?

One modern myth of origins goes something like this: As far back as perhaps the Old Stone Age, there existed a kind of female utopia in which the Great Mother goddess ruled a peaceful people. From Crete to ancient Palestine, archaeologists discovered female statuettes dating from the Middle Bronze Age IIB. Most were naked, huge breasts, broad hips, large buttocks. Figures of pregnant women are found almost universally from Crete to Europe, to the Mideast. Statues of women giving birth, along with many other stylized forms of serpents, butterflies, eggs, water, seem to celebrate the mystery of feminine fertility.[1]

---

[1] For example see Riane Eisler, *The Chalice and the Blade: Our History, Our Future*, (San Francisco, 19870; Marija Gimbutas, *The Language of the Goddess*, (New York, 1989); Merlin Stone, *When God Was a Woman*, (New York, 1976), probably the most popular from a vast library of such creation myths.

During these "good ole goddess days"—the story really picks up speed here—women were generally afforded a higher status in society. It is possible—but why worry about the uncertainty inherent in "possible"—it is for certain, many of these societies were matriarchal. Further, they were matrilineal as well. Worshiping the goddess, they were peaceful, agrarian, non-militaristic, valuing life over the state's power to take life.[2]

But does a goddess figure translate into a higher status for women? John Paul II practically worshipped the Virgin Mary and at the same time would not even listen to suggestions that women be allowed into positions of power within the Church. Further, it is something of a stretch to believe that so many statuettes and terra cotta figurines over such a vast expanse of space and time represent a *single* goddess—for that matter, even a *goddess*.

As in all good origin stories, there is a Fall from grace. The so-called Axial Age (800–200 BCE) and its so-called Aryan migrations, specifically in Greece, brought an end to the female paradise, ushering in a male dominant warrior culture. In the Near East, on the other hand, national states arose, led by Kings like David, and were conquered by the great god-kings of Assyria, Babylon, and Persia. Social relationships became based upon male-only hierarchies dedicated to large-scale organization. Male gods became dominant as did their human counterparts, Kings and their bureaucracies, which included priests and scribes, and which one finds in the Bible. Women were reduced to "male-controlled technologies of reproduction."[3]

Ironically, the modern goddess myth seems to mirror John Paul II's culture of death fantasy. Whereas the feminine goddess gave life, the new male warrior elites developed organizations dedicated to taking it. In passing from a peaceful matriarchy to an aggressive patriarchy, from the culture of life (and love) to the culture of death, Christianity plays a major role. The Lord God (YHWH Elohim) is a man of war.

And all of this comes from the statues of buxom and plump naked women.

Written sources and art require interpretations as we've noted, and there are plenty. It is claimed that the old mythology symbolized a basic human lived experience: the dying God-King (Osiris, if one is Egyptian) is resurrected through the life-giving power of his Goddess-Queen, Isis. The female is the divine power of life, an image found across the world—Astarte, Asherah, Isis, Semele, Gaia, and many more. The feminine power of the universe is called *Shakti* in ancient India and becomes a special branch of Yoga.

The Mesopotamian creation epic, the *Enuma Elish* (When Above) presents one with a story of state-building as the expense of the female. The old goddess Tiamat, partly identified with the waters of chaos, the dragon, or the sea-monster, is defeated by the male warrior god Marduk, who leads the new divinities in a struggle to bring order to the world.[4] In ancient Canaan, the Ugaritic cycle of myths also includes a struggle with a sea-monster who is defeated by the warrior god Ba'al. The goddess Asherah is the consort of

---

[2]Eisler, p. 48.
[3]Eisler, p. 175.
[4]See Alexander Heidel, *The Babylonian Genesis: The Story of Creation*, (Chicago, 1951).

the god El, Lady of the Sea, Mother of Gods (*'asherah* from "to tread," "to go straight"). She appears in the Hebrew Bible over forty times.[5] More will be said of her below.

In Greece, the Aryan invaders brought with them the sky god Zeus, wielder of the lightning bolt. He may have a counterpart of the Vedic god Indra who also commands the lightning bolt (vajra) and slays a dragon. Not to be outdone, the Hebrew god YHWH, the man of war, who appears in Exodus as a pillar of fire, conquers the sea, splitting it (as Marduk does Tiamat) with his divine storm. Modern children of Freud can hardly ignore the sexual symbolism. The female is split open, conquered, penetrated—but that is another myth.

Zeus marries the goddess Hera, but he is not faithful. His many sexual conquests of goddesses and mortal women may have been as an attempt to unite the Aryan male god with the numerous fertility cults of the scattered indigenous villages.[6]

So goes the story. Surely many modern goddess worshipers take their cue from this myth. It is probably a healthy antidote to the one-sexed monotheism of the male Kings. It feels good. Unfortunately, historical argument requires more than good feelings.

As already noted, there is no reason to think that so many female figurines from so many different cultures represent a specific Earth Mother Goddess. For years, scholars have challenged the modern tendency towards religious syncretism, or the soothing homily that beneath their surface differences, all religions are really one. Stephen Prothero's book, *God Is Not One* (2010) is a popular version of this challenge. The Earth Mother Goddess Fertility Religion, Inc., is a similar reading of the past. But there is no historical record of anyone who was brought before an inquisition and burned at the stake for doubting it.

And why fertility? Why sex? It could be the modern obsession with sex, positive (the Earth Mother), negative (the Church). Why saddle ancient people with such obsessions? It could well be a misreading; naked breasts, for example, represent the nurturing of young, not necessarily sex.[7] Wide hips and large buttocks may have something to do with puberty. Most important, as we have said, the worship of a goddess does not immediately translate into a feminine utopia.

Scholars generally agree that ancient Israelite culture is a "subset" of the Canaanite, in which worship of YHWH, El, Asherah and Ba'al were included. It is likely that YHWH, the old tribal god of the Sinai, was identified with El and, at least by implication, such an identification would also signify his marriage. Marriage, perhaps, was something YHWH had not bargained for.

Devotion to a goddess cult may have never completely disappeared. The symbol of a tree or some sort of wooden pole surrounded by animals is often referred to by the

---

[5] William G. Dever, *Did God Have a Wife? Archaeology and Folk Religion in Ancient Israel*, (Grand Rapids, 2008), pp. 100-101.
[6] Pomeroy, *Goddesses, Whores, Wives, and Slaves*, p. 13.
[7] Dever, *Did God Have a Wife?* p. 189.

Hebrews as an *asherah*. It appears to be more of a cult symbol than a recognizable goddess, claims Jonathan Smith in *The Early History of God,* (p. 89).[8] The Tree of Life in the Garden of Eden may well point to this symbol. However, the serpent and the Tree of Knowledge, and by extension Eve, certainly reference goddess symbols. Interestingly, both trees are forbidden and the female susceptibility to the temptations of the snake introduces evil into the world, like the opening of Pandora's box. To paraphrase Freud, not all trees are goddesses. Some, however, especially in Israel, may be.

Inscriptions on large jars found at Kuntillet 'Ajrud near a crossroad leading into the Sinai, dating perhaps to the ninth century BCE, do speak of the YHWH of Samaria and his *asherah*.[9] Archaeologists conjecture that two stone altars found at the fortress of Arad in Judah may also represent YHWH and his consort Asherah[10] Figurines of goddesses (?), naked females holding their breasts (fertility?) between the eighth and seventh centuries BCE, have been found in and around Jerusalem.

Inscriptions use the pronominal suffix for *asherah* which in Hebrew usually refers to a common noun and not a proper name. For example, the name Immanuel, really means "god with us." The name is composed of the preposition *'im*, affixed to the pronominal suffix, *'immanu,* (with us) and *el* at the end. El, god, is a common noun, not a particular god's name, YHWH. On the other hand, over time the construction may evolve into a proper name, Immanuel.

Ugarit mythology indicates that Asherah was a proper name, predating Hebrew scripture. Hebrew writings themselves contain plenty of evidence for her existence, especially the Deuteronomistic history (roughly Deuteronomy through Kings, sixth century BCE). In I Kings 18:19, Elijah bested 450 prophets of Ba'al in a contest of calling upon their respective gods to light fires on sacrificial altars (the prophets of Ba'al lose, of course, and are slaughtered). Along with Ba'al's unfortunate prophets on Mount Carmel are 400 prophets of Asherah, who eat at the table of the Queen Jeze-bel(ba'al). Asherah is no less a proper name than Ba'al. Samuel tells Israel to remove alien gods, the Baalem and Ashtaroth, from their midst. Jeremiah thunders against baking cakes for the Queen of Heaven. Many goddess (?) figurines are pictured with cakes.[11]

Combining the general condemnation of the biblical writers with archaeological discoveries, William Dever postulates a Hebrew folk religion in which a goddess, Asherah, played a significant role. Given the fact that the Deuteronomistic writers, male, urbanized, literate, represent a tiny fraction of the Hebrew population, Dever speculates that the true religion of Israel was everything the biblical writers condemned.

There was a Hebrew goddess and YHWH did have a "wife." She does appear in the Bible, in fact quite frequently. Monotheism as it is generally understood (other gods are not only forbidden, *they do not exist*) is a theological construct imposed upon ancient folk religion much like the difference between the sacred and the profane.

---

[8] 2 Kings, 21:7 does refer to the "sculptured image of Asherah," which seems to indicate a goddess.
[9] Amihai Mazar, *Archaeology of the Land of the Bible, 10,000-586 BCE,* (New York, 1985), p. 448.
[10] Mazar, p. 497.
[11] Dever, *Did God Have a Wife?*, p. 194.

Or...it may have been the hobgoblin haunting the minds of a few androcentric writers.

Monotheism was not originally the religion of ancient Israel. Ancient folk religions did not deny the existence of other gods—YHWH does deny the divinity of the Pharaoh in Exodus, only his powers, especially his war-making abilities. For male priests, however, then and now, a single gendered god existing *alone*, who grants male priests, then and now, exclusive access and the power that flows from it, would be very appealing. Monotheism takes time to evolve, from YHWH alone to YHWH the one and only. It may well have come from the minds and pens of a tiny number of male priests and the prophets.

Still, goddess symbolism persists throughout the bible. One of the most ancient parts of Genesis is Jacob's blessing of his sons in Chapter 49. The blessings include blessings of the *breast and womb* (49:25), the language of the goddess. To avoid the divine female implications, some commentators (as one might imagine their ancient priestly counterparts) treat the terms as simple natural objects. But feminine qualities, once reserved for the goddess, are found throughout the Tanakh and explicitly applied to YHWH. Elite male monotheism absorbs other gods and goddesses as much as it denies them, much as an alcoholic claims never to touch the stuff before seven or eight. Later, especially in Jewish mysticism, God's earthly presence, the female *Shekinah,* once dwelling in the Temple, comes to rest in the Torah itself. The mystical presence of God feminizes the Torah even though it is not supposed to be taught to a woman.

In the Ugarit mythology, as in many ancient tales of the gods, El, Ba'al, Asherah, Anat and divine others all engage in sexual activity. Yam, the sea monster, battles the gods and tries to rape the goddess; there is Mot, the god of death; gods die and are reborn. Sex, life, struggle and death are all part of divine existence. In a sense, such very human experiences are "blessed" when they are lived by gods. Each experience contributes to the whole. Each contributes to the divine symphony, which is the universe. Sex, *eros* in general, is that mysterious fire of reproduction that propels the universe, a fire that burns in gods and humans alike, indeed in the stars themselves.

YHWH has no consort and never experiences divine sex (still speaking in terms of the myth). While he does engage in war, he never dies, even figuratively. Nor is he concerned with death and the underworld (*sheol*). He has no parents, no mother, no father. He is the divine monomaniac who suffers fits of jealously. The very existence of Eve is a challenge to him, because she vies for Adam's attention. It might be said that God gets his identity from Adam's worship. He knows He is God only after he sees His divine image reflected in the object of human worship. Without humans, He is truly alone. And no wonder. He is a truncated god, half a god, but for certain he is male.[12]

---

[12]Speaking of Genesis 3:6, Ratzinger comments: "In that religious setting the serpent was a symbol of that wisdom which rules the world and of the fertility through which human beings plunge into the divine current of life and for a few moments experience themselves fused with its divine power. Thus the serpent also serves as a symbol of the attraction that these religions exerted over Israel in contrast to the mystery of the God of the covenant" (*In the Beginning...A Catholic Understanding of the Story of Creation and the Fall,* 1986, p. 66). It would require an entire book, not a mere footnote, to psychoanalyze these words, and they most definitely cry out for psychoanalysis. In religious terms, keeping to Ratzinger's stated intention, they obviously refer to the goddess cult, but in an almost schizophrenic way. The serpent is wisdom that

God contains other female qualities. The Priestly Source creation story describes the spirit or breath (*ruah*) of *'elohim* (Elohim, the plural of El) hovering over the waters. As Marduk built the world from the body of Tiamat, so too does God divide the waters and set the order of the cosmos. As *'elohim* becomes identified with YHWH, one begins to see a diminishing of the female. At last, in her form of wisdom (*hokmah* in Hebrew, *sophia* in Greek), she becomes a mere attribute of the male god who is now *the* great cosmic deity of creation.[13] The heavenly realm is the sole domain of the male.

So too the Churchly realm. So too His priests. Like Him, they, poor things, never know the joyful wisdom of the human experience of sex (except, as explicated later, in a perverted, destructive way). They reject the formula "YHWH and His Asherah." The religion of *their* book is "YHWH knew not His Asherah."

The one, transcendent, spiritual god occupies the heavenly, superior realm of being. From His throne on high, He orders the world. In philosophical terms, the contingency of the lower earthly realm would revert to chaos without the continual rule of the absolute principle of Being (as Plato in the Timaeus divides the universe into Reason and Necessity). Matter belongs to the lower realm; the spirit, the organizing, rational factor is heavenly. Woman, most specifically in her biological role of reproduction—her "Motherhood" in John Paul II's philosophy—represents this lower realm, the realm of contingency, chaos, coming-to-be and passing-away. The male god is reason, spirit, "higher things." In the sense of ancient anthropology, while humanity is one, humans do not come in two kinds, male and female. Rather, like the descent from heaven to earth, there is a scale of being, an incorruptible spirit to corruptible matter, in which men are the most fully developed human form while women are only partial or imperfect men. Women, so-to-speak, have not reached full maturity.

This cosmic myth, the creation of a tiny group of men, is the dark cellar of the rational myths of Aristotle and Aquinas (and John Paul II, and Ratzinger, and a tiny group of men).

The question still remains if preserving the female goddess in the myth of YHWH would eventually result in Catholic equality for women? Possibly not. Having a Queen like Elizabeth of England or Catherine the Great of Russia did not open the gates of political power for women.[14]

But it might not do any harm to at least acknowledge her presence. *And an institution that included women in its highest positions of power might well react quite differently to child-molesting priests.*

---

rules the world. Is this the feminine wisdom of the earth? Of fertility? But God blessed fertility. Is it the questioning of the male god's authority, hence the rebellion against patriarchy? Earthly wisdom's attraction, on the other hand, seems mystical: for a few moments (?) we are fused (?) with its divine power, hence its attraction. So, the female is fatally attractive in that she tempts us to *fuse* with the *shakti*, or divine feminine power. What is this fusing? The pure joy of sex seems to be a spiritual danger. It is to be eliminated and not integrated into the self.

[13]Rosemary Ruether, *Sexism and God-Talk: Toward a Feminist Theology*, (Boston, 1993), p. 57.

[14]Carole R. Fontaine, *With Eyes of Flesh: The Bible, Gender and Human Rights* Sheffield, UK, 2008), p. 21.

Women are stunted men and are by nature subservient to the male. Patriarchal society is based upon natural law. Women lack reason, they are less spiritual. Women should not be allowed to study the Torah. Rabbi Yehuda prayed: "Blessed be God that he has not made me a woman."[15] That women are inferior to men is a given in Jewish thought from which Christianity grew, as well as the later developments in Islam, and would persist in modern Catholicism. The same may be said for most ancient Near Eastern cultures. Female equality would have probably been beyond the intellectual horizon of most people, perhaps even most women. Those who might have considered the possibility were thought either mad or dangerous.

If society is a microcosmic reflection of the macrocosm, then it cannot be ruled or dominated by women. But this poses a problem for male to male, father to son or brother to brother, inheritance and succession, patriliny, given the unfortunate existence of another natural law. Women are necessary ingredients in the production of sons. What is worse for men, only women know the true identity of the father? Many of the stories of the Patriarchs illustrate the problem. For example, the *berit* passes through Isaac, Sarah's son, not Ishmael, the son of Hagar. The female makes the difference.

Sacrifice, in which worshippers are united in a community, solves the problem. In the act of shedding blood, says Nancy Jay in *Throughout Your Generations Forever*, "atonement is also always 'at-one-*men*-t'" (p. 19). Only the priests officiate and only males are priests. The blood of the domesticated animal replaces the blood of female pollution, but it also establishes a new community, a male to male line of priestly descent. In Genesis, it restores the descent from father to son, creating a male society in no need of the female. Isaac's sacrifice restores the patriliny; Muslims believe that Ishmael was offered. Sarah dies immediately after the Isaac story, as if, having served her use, there is no longer a need for her.[16]

Anticipating what follows, if John Paul's idea of feminine characteristics is most fully realized in motherhood, despite the eloquent bows to female dignity, despite the special pleading (he respects female dignity far more than secular women's liberation), and despite his so-called spiritual vision of sex, the body, and marriage, women still remain a threat to his vision of the patriarchal Church.

Alas, even priests and popes have mothers. Without the female, how does one establish a patrilineal descent of popes and priests within a patriarchal society? God and His Son are male (although, as explored later, the Pope is well aware that Jesus had a mother). The Church hierarchy stands over the flock as God rules over the universe, *in persona Christi*. The hierarchy must be male.

---

[15] Quoted in Elizabeth Schussler Fiorenza, *In Memory of Her: A Feminist Theological Reconstruction of Christian Origins* (New York, 1983), p. 217.

[16] Later, in Genesis 27:3, Isaac calls for Esau to hunt game, sacrifice the game, and prepare his favorite dish so that he might confer the blessing. Rebekah, overhearing the order, tells Jacob to sacrifice kids from the flock, that is, domestic animals. Only domesticated animals were proper for sacrificial ritual. The woman, then, decides in this the descent of the blessing.

The Catholic Church does not have a monopoly on being accused of religious misogyny.

Like the Catholic Church, Islam has often been accused of discrimination against women. Although Islam may have offered protection for women (and better treatment) than in pre-Islamic Bedouin culture, the modern manifestations of Islamic law have not afforded women equal treatment or status with men, theologically or practically. As in early Christianity, "the religion of al-Lah was originally positive for women" according to Karen Armstrong in *A History of God*, (1993, p. 157). The *Qur'an* offered protection to women, such as conferring equal rights in inheritance and divorce as men, prohibition of infanticide of female babies.

Christianity misogyny may have actually influenced misogyny in Islam. If this is so, complaints about Muslim misogyny—and there is plenty to complain about—need to take into account Christianity's bad role model.

Veiling, for example, was actually taken from the Christian Byzantine Empire. Veiling represented the dignity of the aristocratic women in imperial society. From some modern Muslim perspectives, a veiled woman must be treated as a person and not merely a sexual object, that is, not valued according to her physical attractiveness (as defined by men) but by her character, her full humanity.[17]

In modern Western culture, the general use of fashion and cosmetics, while volunteering on the surface—that is, *not governed by written law*—serves as a kind of misogynist veil. Although it is true that a woman is free to choose, the choice carries with it the possibility of punishment. A much stronger social code is at work here, the code of necessity. Does a woman desire recognition? Approval? Admiration? A mate? Maybe even success in her profession? The Western veil is invisible. It is invisible because it has been internalized.

Women do not believe themselves oppressed when they think they are making a free choice. But sometimes the choice is generally the look that men prefer. A woman risks a great deal by refusing to conform. Given the fear of social punishment, which also has been internalized, she really does have little choice in the matter. She is even willing to undergo painful surgery. Women have become something like Buridan's ass, their choice is between two equal stacks of hay.[18] Capitalism, the economic religion of the modern world, has made misogyny into an art form.

One must not forget, however, that these secular veils arise from a system constructed by human beings and are acknowledged as such. They are fallible. If a person believes that God has decreed some rule, or has communicated some general notion that pertains to women, then such decrees or notions are absolute. They cannot even be questioned.

---

[17]See Seyyed Hossein Nasr, *The Heart of Islam: Enduring Values for Humanity*, (New York, 2001).
[18]Equal stacks of hay. Jean Buridan (1295-1360) imagined an ass placed exactly between two identical stacks of hay. The poor ass would starve, having no reason to make a move towards one or the other. The example introduces the Principle of Sufficient Reason. But it demonstrates something else. For anything to *happen*, some asymmetry must be introduced into the system. Nothing happens in a perfect state of equilibrium. The ass starves in the middle of abundance. The Western woman literally starves herself.

John Paul II was, among other things, a philosopher of the human person and human sexuality (see *The Acting Person, The Theology of the* Body, and *Love and Responsibility*). As such, he has been credited with healing the Church's attitude toward sexuality. Ever ready to sing psalms in praise of the saint, Weigel has claimed that John Paul's work "...may prove to be the decisive moment in exorcising the Manichaean demon and its depreciation of human sexuality from Catholic moral theology." (p. 343)[19] Sex will be dealt with later, as will more about "demons." But what about the Sons of God?

In this chapter, we identified that the biblical basis of misogyny is undeniable, yet we identified that ancient Hebrew folk religion did worship a goddess who does makes appearances in the Bible. We also identify that God, as portrayed in the Old Testament, had female characteristics.

---

[19]Weigel wants us to believe that he is writing objective biography. He quotes the Dominican Melchior Cano as the watchword of his project: "Peter has no need of our lies or flattery. Those who blindly and indiscriminately defend every decision of the supreme Pontiff are the very ones who do most to undermine the authority of the Holy See—they destroy instead of strengthening its foundations." (p. 15) A forthright sermon. But does it apply? What is one to do with the statement: "Given the expectations of contemporary biography, a writer almost regrets the absence of detractors and critics of his subject."(p. 119)? The best (or worse) criticism Weigel can come up with is that Wojtyla was almost always late for meetings (same page). A bureaucratic sin to be sure. If these are the watchwords guiding his pen, then how can he write objectively at all? He, like Cano, must not wish to "undermine the authority of the Holy See." But should the evidence demand, it is his duty to do so. Peter may not need praise, but he certainly requires image restoration. Why else the apology? Weigel admits regrets. We hope this book does something to relieve them.

Chapter 7

Was Jesus a Feminist?

We continue our exploration of the institutionalization of misogyny in this chapter. We offer a female-friendly reading of the New Testament Gospels. We critique the Church's interpretation of the views of Jesus on women presented in the canonical Gospels.

No, Jesus was not a modern feminist. He was a first century Jew. Modern categories must be used sparingly and with great caution.

Having said this, the history of Catholic misogyny does appear to be inconsistent with at least one model of the early Church as depicted by many respected historians. This is an important point because it implies that misogyny may have been, to a significant extent, introduced by the Church Fathers such as Augustine and others. A female-friendly reading of the New Testament seems to indicate that Jesus and maybe even Paul accepted women to a certain extent, and were willing to praise them, as Jesus does in Luke 7:44–47 where he extols the virtues of a woman over Simon, the future rock upon which he will build his Church:

> ...Her sins, which are many, are forgiven; for she loves much; but to whom little is forgiven, the same (one) loves little (verse 47).

Apologists often claim that Jesus' statements on divorce were empowering for women of his time. Josephus wrote that Jewish men had previously possessed exclusive rights to divorce, although women were often powerless in marital arrangements and decisions of divorce.[1] In a number of statements attributed to Jesus in the New Testament, he argued against the power of divorce held by men (except it be for fornication, but

---
[1] Josephus, *Antiquities*, 15.259.

not for every cause—because of your hardness of heart, but it was not so from the beginning: Matthew 19:3-9). These can be interpreted as statements in support of the elevation of women:

> He challenged their whole man-made system of superiority, the unjust power of divorce, which they wielded, the cruel inferiority and dependence, which were forced upon women. He declared that in marriage women had the same rights as men.[2]

Thus, if one looks at Jesus' statements here as context-dependent, he clearly spoke of the increase in the power of women in the Jewish institution of marriage (*Mark* 10:11; *Matthew* 19:10). Branscomb concluded that Jesus was an emancipator of women within the context of his day:

> Jesus thus raised woman's place in the family to a point of absolute equality with that of man. In marriage there are equal obligations before God. In this affirmation Jesus made himself one of the great champions of women's causes.[3]

There is evidence, however, that aristocratic women in Palestine did have the power of divorce, the most famous being Herodias from the gospel stories dealing with the execution of John the Baptist.

It is difficult to say how Jesus' peasant audience understood divorce, or how the laws may have varied from Roman society to the occupied lands of Judea, or between social classes. One also needs to question the historical reliability of the Gospels. The Uncertainty Principle of Biblical Hermeneutics cuts both ways. When critics of Catholic dogmas find something in the Gospels, they *imagine* supports their position, abruptly, it is declared "what Jesus said" or "what Jesus meant" without caveat. It could well be that the divorce question arose in certain early Christian communities removed in time and place from the supposed historical Jesus. People required guidance. The question may not have been pertinent in Jesus' day.

It might seem that Jesus sought increased rights for women. If this assertion is anywhere close to historical reality (and close has been all one can ever hope for), then it needs to be seen against the apocalyptic background of the times. In the Kingdom of God, unlike the Kingdom of Rome, there will be no sexual discrimination. "Do unto to others..." was the part of the wisdom tradition position in Judaism. Yet, if Jesus meant to include women and presented this as a universal principle beyond any limited application in space and time, then it is a principle fit for the Kingdom of God. An all-male hierarchy could assume that the golden rule entailed some kind of double standard: one for men, another for women. The "others," other human beings, existed on two different hierarchal links on the human chain, male and female, and therefore required two standards as befitting ancient anthropology. Women's equality becomes an ideal fit only for the world to come.

---

[2] B. H. Branscomb, *The Teachings of Jesus*, (Nashville, TN, 1931), p. 243.
[3] Branscomb, p. 186. On the other hand, Thomas A. J. McGinn insists that we need to consider the Roman context in which obtaining a divorce was easier, even by the standards of 21st century United States. "The Law of Roman Divorce in the Time of Christ," in *The Historical Jesus in Context*, eds. Amy-Jill Levine, Dale C. Allison Jr., and John Dominic Crossan, (Princeton, N. J., 2006), p. 309.

In addition, Jesus may have been "perfectly at home" in the company of Jewish holy men like Honi the Circle Drawer (or Rain Maker), first century BCE (?), and his near contemporary Hanina ben Dosa.[4] They were men of God, capable of working miracles. The Rabbinic sources for these sages are certainly no worse than the Gospels, coming after the destruction of the Temple by the Romans in 70 AD (as we will see later with non-canonical gospels like *The Gospel of Mary*). Having witnessed the destruction of the Temple as well as the failure of the Bar Kokhba Revolt in 133-35 AD, the Rabbis would have certainly had an ambivalent attitude toward eschatological prophets and charismatics who they believed drove the nation into disaster.[5]

A prerequisite of such a sage would have been the proper interpretation of the Torah. Exaggeration, parables, and metaphors were typical of these teachers as they were of Jesus. The tendency to reverse things, to upset the power pyramid, the social hierarchy, perhaps even the natural order is found almost universally among popular sages. And why not? The logic is perfectly clear: to shock the audience out of previously unconscious and unconsidered assumptions is a prerequisite for imparting a new vision, of seeing the world differently, through the eyes of the sage.

Given all this, it is plausible that Jesus' attitude towards women was typical of the Jewish holy man. Because many believed that such radicals brought destruction upon the nation, they and their teachings, and their methods, would be repudiated by subsequent generations of Rabbis. Indirect speech, metaphor, hyperbole, exaggeration, are always in danger of being taken literally. Human beings are not birds of the air or the lilies of the field, and it is foolish to think that such radical minimalist statements should be taken as literal guides to living. Ancient Jewish peasants heard things that modern ears, and even the ears behind ears, can no longer grasp.

Elisabeth Schussler Fiorenza warns that it is also important to realize that ideas about women held by such sages, all men, do not always reflect the historical reality of women (*In Memory of Her*, p. 89). It is not always an easy task reconstructing this reality, or, one should say it is seldom easy. The historian requires women's voices, and these are rare indeed. It is also important to recognize the multiform nature of early Christianity, that what constitutes Catholic Christianity is a variation—*the* variation—that triumphed over the others. The alternatives were later condemned as heresies. Mary of Magdala, for example, might have been the leading apostle who, because of her spiritual acuity, understood Jesus far better than that hothead and spiritually immature Peter.[6] The New Testament portraits of Jesus are end products of such earlier disputes. The others are labeled "late," derivative, or heretical, although in fact, they recall the fluid nature of early Christianity. And so Mary is later misconstrued (intentionally?) with the fallen woman of John 8:1-11.

---

[4]Geza Vermes, *Jesus In His Jewish Context*, (Minneapolis, 2003), p. 127. Also see Vermes, *Christian Beginnings: From Nazareth to Nicea*, (New Haven, 2012). Vermes says that "without a proper grasp of charismatic Judaism it is impossible to understand the rise of Christianity."

[5]Alan J. Avery-Peck, "The Galilean Charismatic and Rabbinic Piety: The Holy Man in the Talmudic Literature," in *The Historical Jesus In Context*, p. 150.

[6]Karen L. King, *The Gospel of Mary of Magdala*, p. 187.

It does seem that among many of the early Christian movements women did play an important, sometimes equal, maybe even a superior role as men. One hears of female prophets and ministers, deaconesses, priests, even apostles: Mary, Salome, Martha, Mary the Mother of Jesus, and others can be counted among the first disciples. They stood at the foot of the cross (Peter deserted, apparently to fight another day), they discovered the empty tomb, they were the first to see the resurrected Lord. Later, the women traveled with Paul as they had with Jesus. According to some scholars, parts of the gospels may have been authored by women, especially Luke, who seems more concerned with women's issues.

It is generally agreed that the major teaching of the historical Jesus was the *basileia tou theou*, the Kingdom of God (the Jesus Seminar translates the phrase as "God's Imperial Rule," in contrast to the Roman Imperium, in *The Five Gospels*, 1993). The proclamation may simply contrast the relative nature of *all earthly kingdoms* with the power of God.[7] Whatever the phrase may have meant to Jesus and his audience, it does appear to be an absolute break from the normal power relationships of the day. Such relationships were based upon the patriarchal family structure. But the *"basileia"* is for the downtrodden, the destitute (*"ptochoi"* in Luke). Women and children, orphans and widows are "paradigms" of the destitute, says Fiorenza (p. 146). In the Kingdom, all such differences are abolished; there will be no giving and taking in marriage. Marriage in the context of the first century must be seen in terms of ancient patriarchy. Therefore, no marriage, no patriarchy.

Fiorenza noted that when Jesus does identify his true family, as in Mark 3:35: "Whoever does the will of God is my brother and sister and mother," he conveniently forgets the most important member of all for the ancient family, the father (p. 147). The new community, the new family upon which the new *kingdom* will be built does not include the father, and by implication the Emperor. An objection would of course point out that God is Father, and it would be quite correct. But in human social terms, the Kingdom realized on earth (or in the Church), it is a different matter. The invisible Father casts no earthly shadow. Also, the divine father could more fully exhibit his goddess qualities in a Kingdom where women are the equal of men.

Paul writes to the Galatians that there is neither male nor female in Christ (Galatians 3:28). In the coming Kingdom, human divine nature will be restored, which Fiorenza understands as being androgynous (p. 205). On the other hand, this apocalyptic future of spiritual rebirth, although "at hand," must still be awaited as the present evil age under the dominion of the *"archons"* (either spiritual or temporal "powers," or both) plays itself out. Therefore, Colossians exhort Christians to patience—while the faithful await the end, they must participate in the old epoch, obedient to the old hierarchal situations: husband and wife, child and father, slave and master. It is also possible that Paul wanted to prevent Christianity from becoming identified with one of the orgiastic cults of the Empire as was happening in Corinth. Hence Paul's famous plea in I Corinthians 7 to the unmarried and widows that they remain as he is and to marry as a last resort (see below).

---

[7] See Christopher Bryan, *Render To Caesar: Jesus, The Early Church, and The Roman Superpower*, (Oxford, 2005).

As an eastern mystery cult (to the Romans), Christianity grew up in the shadow of Isis. Far older than even the Hebrew Bible, the Egyptian Isis appeared in Rome around the second century BCE. Isis, sister-wife of Osiris, mother of Horus, resurrects her husband-brother-king after he is murdered by his brother Set (the variations of the myth are nearly endless). She is a mother, a creator, restorer of life, to her followers she brings the gift of blessed immortality. At last she becomes everything. Her attributes are limitless.

Renderings of the Virgin Mary holding the baby Jesus recall Isis and the baby god Horus. Cleopatra was Isis incarnate, hence the Roman feared Egyptian seduction as in the case of Mark Antony. She was a mother, wife, even whore. She could take on male attributes too. Many of her priests were women. She provided women a measure of equality. In this respect a goddess did raise the status of women in the empire.

She did stand for the equality of women, and one cannot help wondering about the nature of the subsequent history of Western women if the religion of Isis had been triumphant.[8]

Although it may be true that ideas about women do not always reflect real life situations, it is also important to acknowledge that ideas no matter how far removed from reality do have future repercussions. And while politics certainly contributed to the exclusion of women, as did the emerging male dominated power structure of priests and bishops, philosophical assumptions about the nature of reality do have a lasting influence. Ironically, such influences shape present day interpretations, even where the "reality" behind such assumptions is no longer believable. This brings one to the Paul of Romans.

Once again, the scholarly debate over what Paul "really meant" would take make a library and may well never cease because the question is ultimately impossible to answer. The possible implications for Catholic misogyny are, thus, interesting. In other words, how did the leaders of the Church read Paul?

Going by a simple literal reading of the Gospels, women were prominent in the ministry of Jesus. Although women might not share the full fellowship of the twelve apostles (in the canonical Gospels, but not the others), women play significant roles in the story. There seems to be a tension, as later writers or even scribes sought to bring the Gospel story in line with the emerging power structure of their time, which many scholars agree comes later than the actual historical events. Yet, some things cannot be dismissed. As John Paul II himself points out, the story begins with a woman, Mary. Significantly, Mary does not actively cause events to happen, she *passively accepts* God's command. The primal Christian woman is a "handmaiden." In almost Orwellian language, the Pope says that she discovers herself, her "person," by giving herself completely up to God's will (*Mulieris Dignitatem*, 11, p. 14). How one becomes a person by surrendering completely to a spiritual totalitarianism is not clear. It should be noted that this emphasis on "self-giving," on "passivity," on the "feminine genius," when seen from a different perspective

---

[8]Pomeroy, *Goddesses, Whores, Wives, and Slaves*, p. 226.

in a different age and culture—say, the male inquisitors of the witchcraft trials—will not contain the same "Christian feminist" meanings that the Pope intends.

Paul's attitude towards women could be wildly inconsistent, which may again reflect the changing power structure of the Church as it forms the evolving literary canon, especially letters like Timothy and others that are Pauline forgeries.[9] Paul like Jesus is celibate, yet he travels with women and praises their spirituality and teaching, as he does Priscilla and Aquila in Romans 16:3-4 as well as a certain Junia who significantly is called "foremost among the apostles." (Romans 16:7. In the apocryphal *Acts of Paul and Thecla*, Thecla, after Paul's instruction, renounces her coming marriage and by practicing celibacy achieves her freedom from the bonds of patriarchy (her betrothed was none too happy about this turn of events). She is even qualified to teach the gospel.[10] Although Paul favors celibacy, he does admit marriage for those who are not up to it: "it is well for them to remain single as I do. But if they cannot exercise self-control, they should marry" (Romans 7:9).

One might say that this particular incarnation of the Church regards marriage is a form of bondage, living according to the flesh in the old patriarchal society under the present evil archons, in which both men and women are slaves to lust, their own and another's. The unmarried man is free to devote himself fully to the Lord's business, says Paul (I Corinthians 7:32). The married man is divided, he cares for worldly things. Here is the garden story all over again. Eve distracts Adam from devoting his full attention to God. It is not too difficult for us moderns to grasp the strength of that distraction, but poor God, not having a goddess, reacts like a jilted juvenile, jealous and vindictive. And blindly—he cannot see that his own command to be fruitful and multiple might conflict with his need to discover self-identity through human groveling.

After Paul, the problem of women's role in the Church came to a head. The new age, the "Kingdom of Equality," is yet to come and for the time being women must be content with their roles. The pseudo-Pauline I Timothy puts these words into Paul's mouth: "I permit no woman to teach or to have authority over men; she is to keep silent. For Adam was formed first, then Eve; and Adam was not deceived, but the woman was deceived and became the transgressor" (2:11-13).

Thus, one erases the authority of Thelca and all her sisters. The sinful actions of Eve leave a moral stain on all women. The first woman, because of her weakness as a "misbegotten" male, was tricked by the serpent. Like the first woman, all women are weak, passive, and easily tempted, as believers are told *ad nauseam*. Mary, also passive, is the second Eve who surrenders to God, thereby reversing the first Eve's surrender to Satan (if this really is the identity of the "clever" serpent).[11] Surrender is, nonetheless, still surrender. Ironically, Mary is honored for her surrender while Eve is condemned

---

[9]See Bart Ehrman, *Forged: Writing in the Name of God.*
[10]Crossan and Reed, *In Search of Paul*, 2004, reproduce an interesting series of plates from the grotto of St. Paul near Ephesus. The two figures are Paul and Thecla, both of the same height, both with their right hands raised in teaching, both of equal authority. But someone has scratched out the eyes and erased the uplifted hand of Thelca! The female apostle has been repressed; so too the female priest (p. xii-xiii).
[11]The "clever" serpent is actually a pun. the Hebrew '*arum*, clever, is a pun on '*arummim*, naked.

for it. Apparently, it is not the primal character of the woman—her passivity as in John Paul's assertion that life growing in the womb happens *to her* (*Mulieris Dignitatem*, 19, page 23)—but to whom she surrenders. Since the Kingdom of the Heavens is not yet arrived, *women obey your husbands.* After all, as Aquinas knew, Eve did not come from Adam's head.

In *The Literal Meaning of Genesis*, Augustine wondered how it was that Eve knew not to eat of the fruit of the tree of knowledge since she was created *after* Adam had been given the command. Like any good apologist when faced with a problem in scripture, or a contradiction, Augustine proceeded to compose his own bible. That is, he reads "between the lines," letting his imagination wander. The answer is quite simple: Adam told her about it. Apparently some inept scribe must have forgotten this footnote. But no matter. The interpretive rule here seems to be if it is not written in the text, it should have been, Heisenberg be damned. From this added fact Augustine draws a moral. If women wish to learn anything, they need to ask their husbands at home (quoting 1 Corinthians 13:35, Book VIII, 17.36, p. 367).[12]

Read literally, Eve actually changes the command when she repeats it to the clever serpent. She adds, "not to eat *or touch*" in Genesis 3:3. Like the child she is, and according to Church opinion will always remain, she adds "touching" to the what her father has forbidden. Is the writer giving a knowing wink to readers who are parents and can easily identify with such things?

Through the passivity of woman sin entered the world—and with it that dread adversary, death. It is an ironic reversal. From woman comes life. For Augustine and his male heirs the woman brings death. Granted, in some cases the female goddess does indeed bring life *and death*, as does the earth. But here the male god is ultimately the source of life. When Eve bore Cain she said: "I have got a male child with the Lord" (*ish 'et-yehwah*, the phrase "help of the Lord" is not in the Hebrew text). The ultimate power of life belongs to God. Circumcision may represent a jealous God taking back a part of the human creative ability, the human as sub-creator.

Ancient commentators wondered if in fact the passage really refers to Eve having intercourse with Satan.[13] Given Cain's evil nature—he commits the first murder—the word "lord" may have actually meant Satan. The Hebrew *ish*, man, could mean a supernatural being. So, the first woman, as her witch daughters "down through the generations," had sex with the devil.

When Adam "knew" his wife, his knowledge was of her infidelity. The Second Eve, true to her spouse, remains a virgin. She, not Eve, provides the model for the faithful wife, and women in general. The Virgin Mother. Possible, perhaps, in some supernatural realm of fearful male dreams (can a man ever be certain of his wife's fidelity?), an impossibility for the inhabitants of this cave—the mythical complex certainly does require a new hermeneutic.

---

[12]We know already the consequences of female education. It makes them positively dangerous, servants of the devil, or in Ratzinger's case, "radical feminists and lesbians."
[13]James L. Kugel, *How To Read the Bible: A Guide to Scripture, Then and Now*, (New York, 2007), pp. 60-61.

The flesh, according to Paul (or someone else writing by that name) is possessed of a principle in opposition to God's law. Death is the divine punishment. The frail, fleshly body, not able not to sin (*non posse non peccare* according to Augustine), is thereby subject to destruction. Through original sin, death entered the world. In the context of Romans this most obviously means the death of the body.[14] Living according to the flesh means death. But if you live according to the Spirit you put to death the deeds of the body, says Paul in a nice turn of phrase (*Romans*, 8:13). Living according to the flesh means, among other things, sex. Sex is the means by which more flesh (infested with sin) is produced, and thus more death enters the world. The production of life brings death.

Given this "spiritual anthropology," it would seem that Christianity, not modernity, promotes a Culture of Death. The Pope is in danger of falling beneath the knives of his own critique. But the heavenly ladder is always at hand. In those audiences given between 1979 and 1984 and under the title *The Theology of the Body*, John Paul lectured that "concupiscence and the inevitability of death appear together with sin" (p. 183). Thus the act of sex, "fruitful and good" as God intended, is polluted. Before the Fall, sex itself was good and productive in life, according to the Creator's original intention.

Again, the Pope somehow knows such intentions, in this specific case from the fact that God pronounced everything good—which includes, he *assumes*, although it is not mentioned, sex. Interestingly, heaven is not called good either, but one would *assume* it is. Also, "good" (*tob*) simply means in the context of the Hebrew fit to form or serving its purpose, not necessarily perfect or morally good.

Biblical silence invites interpretive anarchy. Since biological sex complete with concupiscence is the only sex humans know, introducing the spiritual vertical plane means that anything goes. Thus concupiscence, the bane of the saint—*goes*.

As will be seen later, the ancient pagan world perceived the human body and its sexual drive as divine, a part of the natural world—the sexual fire burned simultaneously in humans, animals, even the bright stars of heaven, says Peter Brown in *The Body and Society*. Christianity held that the universe had been polluted by human sin. But Christ's resurrection had broken this sinful world. By the imitation of Christ, the body might be sundered from the natural world. By practicing chastity, Christians could bring to an end the reproduction of sinful flesh, and with it, death and human bondage. It is not sex itself that is evil or even the origin of original sin. On the contrary, sex in itself is participation in the divine creative act as it was understood in Judaism. Rather, it is the overwhelming nature of desire, the almost bestial irrationality of lust (see Augustine's *Confessions*, for example) that is sinful and leads to carnal sin.

Therefore, even the married Christian must strive to practice chastity in marriage, which, according to John Paul II, is the only acceptable form of birth control (*Evangelium*

---

[14]This sets up a problem for what God says to Adam in Genesis 2:17: if he eats of the tree of the knowledge of good and bad, on that day he will die. The Hebrew might be translated to mean "as soon as," but it seems certain that the image is of Adam immediately dropping dead. But Adam lives to age 930. Some apologists like to talk about spiritual death, but Paul interprets the words to mean bodily death as above. Another possibility comes from the statement in Psalms 90:4 that a thousand days is like a day to God. Since Adam lived to 930, and a thousand years is a day (930+70=1000), Adam did die on that day, in the later afternoon. When apologists introduce the vertical dimension anything is possible.

Vitae, 1995, 13, p. 10). Chastity within marriage, the Pope argued, respects full personhood; the person is not simply an object to be used but a subject to be respected. Contraception "contradicts the full truth of the sexual act as the proper expression of conjugal love..." (p. 10). The contemporary "hedonistic culture" is based a self-centered concept of freedom, not the freedom of self-discipline. Reason and self-discipline, when trumped by the irrational drive for individual pleasure (at the expense of treating the other as an object) results in sin.[15]

A woman's fertility, her desire for her husband, results in the pain of childbirth as well as the domination of men. Through virginity, the refusal of sex—and such a refusal must be paradoxical or divinely assisted if the irrational sexual desire for her husband is beyond her control as a consequence of the fall—a woman becomes "liberated." She is free from patriarchy. She is free of her biology. She is a free person as long as she remains a virgin. And so, the Virgin Mary becomes the New Eve. Thus John Paul II completes the circle. Virginity is women's liberation. Mary gives birth while remaining a virgin. Female sexual desire actually leads to patriarchy, which implies that women are the cause of their own bondage. The Pope has done three impossible things before breakfast.

Let one not go too far. John Paul adamantly denied that Genesis meant husbands ought to subjugate wives. In the "John Paul Ministry of Truth," the wife finds her relationship with Christ—who is Lord over husbands and wives—the motivation of that relationship which flows from the very essence of marriage and family (*The Theology of the Body*, p. 310). Designed to take the sting out of any misogynist interpretation of Genesis, the statement still admits a hierarchy, the rule of men over women. Christian domination of male over female, however, is holy. Christ is a man, but his love is divine love which, by papal fiat, excludes subjection. Therefore a husband's love—husbands love your wives—if it is like Christ's love, means that wives should not be treated as servants or slaves. Nevertheless, there is no equality of the sexes. A hierarchy, like a mathematical line segment, admits of infinite points. There exist degrees of domination.

But even if she is a virgin and therefore "liberated," a woman is still tempting to men, appealing to their irrational, uncontrollable lust. Interestingly, this feminine temptation is also a passive thing; she cannot control it for it belongs to her nature. A woman, despite her "personhood" using the Pope's language, becomes a passive object of sexual desire. Tertullian of Carthage specifically identified women with sexual temptation, calling women "the devil's gateway." With the long development of priestly celibacy, the

---

[15]Of course, the Pope does not accept the animal nature of human beings—we are specially created, the only species created for its own sake. Furthermore, a purely scientific description of the body is incommensurate with the human being, for "man" expresses "himself" as a person (*The Theology of the Body*, p. 203). Let us try to give some flesh and blood to this "person." Biological science—here the Pope specifies—cannot develop awareness of the body as the sign or visible manifestation of the invisible, in short, a spirit. The Pope by this statement seems to be referring to Aquinas' teaching of the unity of body and soul (against Manichean dualism). Biology then is incomplete, and so much for Darwin. The entire argument is another manifestation of the ad hoc nature of the vertical. Again, we need not deny the existence of the spiritual in order to criticize such visitors from the stars. Abstractions are infinitely empty and thus infinitely serviceable. It is creation ex nihilo, or creation according to what the situation requires. But what are the criteria? Who decides? If it is scripture, then the Heisenberg Uncertainty Principle of Biblical Hermeneutics questions such authority, like the serpent in the garden.

danger of women became even greater since sexual temptation was part of that inability not to sin, even for priests.

John Paul II indirectly acknowledges the problem in *Mulieris Dignitatem*: "*The woman cannot become the 'object' of 'domination' and male 'possession'* (his italics, 10). For humans burdened with sin, this "cannot become" becomes impossible. Without divine help, the grace of celibacy, for example, it is simply beyond the powers of Everyman. The words of the biblical text directly concern original sin and its lasting consequences in man and woman. Burdened by hereditary sinfulness, women bear within themselves the constant '*inclination to sin*,' the tendency to go against the moral order which corresponds to the rational nature and the dignity of man and woman as persons" (10, p. 12). Women are the occasion of sin by simply being. The devil's gateway is without a lock, indeed without a gate.

This chapter began by asking if Jesus was a feminist. Whether he was or not, he has been ripped out of history and made into a symbol. Reified beyond all human recognition, *Christ is the Truth*, he has become an idol.[16] He is the idol of a male-only club, celibate, sexless even, a man who like his Father knew not his Asherah. Yes, he does associate with women, and yes, women do play a role in the story. In competition with Isis, it makes sense to give women a series of bit parts, perhaps with a knowing wink to our male apostles.

Apologists like to cite the story of the various women's visit to the empty tomb as evidence for the resurrection (as if fiction suddenly becomes history). If the apostles believed such a fantastic thing coming from such fools as women, then this is evidence that it happened. Why make it up? How could gospel writers expect to sell the faith when no one in the ancient world believed a woman's testimony?

Apologetics has apparently become high (or low) comedy. The male apostles are still required to verify the empty tomb. But more important is the myth complex itself. Isis brings Osiris back from the underworld; Asherah pulls off the same trick, as do many other goddesses. But notice how even when women are included in a most significant part of the story they are degraded. *Who would believe them?* The ancient prejudice against women, that they are weak minded and untrustworthy, is used by modern apologists as evidence in the founding event of Christianity. If this is so, the whole religion is built upon misogyny.

In this chapter, we continued our exploration of the institutionalization of misogyny. We offered a female-friendly reading of the New Testament Gospels. We critiqued the Church's interpretation of the views of Jesus on women presented in the canonical Gospels.

---

[16]"All theological claims to the formulation of Universal Truth must be put under the strictly theological hermeneutics of 'idolatry.'" David Tracy, *The Analogical Imagination: Christian Theology and the Culture of Pluralism*, (New York, 1981), p. 66.

Chapter 8

Women Priests in the Early Church From *Was to Should Be*

In this chapter, we explore the epistles from the New Testament, non-canonical Gnostic writings, and archeological findings that indicate women clergy served the Catholic Church in its first three centuries, and longer in some cases.

"There is neither Jew nor Greek, there is neither slave or freeman, there is neither male and female; for you are all one in Christ Jesus." Galatians 3:28, New American Bible. This quote typifies the egalitarian spirit of the early Church, if it is interpreted to apply to the visible world and not some invisible future state of being that must remain vague and insubstantial, even if one grants supernaturalism, heaven, the life-to-come, the Kingdom of God. Otherwise, the question may be logically addressed to Paul, in the words of Diogenes: "When did you get back?"

Given the egalitarian nature of Jesus' message, as identified in the previous chapter, biblical scholar Elisabeth Schussler Fiorenza (1982) and many other scholars are correct: women took leadership roles in the early Church. This is clear from the stories presented in the New Testament epistles, non-canonical writings, and archeological finds.

The Christian Church once embraced female leaders. The modern *City of God* can and should return to reliance upon the leadership of women, institutionalized by the ordination of women, as was the case in the first three hundred years of the Church. One of the main arguments against the inclusion of women clergy in the Catholic Church is that the exclusion of women is based on unbroken tradition. This is patently factually false. Literary analysis and archeological finds have shown that women have been accepted as clergy at various points throughout the history of the Catholic Church, particularly in the first three hundred years when ministries better reflected the spirit of the teachings of Jesus and was not yet institutionalized and subverted by Greco-Roman patriarchal values. Women led house-based worship before the institutionalization of the Church under Constantine.

There are a number of instances in which the writers of the epistles of the New Testament reference female clergy who led the early Church, particularly in Rome, Corinth, Philippi, and Ephesus.

An initial caveat is offered for this section: This is an interpretation of the first century epistles of the New Testament. To be fair and consistent with the Heisenberg Uncertainty Principle of Biblical Hermeneutics posited earlier in this book (somewhat tongue-in-cheek), one must recognize that our reading is influenced by our consciousness and our conscientious intention. To modify this caveat, these epistles were presumably written, a few decades not many decades after the discussed events, as was the case for the canonical Gospels. The disputes over the leadership of women are, again presumably, going strong and the issue is far from decided. We will probably never actually hear the opposing voices (they belong to the oral tradition) but we hear echoes of them in the epistles as well as the so-called late heretical gospels, especially those from the Egyptian desert. It is a kind of hopeful fantasy of apologists to declare that later gospels are built upon heretical readings of the canonical four. It is more likely that the so-called heretical gospels (again heresy requires a developed orthodoxy, perhaps up to Nicea) sound similar because they record the disputes that go back to the earliest tradition.

In addition, the translation preferred by the Catholic Church is useful in this chapter. On the title page of the Saint Joseph Edition of The New American Bible, it states that his translation is authorized by the Board of Trustees of the Confraternity of Christian Doctrine and "Approved by the Administrative Committee/Board of the National Conference of Catholic Bishops and the United States Catholic Conference." The *New American Bible* in this chapter for the sake of clarity and fairness, as it is the preferred Catholic translation. With those caveats in mind, it is clear the New Testament epistles identify a number of important female ministers in the early Church, a Church closest to the intention of Jesus if the Catholic Church truly descends from the conferring of the keys to the Kingdom to Peter. Let us for the sake of argument take these claims on face value. Catholic practices since those times represent movement away from the ministry established by Jesus.

Junia was mentioned as an important female minister in Rome referenced in Romans 16:7, as discussed in the Chapter 7: *Was Jesus a feminist?* Unfortunately, and as an indicative example of the efforts of men to later discount the ministerial role of women after the thirteenth century, she was translated into a man in many versions of the New Testament. For instance, in the New American Standard Bible, she grows testicles and a penis: "Greet Andronicus and Junias, my kinsmen and my fellow prisoners, who are outstanding among the apostles, who also were in Christ before me." (NASB) *Junias* is the male form of the name. Before the thirteenth century, she was recognized as a woman in the text of the Bible and recognized as a woman by Catholic Church Fathers such as Chrysostom, Origen, and Jerome. The mistranslation is revelatory of the effort by later Catholic men to erase the legacy of female clergy at the birth of the Church.

The New American Bible, the official translation for Catholics in the United States, returns to the feminine form of the proper noun: "Greet Andronicus and Junia, my relatives and my fellow prisoners: they are prominent among the apostles and they were in Christ before me." (Romans 16:7; New American Bible). A footnote in the St. Joseph Edition further supports the claim when it states: "The name Junia is a woman's name." One ancient Greek manuscript and a number of ancient versions read the name "Julia." Most editors have interpreted it as a man's name, Junias. In his *Homilies on the Book of Romans*, fourth century church father, Chrysostom, preached about Junia and recognized her as an outstanding apostle.

Here it is in black and white: no need to read anything other than the black parts of the page. Paul identified Junia as a minister and an apostle. The Catholic Church should return to the tradition of the pre-institutionalized Church, as it was practiced in Rome. The real tradition of misogyny breaks the illusionary tradition of "the unbroken tradition."

Another key female minister esteemed by Paul was Phoebe. Paul recognized Phoebe as a leader in the Church in Cenchrea, a few miles east of Corinth on the Saronic Gulf off of the Aegean Sea. Paul's important letter to the Christian community was likely delivered by Phoebe. Paul commends Phoebe to the church at Rome, as if to bolster her to the Roman community when she delivered the letter. In Romans 16:1-2, Paul wrote:

> "I commend to you Phoebe our sister, who is [also] a minister of the church at Cenchrea, that you may receive her in the Lord in a manner worthy of the holy ones, and help her in whatever she may need from you, for she has been a benefactor to many and to me as well." *New American Bible* (NAB)

Here Paul identified Phoebe as *diakonos* in Greek, which is usually translated as minister (clergy). Officially the Catholic Church translates *diakonos* as minister: "*Minister:* in Greek *diakonos*" (p. 241, Saint Joseph Edition of the *New American Bible* New Testament, footnote to Romans 16:1). In the *New American Bible* in this chapter, as it is the preferred Catholic translation, Paul writes, she has the stature of the "holy ones."

Commentary from Theodoret of Cyrrhus (393-460 AD) on Romans 16:1-2 adds valuable perspective:

> Such was the significance of the church at Cenchreae that it had a female deacon [i.e. minister], honorable and well known. Such was the wealth of her accomplishments that she was praised by the apostolic tongue... I think what [Paul] calls patronage (*prostasia*) is hospitality(*philoxenia*) and protection (*kēdemonia*). Praise is heaped upon her. It seems that she received him in her house for a little time, for it is clear that he stayed in Corinth. He opened the world to her and in every land and sea she is celebrated. For not only do the Romans and Greeks know her, but even all the barbarians. (Hill, 2007)

Clearly, women were ministers in the early Catholic Church (and should be again). Phoebe traveled widely and brought the Gospel to foreign lands where she effectively ministered as an apostle-evangelist. Tradition holds that it was Phoebe, who carried Paul's letter to the Romans.

Paul's writings refer to women leading the Church in Philippi. In Philippians 4:2-3 Euodia and Syntyche are identified as "Chiefs of the Church." Paul wrote:

> "I urge Euodia and I urge Syntyche to come to a mutual understanding in the Lord. Yes, and I ask you also, my true yokemate, to help them, for they have struggled at my side in promoting the gospel, along with Clement and my other co-workers, whose names are in the book of life." (New American Bible)

Here Paul recognizes these women as genuine "suzuge" which probably means "fellow-workers," or yokemates. The Church is not mentioned except once where its obvious meaning is the community. Nonetheless, to mention women as fellow workers is to give them a significant role.

Another important leader in the Church of Philippi was Lydia. The author of Acts suggested she led first Church in Philippi. Lydia may have also been the first convert in Europe. The author of Acts wrote in Acts 16:14:

> One of them, a woman named Lydia, a dealer in purple cloth, from the city of Thyatira, a worshiper of God, listened, and the Lord opened her heart to pay attention to what Paul was saying. After she and her household had been baptized, she offered us an invitation, "If you consider me a believer in the Lord, come and stay at my home," and she prevailed on us. *New American Bible* (NAB)

This indicates Lydia is head of her household. Thus, she would also be in charge of spiritual services in her household.

Lydia is again recognized in Act 16:40: "When [Paul and Silas] had come out of the prison, they went to Lydia's house where they saw and encouraged the brothers, and then they left." (NAB) These passages indicate Lydia led an early Church in Philipi.

Other female church leaders are mentioned in the New Testament, including Philip's daughters. In Acts 21:8-9, readers are told that Philip had four unmarried daughters who prophesied: "On the next day we resumed the trip and came to Caesarea, where we went to the house of Philip the evangelist, who was one of the Seven, and stayed with him. He had four virgin daughters gifted with prophecy" (New American Bible). The fourth century church historian Eusebius described these women as "mighty luminaries" and ranked them "among the first stage in the apostolic succession." Eusebius also quoted Papias, an early church writer alive at the time of Philip's daughters. Papias said that people traveled great distances to visit these prophetesses and listen to their accounts of the early church. (Bruce, 1951, p. 387). It should also be noted that this minister of the early Church had daughters. He was married, which will be important in the chapter on married clergy through the first thousand years of Catholic Church history.

Ben Witherington (1988, p. 152), in writing about Philip's daughters, quotes E. Earle Ellis as saying: "Although prophecy is a possibility for any Christian, it is primarily identified with certain leaders who exercise it as a ministry." By all accounts, Philip's daughters were highly respected prophets and *leaders* in the early church.

Paul also identified Priscilla as a Church leader in Ephesus in Acts 18:26. Acts 18:24 identifies a mistaken teacher: "A Jew named Apollos, a native of Alexandria, an eloquent speaker, arrived in Ephesus. He was an authority on the scriptures" (New American Bible). Paul describes how a female minister in Ephesus, Priscilla, had to set this preacher straight in Acts 18:26: "He [Apollos] began to speak boldly in the synagogue; but when Priscilla and Aquila heard him, they took him aside and explained to him the Way (of God) more accurately" (New American Bible).

Christians also met and worshipped in the home of Priscilla and Aquila, a married couple of ministers in Corinth, according to 1 Corinthians 16:19. Paul called it "the church in their house," reflecting the house based nature of the early Catholic Church movement. "Sunergous" is the term used in the text for Priscilla and Aquila, or servants of the Catholic movement. It is valuable to note Paul refers to them as a serving couple, and does not celebrate the husband more than the wife when he refers to this ministerial team.

This ministerial couple is also mentioned in Romans 16:3-6: "Greet Prisca and Aquila, my co-workers in Christ Jesus, who risked their necks for my life, to whom not only I am grateful, but also all the churches of the Gentiles; greet also the church at their house" (New American Bible).

Chloe was also recognized as another female leader in the early Catholic ministries. In 1 Corinthians 1:11, Paul recognized that when he wrote "For it has been reported to me about you, my brothers, by Chloe's people, that there are rivalries among you" (New American Bible). Chole is recognized by the writer as a leader in that Christian community.

Nympha was another leader noted in Colossians 4:15. Paul wrote:

"Give greetings to the brothers in Laodicea and to Nympha and to the church in her house" (New American Bible). Here again, the Catholic scholars recognize the efforts of many translators to minimize the role played by female ministerial leaders. The footnote in the St. Joseph edition states, "4, 15: *Nympha and...her house*: some manuscripts read a masculine for the house-church leader, "Nymphas and...his house" (St. Joseph New American Bible, New Testament, p. 313).

Another female Church leader, possibly Apphia, was noted by the author of 2 John 13, who refers to her as "the chosen lady." In 2 John 12, the writer hopes to visit the community: "Although I have much to write to you, I do not intend to use paper and ink. Instead, I hope to visit you and to speak face to face so that our joy may be complete." In 2 John 13, the writer recognizes a woman leads the Church to which he is addressing his letter: "The children of your chosen sister, send you greetings"(New American Bible). The commentary in the St. Joseph New American Bible, New Testament on this letter acknowledges, "The Second Letter [of John] is addressed to the 'chosen lady' and 'to her children'" (p. 379). Clearly, a woman leads the Church and is recognized as such by the writer (presumably John or someone by that name). Unlike certain modern popes, John does not complain, condemn or in any other way reject a female leader of the Church. On the contrary, a female leader (priest?) appears quite natural to him.

A number of women ministers are recognized by the writers of the New Testament epistles in a number of communities, including Rome, Corinth, Philippi, and Ephesus.

They include Junia, Phoebe, Euodia and Syntyche, Priscilla, Philip's daughters, Lydia, "the chosen lady" or "the chosen sister" mentioned in 1 John, Nympha, and Chloe. There may be others mentioned in other places in the epistles, including Apphia (Philemon 2), and a female leader in the church in Thyatira in Asia Minor mentioned in Revelations 2:20-24. These identified female ministers were leaders in the growing Christian movement.

Other writings from later Catholic writers indicate these female ministers and leaders may have served into the fifth century. In his analysis of writing from Church father Gelasius, Professor Giorgio Otranto, University of Bari, Italy (1991) concluded, "In sum, we may infer from an analysis of Gelasius' epistle that at the end of the fifth century, some women, are ordained by bishops, were exercising a true and proper ministerial priesthood in a vast area of southern Italy." Writings from the Church reveal women performed priestly functions.. The New Testament epistles reveal what seems to be an early tradition of inclusion of women ministers and leaders. If it is truly concerned with the "tradition," the Catholic Church ought to return to the standard established by the people who were closest to the ministry of Jesus.

The ministerial and leadership roles of these women naturally flow from the house-based early Catholic Church movement. The discussion of female priests necessitates the recognition of the historical context surrounding the non-institutionalized nature of the early Catholic Church, recognizing that these Churches were house-centered Churches, and that the custom was that the woman was the head of the domestic realm. Thus, women would have led many if not most of these house Churches. Kevin Giles (1992) offered this explanation:

> It is now accepted that most, if not all, of the early congregations were house churches... The 'head' of such a household would naturally be recognized as having oversight of the new church. His [or her] social standing would give him [or her] pre-eminence in the group; his [or her] close association with the apostle who founded the church... would add to this. And as time passed, the fact that he [or she] was the first (or one of the first) converts would further enhance his [or her] position in the group. (p.31)

It would have been natural, given their leadership when Christian services were held in households, "Women also probably blessed the bread at the Eucharist" (Raab, p. 34).

Archeology also reveals the important role women played as leaders in the early Church. In her book, *When Women Were Priests*, Torjesen (1993) identifies a number of archeological artifacts that indicate women were important leaders not only in the Church, but also in the Jewish community between 5000 B.C.E. and 300 A.D. In the

Roman basilica dedicated the saints Prudentianna and Praxedis, there is a mosaic that portrays Bishop Theodora. The inscription identifies Theodora as *episcopa*, the Latin form of the feminine title bishop. There is an evident attempt to deface the last letter of the inscription in an attempt to obfuscate the leadership of Bishop Theodora celebrated in the mosaic. This becomes metaphoric for the attempts, after the fourth century, to hide the leadership women played in the first three hundred years of the Church. The record is clear.

The Catholic Church can no longer discriminate against women by marginalizing their roles in service of the Catholic Church. Catholic leaders must acknowledge the standards established by those closest to Jesus and return to the egalitarianism that guided the birth of the Catholic faith.

In the Greek Chapel in the Pricilla Catacomb in Rome, there is a fresco from the early third century that depicts a woman breaking bread in a Eucharistic celebration (Torjesen, 1995, p. 52). In another fresco, *The Celestial Banquet*, located in the catacomb of SS Pietro e Marcellino, a female is depicted leading an *agape* feast (Torjesen, p. 154). In these archeological findings, women are performing the Eucharistic ceremony in the early Church.

Archeological findings also identify women as ministers in the early Catholic Church. An inscription on a tomb in Egypt from the second or third century states, "Artemidoras, daughter of Mikkalos, fell asleep in the Lord, her mother Paniskianes being a [*presbytera*] elder" (feminine form). There is a memorial for "Ammion the [*presbytera* {femine form}] elder" set up by the Bishop Diogenes in the third century". "Kale the *presbytis* {another feminine form} elder" is identified in a fourth- or fifth- century epitaph. These archeological finds prove female priests served the Church for centuries before the Church fathers moved away from the standards established by Jesus, the apostles, and Paul, or more conservatively (a funny word for us, huh?) the people who were either the major players in the drama or wrote the texts (and went by those names).

There are many benefits of a Catholic return to the ordination of women. The most important of these is that women within the clergy and in leadership positions would alleviate the atmosphere in which molestation of children can occur and in which conspiracies to cover up these crimes can so easily occur. One of the most relevant conclusions Raab draws is, "Issues that particularly affect women-such as rape, poverty, and domestic violence-would also receive greater attention" (p. 235). Certainly, sexual abuse of minors deserves greater attention. Ordination of women priests will transform the environment in which such abuse occurs and conspiracy to cover such acts up are accepted.

Raab (2000) analyzes the debate over the impending ordination of women as Catholic clergy from a psychological perspective. Particularly valuable is her inclusion of experiences in the Episcopalian Church since women began to be ordained in 1977. Raab affords much attention to how the atmosphere in the Episcopal Church has been affected, the changes in the experiences in women during the rituals within the

Episcopalian services, particularly during the sanctification of the Eucharist. Raab also considers how the inclusion of women priests expands and transcends the identification of God as exclusively male. She then uses her psychological approach to consider the question of "what difference women priests would make" (p. 1) in the Catholic Church. Raab also explores the implications of such eventuality as it relates to "underlying concerns of gender, symbolism, and power" (p. 3). Obviously, Raab iterates throughout her work, when women serve as deacons, priests, and bishops in the Episcopalian denomination, women in congregations feel closer to God. Nevertheless, "Ordination remains out of bounds for Catholic women, despite their lengthy history in involvement with church ministries, a shortage of priests, and a recent Gallup poll showing that in 1992 Catholics favored women priests by a margin of 67 percent" (p. 25). According to a poll conducted by Quinnipiac University released March 8, 2013, 62% of Catholics in the United States support allowing females to become Catholic priests. Several bishops in the United States have vocally supported the ordination of women priests in the Catholic Church.

The Catholic Church has moved forward on including women more in areas that for a long time were sacrosanct prohibitions. Until the early 1960s, women were forbidden to approach the altar. Women can now perform such services as altar servers, lay Eucharistic ministers, and lectors who read scripture during mass.

Anne Carr has argued that allowing women to be priests would open the authoritarian patriarchal "male-dominated club" to a "spiritual service of unity" (p. 40). Rabb argues the inclusion of female priests would create a more egalitarian Catholic Church. The inclusion of female and married priests would dismantle the "clerical caste" (Raab, p. 26).

There are myriad advantages to the inclusion of female clergy, as is evidenced from the experience of other Christian denominations. Mainline Protestant denominations in the United States have included female clergy since the 1950s. Lutheran churches have adopted female clergy. Most notably are the experiences of the Anglican Church in England and the Episcopalians in the United States.

In *Women Priests: The First Years,* Wakeman (1996) presents an edited collection of essays by women clergy in the Anglican Church. There are several benefits identified by these women that result from a more inclusive clergy. First, women in congregations feel that seeing women leading the rituals as just and natural. Second, the feminine aspects of God are brought to the fore in the minds of the worshipers. The threads of Christianity that emphasize the nurturing feminine side of the Creator, the Cosmic Lover, come to the surface in the worship experience when women lead the service.

The institutionalized Catholic Church, a creature of time and space, has made attempts to take the sting out of a first century Jewish mystic's radical view of the human condition in which men and women are people, humans, spiritual beings and worthy of equal dignity, at least according to this version of Schrodinger's cat.

The solution? Believers may all be Semites, as Pope Pius XI said, but if the faithful are followers of Jesus, believers are first of all mystics, for whom the distinctions of language, culture, gender, etc. are mere words that signify but do not identify. Thus, females should once again be Catholic deacons, priests and bishops.

Women have long been leaders and ministers of the Quaker and Unitarian denominations. Women are leaders and ministers in the Episcopal Church, the Methodist Church, the Presbyterian Church, the Jewish faith, most mainline Protestant denominations and a number of other international Christian denominations. It is time for the Catholic Church to join the Christian community in embracing sexual equality in the clergy. It is time for the Catholic Church to return to the egalitarianism that exemplified the birth of Christianity.

In sum, Torjesen (1993) is correct: "The last thirty years of American scholarship have produced an amazing range of evidence for women's roles as deacons, priests, presbyters, and even bishops in Christian churches from the first through the thirteenth century" (p. 2). The Catholic Church, from school children, the laity, female orders, deacons, priests, bishops, cardinals, and the pope, should return to the true Catholic Church and ordain women clergy.

From this chapter, it is clear women clergy played an important role in the early Church. The canonical New Testament writings identified female ministers and "apostles," as Paul referred to them. Second, the historical context of the early Church and identified that as non-institutionalized house Churches, women played a leading role. Archeology corroborates the role played by female priest in the early Catholic Church. Thus, women clergy were a common feature of the early Church, and should be once again.

Women should once again be ordained ministers and considered apostles. Mother Teresa should have been ordained a minister of the Catholic Church and considered a modern-day apostle, as opposed to Father Geoghan of the Boston area, who may have molested over 130 children. One could say that a new day should dawn in the Church, but that would be incorrect. If the Church is true to *tradition,* ought it not wish to return to what appears quite obvious in the New Testament?

In the historic *mea culpa* in March of 2000, the John Paul appeared to promise corrective action in response to accusations of discrimination against women in the Church. After the recognition the persecution of women, John Paul II suggested a new approach: "Forgive us and grant us the grace to heal the wounds still present in your community on account of sin, so that we will all feel ourselves to be your sons and daughters." The Catholic Church should enact what was promised by John Paul. The Catholic Church should embrace female ministers for the practical sake of ending sexual discrimination and for the theological and moral goal of destroying an environment in which children are raped, and the rapists are protected. *The all-male priestly caste must come to an end.*

In this chapter, we explored the epistles from the New Testament and archeological findings that indicate women clergy served the Catholic Church in its first three centuries, and longer in some cases.

Chapter 9
Did Jesus Have a Wife?

We continue alternate exploration of the views of Jesus on the issue of married clergy in this chapter. We examine versions of Christianity the Church declared heresy. The celibate Jesus is an interpretation of the Gospels that favors a certain patriarchal outlook. We argue that the historical Jesus may have been quite different.

Women are easily seduced by heresy. They might even assume positions of power in such heretical movements as Gnosticism.

Gnosticism is an umbrella term—an arbitrary scholarly creation which many think ought to be allowed to go out of style—for diverse religious philosophies opposed in some way to the "proto-orthodoxy" of the apostolic Church.[1] One very general form of so-called Gnosticism (we will continue using the term for convenience) viewed Jesus as a purely spiritual being, an emissary from the High God, the *Pleroma* or Fullness, the God-Beyond who *was not the blind creator god of Genesis*. This blind, lower god, creator of the material world, was the offspring of a cosmic disaster. The divine history of the universe is related by the Gnostic Scriptures in many complex variations. The Demiurge is ignorant and believes himself supreme. "I am God and there is no other God beside me" according to *The Apocryphon of John*[2] is a declaration of sheer ignorance.

Jesus came from the *Pleroma* to remove this ignorance among humans by teaching them to realize their true spiritual selves, which in the second chapter of "cosmic-disaster-the-series" had been cast down into the evil prison of matter. Again, this imprisonment of the spirit in the darkness of matter rests upon a complex, sometimes contradictory

---

[1] Bart Ehrman, *Lost Scriptures: Books That Did Not Make It Into the New Testament*, (New York, 2003), p. 179.
[2] For the Gnostic Scriptures, we use *The Nag Hammadi Scriptures: The International Edition*, ed. Marvin Meyer, (San Francisco, 2007). *The Secret Book of John*, p. 116.

mythology. The original Fall, however, did not occur on earth, but in the cosmic realms of the spiritual universe. As Hans Jonas said:

> "Almost all the action would be in the heights, in the divine or angelic or daemonic realm, a drama of pre-cosmic persons in the supernatural world, of which the drama of man in the natural world is but a distant echo."[3]

Jesus had come to awaken the spirit in men *and women*. Such an awakening would result in immortality. "Whoever finds the interpretation of these sayings will not experience death," says Jesus in the *Gospel of Thomas* (p. 139). Salvation, therefore, comes not through the person of Jesus or his death, but through an intuitive self-realization (gnosis) made possible for every human being through his teachings. This is heresy flying in the face of the orthodox understanding of salvation by means of Christ's death and resurrection.

It also rejects the emerging patriarchal hierarchy of bishops, as Elaine Pagels has shown.[4]

In Gnosticism, women seem to be the spiritual equals of men, sometimes their understanding as in the case of Mary of Magdala is superior.[5] They too are able to gain insight and achieve salvation; at times, they are superior to men. Having experienced the truth on a spiritual level, women can author gospels, as shown by the Gnostic Gospel of Mary. In the Gospel of Thomas Jesus said:

> "When you make the two one, and when you make the inside like the outside and the outside like the inside, and the above like the below, and when you make the male and the female one and the same...then you will enter the kingdom" (pp. 142–143).

In Gnosticism, women are able to overcome—free themselves—from their biological condition, *as it was understood by the ancients.* Again Thomas:

> "Simon Peter said to them, 'Let Mary leave us, for women are not worthy of life.' Jesus said, 'I myself shall lead her in order to make her male, so that she too may become a living spirit resembling you males. For every woman who will make herself male will enter the kingdom of heaven" (p. 153).

That a woman becomes male must be seen in the context of ancient anthropology in which, according to Aristotle and Aquinas, women are incomplete men. The fact that a woman may be made male means an overcoming and transcending of her inferior nature. Note, also, that in the final line a woman can make herself male. By following Christ—"I myself shall lead her"—she can become a living spirit, just as the males may free themselves from the world of death by "following Christ." If the woman can do everything the man can do, and achieve this living spirit status, what, then, is to prevent her from becoming a priest? What is to prevent her from performing the Eucharist *in persona Christi*?

---

[3]Hans Jonas, *The Gnostic Religion: The Message of the Alien God and the Beginnings of Christianity*, (Boston, 1963), p. xiii.
[4]Elaine Pagels, *The Gnostic Gospels*, (New York, 1979).
[5]Karen L. King argues that there was a pre-Pauline conflict between Peter and Mary for leadership of the apostles and ultimately the Church. *The Gospel of Mary of Magdala*, p. 176.

A great deal of Christian doctrine was created in response to heresy. It may be something of an irony, or a bad joke on orthodoxy, that if Buddha had it right and everything in the world lacks essential being, an absolute self or essence—the Buddhist principle of *patityasamutpada* (interdependent origination)—than any existent thing *is* its causes and conditions. Orthodoxy *is* heresy just as form is emptiness in the *Heart Sutra*. Nothing stands apart. Nothing exists "from its own side" according to Buddha. Lacking a Christian atman, *Christianity could not exist without heresy*. They are both empty (*sunyata*) of essence, of Self, and so they are both full. Christianity is heresy; heresy is Christianity. The equality (or superiority) of women in Gnosticism is their inequality in orthodox Christianity.

There may also be sociological reasons for an all-male priesthood. If the Eucharist is understood as a sacrifice in which Christ is both victim and priest, then the human priest who presides over the sacrifice mediates between God and the faithful. The hierarchy of the universe is reflected in the hierarchy of the Church. The priest stands in for God. Sacramental practice implies a social structure.

Sacrifice, according to Nancy Jay (quoted earlier in this book), is also "at-one-men-t," that is, a social bond. Faced by heresy, persecution, economic necessities, the Church developed a "sacrificially maintained social structure" to preserve itself.[6] Priests became patrilineal successors to the male apostles. A priest stands as a son (like Christ), but the inheritance must pass through the apostolic tradition and not through the biological woman. It is no wonder, then, that a Mother Church gave birth to an all-male hierarchy. And it is also no wonder that the institution required male only apostles who were actually caliphs of a male founder. Ritual purity determines the succession. The reproductive powers of women, according to the Church Fathers, are especially polluting. The pure blood of Christ replaces the pollution of the female. A male dominated sacrament, not a flesh and blood mother, preserves the patrilineal descent from the apostles. Priests give birth to priests.

Aquinas may have revealed more than he knew. The sacramental significance of Eve coming from Adam's rib, the blood (Eucharist) and water (baptism) coming from the side of Christ "sleeping on the Cross," builds the visible community and its patriarchy. Aquinas even admits to this when he concludes "on which the Church was established" (Article 3). It is almost as if he had read Jay before he wrote. The Eucharistic sacrifice, she concludes:

> can expiate, get rid of, the consequences of having been born of woman (along with countless other dangers) and at the same time integrate the pure and eternal patrilineage. Sacrificially constituted descent, incorporating women's mortal children into an "eternal" (enduring through the generations) kin group, in which membership is recognized by participation in sacrificial ritual, not merely by birth, enables a patrilineal group to transcend mortality in the same process in which it transcend birth. In this sense, sacrifice is doubly a remedy for having been born of woman.[7]

---

[6]Jay, pp. 113–117.
[7]Jay, p. 40.

As a bonus the priesthood transcends death. As seen above, women are the source of life *and* death. Rather than accept the sacred nature of this fact, as, say, some of the goddess religions, the Church frantically struggles to transcend it. The consequences for women are disastrous. If women became priests, the entire worm-eaten structure would collapse. They might not stand in the person of Christ, but in the feminine genius of, say, Isis.

John Paul II's "new feminism" makes an interesting contrast. Motherhood, writes the Pope, expresses the special dignity of the woman, who while sharing equally with the man in common humanity (the image of God), through Motherhood participates in "a special communion with the mystery of life" (*Mulieris Dignitatem*, 18, p. 22). This unique contact with life, the developing child in her womb, has a profound effect on her personality: she is "more capable than men of paying attention to another person." In the biological sense, Motherhood is also passive: the generation of life "takes place" within her body, in that it happens to her (p. 23). Let one call this 'holy passivity" as opposed to the unholy kind that tempts men. Unholy or holy, it remains passivity.

Now the Virgin Mary, who gave herself completely to God in selfless devotion, God's Mother *(theotokos)*, is the archetypal passive woman. In Mary, the dignity of woman is fully realized. But seen from a different angle, say the crooked angle of modern self-serving autonomy that the Pope so despises, one may reasonably ask if it is possible that a woman might desire to achieve her "personhood" through, say, the priestly, spiritual duties of administering the Eucharist? In giving herself to the Church, selflessly, becoming a priest, she too participates in the mystery of "eternal life." Her participation in the spiritual may be Motherhood in the superior life of the eternal. Naturally, this would make her active and dominant in our world, standing over the male, as if Eve had come from Adam's head, and open the depressing (for the Church) possibility of matriarchy. Spiritually, she might become, like the Gnostic Mary, a man. The Pope's celebration of Motherhood, biological, spiritual, or whatever theological rabbits happen to pop out of his vertical crown, is profoundly misogynist. It turns out to be not a contrast at all. It is an up-dating of misogyny.

Within the priestly community of the Church, the woman is still, despite her newly exalted femininity, a prisoner of her biology. She is promoted upstairs in order to be denied power. She cannot become an active male as she does in the Gospel of Thomas. She cannot gain the upper offices of the Kingdom of Heaven on earth and become, heaven help us, Pope. John Paul II warned that the modern idea of "women's rights" must not under any condition lead to "masculinization" of women (10, p. 12). This apparently means activity and authority, that is, becoming a pope. Taking Thomas symbolically, as the Pope does Genesis, the woman cannot become male like you males, which means her special dignity denies her the privileges of the priesthood. But real equality, like real women, exists on the horizontal plane and needs to realized not in symbols but in action.

The priest stands in for Christ, he is *persona Christi*, a man like our Lord. Yet, as the Archbishop of Canterbury once pointed out to the Pope, Christ redeemed *all humanity*, which must include women. If the priesthood bears a representative nature, it must represent this complete redemption.[8]

In the Gnostic *Gospel of Mary*, Peter asks Mary Magdalene to "tell us the words of the Savior, which you remember" (p. 737). It is an interesting scene. The woman has in fact become the teacher of the chief apostle. It is, of course, this apostle who bequeaths to the Pope his authority to make, among other pronouncements, authoritative statements on the "special dignity" of women. In the Gnostic gospel, Peter is skeptical. Like any Catholic priest, then and now, he wonders if Jesus really spoke such words to a woman. Why not to men? Levi answers:

> But if the Savior made her worthy, who are you indeed to reject her?
>
> Surely the Savior knows her very well. That is why he loved her more than us. Rather, let us be ashamed and put on the perfect man and acquire him for ourselves as he commanded us, and preach the gospel, not laying down any other rule or law beyond what the Savior said. (p. 745)

Levi's first two sentences played very well in Dan Brown's *The Da Vinci Code*. If one understands *know* in the biblical sense, Jesus may have known her very well indeed. But this may go too far. Here, the gospel speaks of spiritual knowledge, that the woman, Mary understands Jesus far better than the men. In Gnosticism, contrary to Brown, Mary is not the wife of Jesus in the physical sense. Her status is far greater than this. *She is Jesus*. She has achieved "the perfect man."

Like the canonical gospels, the debate over the historicity of the Gnostics—if they contain anything that takes one close to the historical Jesus—will continue. Whether or not they come later, they are, like the canonical gospels, an interpretation of Jesus and as we've indicated may represent Church disputes in the earliest phase of Christianity. Some assume religious systems, unlike anything previously discovered in the ancient world.[9] In some versions, the material world is the creation of a blind, ignorant lesser demiurge:

> I am God and there is no other but me...
>
> You are wrong "Samael"—which means "blind god." (*On the Origin of the World*, p. 206).

Human beings are prisoners of ignorance, like Samael. Human beings know not of the High God, who exists beyond the created world, beyond earthly minds, beyond all earthly categories of thought. The High God cannot be just another being among beings, even though one says he is omnipotent, omniscient, eternal, that is, the greatest Being.

---

[8]Cited in Weigel, pp. 520-521.
[9]Ehrman, *Lost Christianities*, p. 115.

But he cannot be called *greatest*. He cannot be called by any name or limited by any category. And so in the treatise *Thunder, Perfect Mind* the reader is told:

> For I am the first and the last.
> I am the honored and the scorned.
> I am the whore and the holy.
> I am the wife and the virgin.
> I am the mother and the daughter.
> I am the limbs of my mother.
> I am a barren woman
> who has many children.
> I have had many weddings
> and have taken no husband. (p. 372)

Here, the gender is female. In the next stanza the reader is told that "I am the bride and groom...I am silence that is incomprehensible" (p. 373). Language, including gender specific language, is inappropriate to God. God is the bride and groom, Father and Mother. Does this imply that the *imago Dei* exists in everyone, *equally*?

In the eyes of the church fathers, this was rank heresy. And not merely in the realm of ideas; images of God, or lack of images, influence power relationships. Once women saw themselves as symbols pointing upwards to the God Beyond, there was no telling what other strange ideas might pop into their feeble brains. Tertullian exclaims:

> These hysterical women—how audacious they are! They are bold enough to teach, to preach, to take part in almost every masculine function—they may even baptize people![10]

It has been noted that the Gospel of Thomas (114 verses) seems similar to the postulated Q Source, roughly 235 verses that occur in Matthew and Luke, but are not in Mark, the source of the other two synoptic gospels. Neither Q nor Thomas contain death and resurrection stories, which for Pauline Christians are everything. That there may have existed other Christianities *before* the emergence of orthodoxy is a good possibility. It is obvious that Paul writes in order to combat "false teaching" which indicates that disputes over what Jesus taught and his identity were raging perhaps two decades after the crucifixion.

In the Gospel of John, Thomas is a doubter. He does not believe in the physically risen Christ. The Gnostic Jesus, a spiritual emissary from the God Beyond, stands in opposition to the "physically" risen Christ, even though Paul says that "flesh and blood" (*sarx kai aima*) cannot inherit the Kingdom (I Corinthians 15:50). Apologists try to sidestep the issue by saying that this phrase, flesh and blood, refers to "mortal corruptibility." Well sure, mortality is the very nature of contingent composite bodies. This is hardly news. The turn to abstraction does little to resolve the issue. Further, the so-called "incorruptible" flesh and blood risen Christ is able to pass through doors, disappear and reappear, and, ultimately, levitate. Of course, without a body he is danger of becoming

---

[10] Quoted in Elaine Pagels, *Beyond Belief: The Secret Gospel of Thomas*, (New York, 2005), p. 159.

a mere ghost (Docetism—his body was a disguise worn by the spirit, a Gnostic-like position), and there is nothing unique about that.[11]

Orthodoxy is defined by its victory. The victory was also over women. It set up a male only club as an alternative to the priestesses of Isis. Later, after the so-called conversion of the Emperor Constantine in 312, the image of Christ becomes more martial, Christ savior is also Christ Conqueror as befitting the god of the Emperor and his Empire. Women need to remain in homes as mothers, hopefully mothers of soldiers.

The Church fathers viewed women with suspicion and fear, and as a result treated them like dangerous snakes. John Paul II, on the other hand, talked about personhood and dignity, and the special glory of the mother. But his ideal woman is still passive. Motherhood happens to her, her passive eggs like Aristotle's unformed matter are fertilized by the active "male" sperm. Despite every denial, she is still defined by her biology.

Because of that biology, she is all too often a distraction from the spiritual path. Jesus, like all humans in everything but sin, never strayed from that path. He was obedient unto death. The woman, Mary could well have been his "last temptation." The Gnostic Jesus "kissed her often on her mouth" (*The Gospel of Philip*, p. 171).[12] The orthodox Jesus resisted the temptation and remained celibate. Like his Father. And his priesthood like him. Who knows about the Jewish holy man? But Jesus the Jew, devoted to Torah, not living in Qumran, a wandering teacher, would have seemed weird, odd, to those lost sheep of Israel had he not been married.

We examined versions of Christianity the Church declared heresy. The celibate Jesus is an interpretation of the Gospels that favors a certain patriarchal outlook. We argued that the historical Jesus may have been quite different.

---

[11] See the discussion in Robert M. Price, *Jesus is Dead*, (New Jersey, 2007), pp. 178-179. Also see Kris D. Komarnitsky, *Doubting Jesus' Resurrection: What Really Happened in the Black Box? An Inquiry into an Alternative Explanation of Christian Origins*, (Utah, 2009).

[12] Let not kissing be carried too far (or knowing for that matter). Kissing was a symbol by which the perfect received grace from one another, by which the perfect conceive and give birth. That Jesus kissed Mary means that he passed to her the pure spiritual teaching. A spiritual woman is pure, chaste widows, devoted wives. Karen L. King, *The Gospel of Mary of Magdala*, pp. 146, 181.

Chapter 10

Married Priests, Bishops, and Popes in The First Thousand Years of the Catholic Church

In this chapter, we establish the wide acceptance of married priests and bishops in the early Catholic Church. Virtually all sources agree that married clergy were accepted through the first thousand years of the Catholic Church.

Many ordinary Catholics are undereducated: the current requirement for celibacy for priests, bishops, cardinals, and popes is relatively new, yet another of those "deeper theological truths" supposedly mined from that infinitely malleable abstraction labeled tradition. The Catholic Church never disputed the inclusion of married clergy for the first thousand years of Church history. This is clear through a reasonable reading of the New Testament epistles and explication of the debate within the Catholic Church for its first 1,500 years. This debate re-emerged after Vatican II and should be encouraged to rage today.

A balanced reading of the New Testament reveals that married clergy were accepted as the norm in the original Christian movement established by Peter, Paul, and the so-called apostles. For instance, it is clear that Peter was married, as is evident in Mark 1: 30-31: "Simon's mother-in-law lay sick with a fever. They immediately told him about her. He approached, grasped her hand, and helped her up. Then the fever left her and she waited on them" (*New American Bible*). Clearly, Simon, later named Peter, the first apostle called by Jesus, was married. The passage is clear: The mother of Peter's wife was ill. The other apostles were all likely married, with the possible exception of John.

The writer of the first letter to the Corinthians, presumably Paul, also wrote that Jesus left no command that those who serve God are prohibited to marry. 1 Corinthians 7:25

states, "Now in regard to virgins, I have no commandment from the Lord" (*New American Bible*). Jesus did not prohibit those who followed him or lead the early Church movement from marriage.

The writer's first letter to the Corinthians further emphasized the right for priests and leaders of the early Catholic Church to be married. 1 Corinthians 9:5 states: "Do we not have the right to take along a Christian wife, as do the rest of the apostles, and the brothers of the Lord, and Cephas?" (*New American Bible*). Paul here appears to be defending his right to have a wife. Preeminent Catholic biblical scholar Raymond E. Brown (1997) wrote, "From 9:4-6 we learn that other apostles (for Paul this need not mean the twelve), the brothers of the Lord (including James) and Cephas (Peter) were accompanied by Christian wives" (p. 521) The writer of 1 Corinthians clearly communicates that the other apostles were married, as were relatives of Jesus serving in the early Christian movement—and, as we've seen, possibly Jesus himself.

The first priests in the Catholic Church movement were married according to the New Testament epistles. Titus 1:5-6 offers marriage as a standard for presbyters or ministers (priests): "For this reason I left you in Crete so that you might set right what remains to be done and appoint presbyters in every town, as I directed you, on condition that a man be blameless, married only once, with believing children who are not accused of licentiousness or rebellious" (*New American Bible*). The commentary offered in a footnote in the St. Joseph Edition states, "The terms *episkopos* and *presbyteros* ("bishop" and "Presbyter") refer to the same persons" (p. 333). Thus, not only could (or should, based on one's particular interpretation) priests be married, according to the Catholic translation of the New Testament, but so could (or should) bishops.

The writer of the Letter to Timothy 3:1-5 has an even stronger suggestion that a bishop *should* be married:

> This saying is trustworthy: whoever aspires to the office of bishop desires a noble task. Therefore, a bishop must be irreproachable, married only once, temperate, self-controlled, decent, hospitable, able to teach, not a drunkard, not aggressive, but gentle, not contentious, not a lover of money. He must manage his own household well, keeping his children under control with perfect dignity; for if a man does not know how to manage his own household, how can he take care of the church of God? (*New American Bible*)

The last part of this passage suggests a prerequisite for becoming a bishop is that a person can manage a household including their spouse and children.

Thus, the standard that priests and bishops could (or should) be married is clearly articulated in the New Testament epistles. This standard that priests and bishops could choose to marry was the *modus operandi* of the Catholic Church for the next thousand years. As Jesuit scholar John O'Malley (2002), professor of Catholic Church history at the Weston Jesuit School of Theology, wrote:

> Beginning in the third century there is indisputable evidence that even in the West many priests and bishops in good standing were married. The following list of bishops is but a small sample that I have randomly selected: Passivus, bishop of Fermo;

Cassius, bishop of Narni; Aetherius, bishop of Vienne; Aquilinus, bishop of Evroux; Faron, bishop of Meaux; Magnus, bishop of Avignon; Filibaud, bishop of Aire-sur L'Adour was the father of St. Philibert de Jumiages, and Sigilaicus, bishop of Tours, was father of St. Cyran of Brene. (p.9)

The historical record is clear. There were married priests and bishops for the first thousand years of Catholic Church history. Popes were also married. Kowalski (2005) presented a list of popes who were sons of priests, bishops and popes throughout the first thousand years of the Catholic Church:

These include the following sons of priests: Pope St. Agapitus (535-36), Pope Marinus I (882-84), Pope Bonaface VI (896), and Pope John XV (985-96); the son of a Bishop: Pope Theodore I (642-49); AND SONS OF Popes: the martyred Pope St. Silverius (536-37) son of Pope Hormisdas (514-23), and Pope John XI (931-35) son of Pope Sergius III (904-11). p. 12

The historical record is clear, even as most Catholics are unaware of the relatively new historical development of a requirement for clergy to remain unmarried and celibate.

There was a growing debate about celibacy as a requirement for clergy in the Catholic Church throughout the first millennium. Such debate arose at the Council of Nicaea in 325, but it was reported that the celibate and highly respected monk Paphnutius arose and spoke in favor of the personal judgment of each individual clergy member on the matter of celibacy. Paphnutius called sex between a priest and "a legitimate wife chastity" (Bilaniuk, 1968, p. 40). That ended the debate at the Council of Nicaea. Married priests and higher clergy were accepted.

Debate about required celibacy for Catholic clergy arose numerous times throughout the first millennium of the Church, but some geographical areas placed new restriction on clergy although others did not. Yet, married clergy have been prevalent. Married clergy were accepted without apology in the Catholic Church for its first millennium.

Married priests were banned between 1073 and 1139. As Spoto explained: As for the clergy, since early Christian times, ministerial celibacy had been an honored option but had not been required. It was mandated only a century before Francis, during the papacy of Gregory VII (1073-1085), who went so far as to urge the laity to revolt against married clergy and who called for priests' wives to be hunted down and banished (or worse). By the time of the Second Latern Council, in 1139, the wives of priests were proclaimed to be disreputable concubines, and their children were kidnapped to become Church slaves. There was massive resistance against this ruling, but Rome prevailed, at least legally. As a tactic for restricting ecclesiastical solely by the clergy and for disenfranchising the laity, it was brilliantly successful. But compulsory celibacy also severed the ministerial life from the people, who became completely subordinate to a priestly caste, themselves considered lower than the lordly pope (p. 8).

Thus, a ban on married priests was not institutionalized until a thousand years of married priests, bishops, and popes in the Catholic Church. It should be no surprise that

Pope Gregory VII, former Cardinal Hildebrand, was a reformer who held that the Roman pontiff was more powerful than Emperors, that he alone can be called universal. Peter Damian is said to have called Hildebrand a "holy Satan."

The debate did not reach the conclusion that established the standard that is accepted in the Catholic Church on this issue. It was not until 1563 at the Council of Trent that Catholic authorities declared:

> If anyone says that clergy in sacred orders or regulars with solemn vows of chastity can enter into marriage and that such a contract is valid, despite Church law or vow...and that those who do not feel they have a gift of chastity even though they vowed to keep it, can enter into matrimony, let him be an anathema" (Cannon 9).

The authors of this book proudly stand as anathemas. The Council of Trent continued, "If anyone says...it is not better and more blessed to remain in virginity or in celibacy than to marry, let him be anathema" (Cannon 10).

These conclusions of the Council of Trent seemed to end the debate.

There has been a re-emergence of leaders within the Catholic Church willing to express their opposition to the ban on over this issue. There have been a number of occasions in the last fifty years in which Catholic Church leaders have suggested that the ban on married Catholic clergy be reconsidered. Kowalski (2005) identified a number of these leaders who have spoken in public in support of allowing Catholic clergy to marry. At the Synod of 1971 in Rome, "Many cardinals expressed themselves in favor: Alfrink in the Netherlands, Suenens in Belgium, Malula in Zaire, Arns and Lorscheider in Brazil, Koenig in Austria, and Vidal in the Philippines" (p. 21). There have been a number of other Synods on Married priests. Kowalski (2005) identified a number of other Catholic leaders who have expressed support for return to accepting married Catholic priests, some of these synod settings. These include Bishop Jan van Cauwelaert of Belgium (1971); Cardinal Justin Darmojuwono of Jakarta (1980); Bishop Guy Riobe of Orleans, France (throughout his life and on his deathbed in the early 1980s); archbishop of Sao Paulo in Brazil Cardinal Evaristo Arns (1985); Bishop Michael Vincent Rowland of Dundee, South Africa (1985); the archbishop of Turin Cardinal Michele Pellegrino (1981); archbishop of Mariana Luciano Mendez de Almeida (1987); Bishop Jacques Gaillot of Evreux (1988); Bishop Pascasio Rettler, O.F.M. of Bacabal, Brazil (1989); Bishop Ladislao Bernaski (1996); New York Cardinal John Joseph O'Connor (1990); Archbishop Rembert Weakland of Milwaukee (1991); Bishop Patrick Power of Canberra-Goulburn (1996); Cardinal Basil Hume of Westminster (1998); Bishop Reinhold Stecher of Innsbruck (1998); and Auxiliary bishop of the Baltimore Archdiocese Francis Murphy (1999). Many Catholic leaders recognize it is time to return to acceptance of married Catholic priests.

These Catholic leaders offered many moving statements in support of married priests. In particular, Bishop Murphy (1999), on his deathbed, wrote a letter to the International Federation of Married Priests that is particularly moving:

> A great sorrow for me over the years has been the way the process has laid all the responsibility for change on the individual priest, while the church as an institution

has not been willing to review its own procedures or policies. I feel such a profound loss to the church, to the believing community, from this intransigence on the part of the institution to address the issue of a married history head-on, honestly, and creatively...In the end a renewed Church for the New Millennium will be born, shaped in a large measure by your experiences and those of other faithful who carry the wisdom of the Spirit and the yearning of the community for wholeness and new life."

This book is an effort to contribute to the vision articulated by Murphy. This movement will alter the current environment of the Church, attractive to potential pedophiles and tolerant of sex between boys and unmarried clergy.

A single personal experience does not prove much, but does count as a piece of evidence on the issue at hand. One of the authors of this book, John McHale, experienced the terrarium-like atmosphere in which pedophilia exists, was tolerated, and even protected. McHale spent his freshman year of high school at a Catholic seminary, at which young men studied with a consideration of entering the priesthood later in life. The living situation was one of a boarding school. Students slept in large dormitory rooms and lived in a communal environment.

Sexual relationships between McHale's classmates and men of the clergy were common. McHale suspected that at least 4 of his 14 fellow freshmen were engaged in sexual relationships with priests and brothers. McHale is positive this was the case for three of his classmates. In one instance, McHale saw a fellow 14 years old student dressing as he left the bedroom of a Brother, who was also dressing in the background of his room. Neither the Brother nor the student attempted to hide the contact that necessitated undressing. Such relationships were accepted.

McHale teased the boy who was dressing on his way out of the Brother's room. McHale was later called to the office of the Director of Seminarians for a disciplinary discussion. The Director of Seminarians, whom which McHale never suspected, nor does McHale believe now was involved in such relationships, verbally scolded McHale for hazing the young man involved in the apparent sexual relationship. In particular, the Director of Seminarians accused McHale of having a similar relationship with a priest, the English teacher at the seminary, who was known by McHale and the Director to have sexual relations with other seminarians.

In hindsight, what seems peculiar, even shocking to McHale, is the fact that sexual relations between students and male clergy were accepted and even condoned. Again, McHale was verbally disciplined for giving the 14 year old student a hard time for having a sexual relationship with an adult. Even though McHale is convinced the Director of Seminarians was not involved in such relationships, the authority accepted that such relationships were common, and prohibited McHale for speaking out about them. The culture was one in which these illicit, illegal sexual relationships were common and accepted.

McHale is convinced that if a woman or a married priest was the Director of Seminarians, this culture would have been exposed and stopped. The communal bubble of males, the closed environment in which sexual relationships between male clergy and adolescent boys was accepted as normal, would be cracked wide open.

McHale, although given openings to engage in such relationships with the English teacher, he deeply respected, and loved, had not "taken the bait" or accepted the subtle invitations to commence a sexual relationship with the priest. The thought made McHale uncomfortable. This was not the case with McHale's best friend at the seminary, who had become involved in a sexual relationship with the beloved priest who taught English.

McHale never felt pressure to engage in sexual relations with male clergy at the seminary, although he once felt uncomfortable in the infirmary for a mild illness, when he was sensually massaged on the arms and shoulders by the Brother who ran the infirmary. McHale was uncomfortable with the sensuality of the massage/caressing by what he considered a 'dirty-old man' and demanded the Brother stop it. The Brother stopped.

McHale left the seminary at the end of his freshman year only because there was no debate program. McHale begged the priest who taught English to start a competitive speech program, but to no avail. McHale liked the seminary, appreciated the rigor, and spiritually flourished in the religious environment.

McHale is convinced in the deepest sense possible the presence of married and female priests would have opened the closed atmosphere which attracted clergy who were attracted towards sexual activity with adolescent boys. The presence of married and female priests would have also disrupted the atmosphere in which statutory rape was accepted, protected, and even condoned.

Although this is just one personal experience, it reflects the atmosphere that would be disrupted with a more diverse clergy. Transparency is good in any authority-subordinate relationship. Conspiracies to cover up crimes is not healthy. Open environments with diverse perspectives alleviate group think. Lack of diversity creates closed environments which mat attract certain types of people. Repression is not healthy. More diversity at the seminary would have been healthy.

On Holy Thursday, March 17, 2002, John Paul II attempted to address the sexual abuse scandal in a letter to the priests. The audience of the letter, priests of the Catholic Church, influenced its tone, but the pope and his advisers are savvy enough to realize that the press and the public would be secondary audience. In this letter, John Paul committed the church to corrective action:

> As the Church shows her concern for the victims and strives to respond in truth and justice to each of these painful situations, all of us – conscious of human weakness, but trusting in the healing power of divine grace – are called *to embrace the "mysterium Crucis"* and to commit ourselves more fully to the search for holiness.

John Paul also prayed to God for the strength to engage in authentic corrective action: "We must beg God in his Providence to prompt a whole-hearted reawakening of those ideals of total self-giving to Christ, which are the very foundation of the priestly ministry." In this way John Paul sought to communicate that the church members and leaders would vigilantly guard against such crimes. The Catholic Church can and should fulfill John Paul's promise of corrective action and return to the standards which WERE "the very foundation of the priestly ministry."

If pedophilia is an abnormal condition, then it almost goes without saying that the condition of marriage, or some other "normal" relationship, would not alter the priest's propensity to engage in this activity. Married priests who were pedophiles would remain pedophiles. The question posed here is not the condition (which is a medical question in the end) but the institutional habits that allow easy access to unwilling victims without consequences. In short, the problem, once again, is power over people's lives.

The Catholic Church must return to the practices of its roots to allow an outlet for sexuality, which repressed, may come out in perverted forms. The Catholic Church must also return to the standards establish in the early Church to alleviate an environment that attracts potential pedophiles and in which conspiracies to cover up such crimes can be coordinated. Return to the acceptance of married Catholic priests (and acceptance of female priests) would alter the groupthink, which currently dominated throughout the hall of Catholic power. Once again accepting married (and female priests) would encourage a transparency currently lacking in the exercise of power within the Catholic Church.

The modest proposals based on the original Christian tradition on married and female clergy would also replenish an aging and shrinking priesthood. It would also revitalize the faith of many Catholics who find the Church's official position on these issues antiquated and unjust. 62% of Catholics in the U.S. support marriage for Catholic priests, according to a Quinnipiac University poll released March 8, 2013. Returning to the thousand year standard of allowing Catholic priests would revitalize the Church.

The Catholic Church has allowed married Episcopalian and Lutheran ministers to become priests after they converted to Catholicism. "By 1990 over forty had been ordained in the United States; by 2002 over a hundred" (Kowalski, 2005, p. 26). Kowalski further identified "Married ministers from the Lutheran, Methodist, Presbyterian communions have also been ordained as Roman Catholic priests in the United States" (p. 26). The leadership should extend this standard to Catholics.

In this chapter, we clearly established the wide acceptance of married priests and bishops in the early Catholic Church. Virtually all sources agree that married clergy were accepted through the first thousand years of the Catholic Church. We then identify the support throughout Catholic Church leaders for a return to this tradition. We offer personal perspective which justifies such a return to voluntary celibacy for Catholic priests. Finally, we highlight such changes would constitute substantive corrective action that would fulfill John Paul's image restoration discourse. We argue the Catholic Church should again open this option for the health of the Church and to create an atmosphere less attractive to pedophiles and subsequent conspiracies to cover up atrocious crimes against children.

Bishop Ulrich of Imola in Italy in, in response to calls to prohibit marriage by Catholic Clergy in 1060, wrote, "Can't you see, as the common judgment of all sensible people holds, that this is violence, when one is compelled to enforce special decrees on a person against the evangelical customs and dictates of the Holy Spirit?" (in Barstow, 1982, p. 107). In Part III, this book will explore the implications of such violence.

Chapter 11

Witchy Women

In this chapter, we explore how women as they are defined by the Church, past and present, are at the same time creatures of weak wills and insatiable lust. Therefore, they are subject to demonic possession and witchcraft. We show how John Paul's views and Pope Benedict's views must logically result in a lower regard for women or men who are married to women.

In every Mass, the Catholic priest standing at the altar projects an ethos of male domination. The image contains an entire universe of misogynistic attitudes. The practical results are predictable.

Women have been denied access to positions of power within the Catholic Church. They are prohibited from becoming priests. This has excluded women from ascending to positions of leadership. They cannot hope to become bishops or cardinals. Women have not even been allowed to become deacons, a role that Catholic lay males can attain in the priestly orders. The official policy of the Catholic Church before twentieth century reforms of the liturgy held that the female person may not approach the altar under any circumstances. As we've already heard, even the use of the pronoun "she" is prohibited.[1]

A woman's natural tendency toward gullibility resulted in service to Satan, which in the lexicon of the Church was witchcraft. The Great Witch-hunts, which began in 1485, were full of instances of the torture of women who had been accused of witchcraft. To be fair, Innocent VIII's Bull of 1484 (*Summis desiderantes affectibus*) accuses *both sexes* of witchcraft. Nevertheless, the overwhelming majority of those accused of witchcraft in the 1500s, 1600s, and 1700s were women. Targets of accusations of witchcraft were often women who peddled natural and herbal cures and who were in a weak social position.

---

[1] Fox, *The Pope's War*, p. 187.

This was especially true of older women with no family support or women who were unmarried and lived alone ("when a woman thinks alone, she thinks evil").

The mother of the great astronomer, Johannes Kepler, is a good example. Her husband had deserted her; she lived alone, was quarrelsome and was known to have a sharp tongue.[2] For a host of reasons, including village politics, she was accused of witchcraft, threatened with torture, and put on trial. Not even Kepler, the Emperor's favorite, could spare her such indignities.

Torture was often used by Church officials to obtain confessions, and death by burning or hanging was often the fate of the unrepentant. *The Malleus Maleficiarum* says that besides being unable to weep, witches are insensitive to the pains of torture (p. 223). Unfortunately, such an assumption might result in *no convictions.* To solve this problem, the good Dominican authors decided that the devil might allow a witch to weep or cry out since deception is, after all, proper for a woman (pp. 227–228).

It is impossible to say exactly how many women perished. Recent estimates range roughly 30–60,000 victims in about 300 years, but other claims reach as high as 9 million in 500 years.[3] Catholic persecution of witches was officially suspended in 1657, yet continued into the eighteenth century and nineteenth century.[4]

It is important to note that Catholics did not have a monopoly on rooting out these dangerous old women and milkmaids, just as misogyny has been present in other religions as addressed earlier. Trials of witches occurred in Protestant controlled regions as well. Many of the confessions of involvement in black Sabbaths may have just been a way to stop torture. Carlo Ginzburg has suggested that many of the black Sabbaths or the sexual rituals presumed to be part of these ceremonies may have never occurred, but were extensions of the imagination and fear of the inquisitors, or better, misunderstandings of ancient fertility traditions of the country people.[5]

To be fair to the Church, witchcraft may have simply been a byproduct of village life. Unexplained misfortunes required a cause. A mean looking old woman with an evil glint in her eye, that bad feeling one suddenly acquires in her presence, her secretiveness, may all contribute to the charge of witchcraft. On one level, there is nothing overtly religious about it. The critic is certainly entitled to play the game of "distinct but not separate." Yet, centuries of Church teaching about women's dangerous attractions, the story of Eve and the Serpent, and a host of other saintly tales, predisposed villagers to look for the devil's minions in the company of the female. After all, where would such evil and supernatural powers come from if not Satan?

Misogyny associated with the Witch Craze may have deeper roots. It is possible to see the persecutions as a symptom of a problem that goes to the heart of the Christian world-view, more profound than any theological prehistory of primal gardens with

---

[2] James A. Connor, *Kepler's Witch: An Astronomer's Discovery of Cosmic Order Amid Religious War*, (New York, 2004), p. 14.
[3] John R. Mabry, *The Monster God: Coming To Terms with the Dark Side of Divinity*, (Winchester, UK, 2008), p. 100.
[4] See Cullen Murphy, *God's Jury: The Inquisition and the Making of the Modern World*, (Boston, 2012).
[5] See Carlo Ginzburg, *The Night Battles: Witchcraft and Agrarian Cults in the Sixteenth and Seventeenth Centuries*, trans. J. Tedeschi and A. Tedeschi, (Baltimore, 1986) and Ginzburg, *Ecstasies: Deciphering the Witches Sabbath*, trans. R. Rosenthal, (New York, 1991).

talking snakes. In fact, *the historical example of witchcraft may hold the key to the entire apology.*

Why, after so many centuries of the Catholic Middle Ages, does witchcraft, witch-hunting, trials, torture, hanging and burning of women become so prominent in the fifteenth through seventeenth centuries? At the very moment Europe begins the long journey toward the scientific world-view, the Church goes into near hysteria over the existence of witchcraft. Specifically, an almost voyeuristic obsession with the sexual relations between devils and women seems to haunt the minds of the inquisitors, if not quite a few priests, monks, and bishops.

Probing the theories behind the investigations of women's sexual encounters with devils, Walter Stephens found that misogyny was not "the whole story."[6] Rather, the theorists were most concerned with the *reality of the spiritual world.* Did not the empirical evidence of demonic sex correspond to the real existence of demons? If one could show objectively—and what could be more empirically intimate and material than sex?—that demons did truly exist in reality, the entire spiritual world, the stories in scripture, the miracles, even the miracle of the Eucharist, could be firmly established on empirical grounds. The interest in sex, says Stevens, was not pornographic as such, though it seems so, but metaphysical (p. 26). It was meant as a kind of self-help program, a means of resisting a terrible temptation that threatened the Christian's spiritual health.

And what was this temptation? Stevens provides a beautifully simple yet profound answer: *it was the temptation in themselves to skepticism of the supernatural* (p. 27).

Thanks to Aquinas, the fourteenth century heralded the triumph of Aristotle in the schools. Aristotle's natural philosophy relied upon natural causation, the four causes operating in change. Yet to be Christian, then and now, is by necessity to accept the reality, indeed superior reality, of the spiritual world, that infinitely pliable vertical dimension. But what if, as almost a side effect of the growth of scientific knowledge, "super-nature," the metaphysical world, begins to lose significance within science and the search for scientific knowledge? What if everything can ultimately be explained by natural laws, including the so-called mysteries of faith? Church doctrine in general, the scriptures, their fantastic stories, Virgin births, assumptions into heaven, and the like, become susceptible to skepticism—not the skepticism of the village atheist (or Polish communist), but a deep skepticism that begins to grow *within us*, in the believer, perhaps in a philosopher like young Karol Wojtyla.

George Weigel warned against amateur psychoanalysis practiced from afar in regard to suggestions that John Paul II's views on women may be somehow connected to the loss of his mother at an early age (p. 29). None of this, Weigel sternly admonishes, is of any use to "serious students" of Karol Wojtyla. A less serious student, however, cannot help but be suspicious, especially when examining statements in *Evangelium Vitae,*

---

[6]Walter Stevens, *Demon Lovers: Witchcraft, Sex, and the Crisis of Belief,* (Chicago, 2002), p. 4.

John Paul II's Encyclical Letter on the Value and Inviolability of Human Life from 1995. Attacking the so-called "culture of death," the Pope says of the Virgin Mary:

> "The one who accepted 'Life' in the name of all and for the sake of all was Mary, the Virgin Mother; she was most closely and personally associated with the *Gospel of Life* [Pope's italics]. Mary's consent at the Annunciation and her motherhood stand at the very beginning of the mystery of life which Christ came to bestow on humanity (cf. *John* 10:10). Through her acceptance and loving care of the Incarnate Word, human life has been rescued from condemnation to final and eternal death... As the Church contemplates Mary's motherhood, she discovers the meaning of her own motherhood and the way in which she is called to express it. At the same time, the Church's experience of motherhood leads to a most profound understanding of Mary's experience as the *incomparable model of how life should be welcomed and cared for* [Pope's italics] (102, pp. 77–78).

Babies, human and animal, show signs of profound distress at the sudden absence of the mother. A mother's love in some ways begins with the perfect protection of the womb and continues on with the physical intimacy of infant care and devotion. The mother is in nearly constant physical contact with the child, soft, comforting, warm, kissing and cuddling the baby, her love is unconditional. In some modern societies, the father's love is distant, stern, and packed with conditions. It demands obedience to rules and commands. It disciplines and punishes.[7] The abrupt loss of a mother's love had to have a profound influence on the future Pope's developing assumptions about the world. "Serious students," especially those writing biographies meant to be taken seriously, cannot ignore such things.

Unlike human mothers, the Mother Church, symbolized by the Virgin Mary, never dies. Her maternal love is always present. Yet, it is not the tactile love of real physical contact. It is distant, removed, intellectual. It knows nothing of the chemical messengers, the neurotransmitters, that rush through the body at physical contact, the chemical ecstasy that seemingly fires every cell, that accelerates the heart-rate, quickens the breathing, and overwhelms the senses. The absence of such early experiences, or their sudden disappearance, serving as the dress rehearsal for more powerful and compelling adult contacts, may leave a terrible void in the personality. In this case, the Pope knows from experience that women are weak and passive, because *they die*. Their love cannot be trusted. Mothers die unexpectedly. Only the Mother on High, the Virgin Mary, deathless and ascended into heaven, only such a love abides. But at a price.

As one might expect of cool intellectual love, John Paul II fences his "love" of Mary with rational arguments for the uniqueness of the human being. Man is the only

---

[7] See Erich Fromm, *The Art of Loving*, (London, 1957); Diane Ackerman, *A Natural History of Love*, (New York, 1994). The evolutionary origins of love are probably found in the parental care of young, and are not confined to primates, Robert N. Bellah, *Religion in Human Evolution: From the Paleolithic To the Axial Age*, (Cambridge, MA, 2011), pp. 69–71.

creature capable of morality, he says in *Love and Responsibility*. In man, cognition and desire acquire a spiritual character (pp. 22–23). Unlike animals, he goes on, humans possess the power of self-determination based upon reflection; humans are able to act from choice, from free will, which requires an ethical base (p. 24).[8] Therefore, morality requires one to act towards other humans as *persons*, subjects for themselves, and not objects to be utilized for our purpose. Reducing the human person to a mere object of sexual gratification—as if the person were sex and body alone—violates human dignity (p. 180). But how may one insure that even in marriage a person has not simply become a means to the end of self-gratification?

Again, John Paul II seems to think that the woman in her passive nature is more susceptible to being used. The two, he says, must "*share the same end*" (John Paul II's italics), which in marriage is PROCREATION (our caps). And he naturally means, perhaps all-too-naturally, motherhood for the woman. And Mary is the "incomparable model" through which the Church also contemplates its own *spiritual* motherhood (given that the Church cannot be a biological—merely objective—mother, which, again, introduces the terrible memory of a young boy's loss).

Since women can easily become mere objects of sexual pleasure, the Pope's "new feminism" affirms, in his opinion, the true genius of women: "You are called to bear witness to the meaning of genuine love, of the gift of self...Motherhood involves a special communion with the mystery of life as it develops in the woman's womb..." (1995, 102, p. 75). The faithful are back to motherhood, back to the Virgin Mary. John Paul moves easily from rational arguments to supernatural assertions. Like any good scholastic, John Paul slides almost imperceptibly into "the mystery of life," which proceeds from the Creator in whose image humans are all formed (according to the P-Source). Humans (not the beasts) ultimately receive their dignity as humans from this spiritual source. And this means that humans are greater than any modern (or communist) humanism, which by locating people solely in the natural world, "created from the animals," reduces them in the end to use-value.

The contemporary morally permissive outlook violates human dignity, most especially in the case of women. If supported by the financial and legal resources of the state, as is women's liberation based upon contraception or abortion, Catholics must legitimately inquire whether this is yet another form of totalitarianism beneath the pseudo-benign mask of democracy, John Paul II warned in his little book-length homily, *Memory and Identity: Conversations at the Dawn of the Millennium* in 2005 (p. 48).

---

[8]But are beasts incapable of ethical choice? Darwin had argued that animals display in rudimentary form the mental factors, including emotions, reason, and morality, which are found in humans (see Chapter Four of James Rachels, *Created From Animals: The Moral Implications of Darwinism*, 1991). For examples of various ethical choices in the animals see Rachels and also Steve Jones, *Darwin's Ghost*, 2000, especially Chapter 7. An article in *Time*, "Honor Among Beasts", (July 11, 2005), shows how such formerly human moral codes such as altruism, empathy, fair play, exist *in dogs*. "...animals have at least rudimentary versions of what we call morality" (p. 54). And maybe such ethical choices extend to other species: dolphins have been known to rescue drowning people. We will discuss modern research on primates in the following chapters.

Could it be that despite all the philosophical arguments of *Love and Responsibility* and *The Theology of the Body*, John Paul II like the witch theorists must battle a haunting skepticism within himself: maybe humans are creatures of the natural world evolved from earlier forms? The rudiments of morality may be perceptible in our animal kin. Maybe the stories told thousands of years ago are simply that—stories. We wonder about a Pope who believes that the Virgin Mary intervened that 13th day of May, 1981, to deflect Mehmet Ali Agca's bullet and save his life. One can be skeptical of a Pope who believed that the Third Secret of Our Lady of Fatima predicted him and his assassination attempt.[9] One should question a man who believes that there are no accidents in life; that *everything happens according to divine purpose,* which is John Paul II according to Weigel (p. 440). One wonders about a Pope who has made more saints than all the popes put together since the seventeenth century, and made it easier to become a saint by, in 1983, abolishing the office of the Devil's Advocate (*Divinus Perfectionis Magister*), the "skeptical" lawyer who investigated the claims of saintly miracles. John Paul, like one of those witchcraft voyeurs, frantically resisted the skepticism of the modern "age of suspicion" (our term) *within himself.*

"Created in the image of God" is the biblical story that underpins his outlook. Be it understood as spiritual, moral, psychological, or whatever new theological category is current, an individual who has studied the secular sciences of archaeology, literary analysis/source theory, history, physics, biology, evolutionary psychology—rational science—might legitimately question the relevance of such an assertion for such knotty problems as contraception, abortion, or women's liberation. Stevens illustrates the problem in terms of the witch theorists:

> "Their natural philosophy was driven by the desire to defend God and the Bible.
>
> Science, which has evolved from natural philosophy, has no such bias. This makes the problem of spiritual reality even more acute for the modern would-be believer. Today, it is clearer than ever that the loud declaration that 'these things definitely happen' is often a coded way of protesting that 'these things *cannot not* be happening. Because the Bible says they do...'" (p. 179).

By necessity, witchcraft theorists must believe certain misogynistic truths about women; they are passive, easily tempted, materialistic. Paradoxically, in the light of John Paul II's assertions, the inquisitors understood intimate physical connections to life to mean that women were more material and less spiritual, easy prey to demons. In the end, their sexual desires were declared insatiable. Tradition told the holy priests that women had always been so. No man, however virile, could satiate a woman's lust by any means, said Andreas Capellanus in the twelfth century.[10] Notice how sexual insatiability clashes with a woman's passivity. No matter. Both could be adopted by the Renaissance witch-hunters as empirical evidence for a supernatural world. In such a world, there is no falsification.

---

[9] John Cornwell, *The Pontiff in Winter: Triumph and Conflict in the Reign of John Paul II*, (New York, 2004), pp. 90-91.
[10] Andreas Capellanus, *De Amore*, (1185), quoted in *Woman Defamed and Woman Defended*, p. 123.

Weigel, in his own Gnostic-like assertion, claims that anyone who "knows" or has met John Paul II knows that he is not misogynist; the thought is "completely crazy" (p. 852). Yet, if the analogy holds, like the witchcraft theorists the Pope's resistance to his own possible doubts of spiritual reality operating in the empirical world causes him to become misogynist. His misogyny, which may be completely crazy but real nonetheless, rests upon the need to accept, without the nagging little voice of modern suspicion, the hermeneutical truth of the biblical story of the creation of humans for their own sake, of human sin, of the Virgin Mother Mary, of ultimate supernatural salvation—human life rescued from "eternal death."

John Paul II sincerely wants to be a feminist, but ends up becoming a new feminist, which is really an old Catholic misogynist. This tragedy comes from his need to know and believe the reality of the Christian *mythos* and to defend it against skepticism. It may well be that all the sophisticated philosophical critiques of "naturalism" come from such nagging doubts. But even the best logical demonstrations are not enough to resurrect visions of Zeus and Hermes, and the once populous realm of spirits. Stevens once again makes the point when he asks:

> "To what degree does Christian morality continue to be invoked, even in post-Christian, secularized form, to reinforce belief in spirits and human immortality?" (p. 371).

In this chapter, we explored how women as they are defined by the Church, past and present, are creatures of weak wills and insatiable lust. Therefore, they are subject to demonic possession and witchcraft. We showed how John Paul's views and Pope Benedict's views must logically result in a lower regard for women or men who are married to women.

Chapter 12
Big Brothers, Little Sisters

We examine John Paul's obsession with the Virgin Mary in this chapter. We also examine and critique the tendency of the Church to leave people in "spiritual infantilism."

In order to preserve the male patriliny of the priesthood, the scriptures are called upon to deny women access to positions of power within the Church. The *Catechism of the Catholic Church* states that Jesus chose men (viri) to be his twelve apostles, and this original "college" is the origin of the college of bishops and the priesthood (pp. 439–440). In 1994, John Paul II declared that the Church has no authority whatsoever to confer priestly ordination on women, and in 1995, the Congregation for the Doctrine of the Faith officially clarified the declaration, calling it "infallible."[1] As Christ is the bridegroom of his spouse, the Mother Church, and the Eucharist is the sacrament of our redemption, in which he poured out his blood (and not the polluting blood of the female), the priest stands *in persona Christi*. This time the symbol is of the priest as bridegroom. This gift gives definite prominence to the spousal meaning of God's love.

How easily John Paul passes from historical assertions (which as we've seen are highly questionable) to spiritual truths. New Testament scholarship at the very least questions the validity of such a position. The growing consensus holds that the so-called original apostolic Church is a historical fiction, a creation of men like Eusebius in the struggle to achieve supremacy over other Christianities. We've already discussed the tension between Peter and Mary of Magdala, *a female apostle*. From questionable history, one lurches into spiritual symbolism (the Church as God's spouse), to community

---

[1] John-Peter Pham, *Heirs of the Fisherman: Behind the Scenes of Papal Death and Succession*, (New York, 2004), p. 165. In July of 2010, Pope Benedict XVI declared the ordination of women a "grave crime," on par with clerical abuse of minors.

building and assertions of institutional succession; but in the end, when one comes back to real empirical power, women cannot be priests.

Nonetheless, there have been movements in the history of the Catholicism in which women gained position of some power within the Church or aspects in Church activity. Despite their marginalization within the organization, women have influenced the development of the Catholic Church at various points, even if all too few. The first female influence on power may be the most significant: It is said that Constantine's wife influenced his decision to accept Christianity as the official religion of the Roman Empire.

Female saints certainly played important roles in various ages, especially in Catholic mysticism. Women have played an important part in the Catholic missions, especially in the nineteenth century. Today, women do the most of the labor necessary to keep Catholic institutions operating.

When considering instances of discrimination against women, it is important to note that the Catholic vocation of the nunnery empowered women to choose a lifestyle other than that of a household servant and caregiver for children in patriarchic family arrangements. Although more limited than the roles available to men, it was an option. In the Catholic Church's defense, this option was abandoned by most Protestant denominations that split from the Church. But what the Church gives, it takes away. A male priesthood remains the rule. No priestesses.

Pope John Paul II prepared the way for his millennial *mea culpa* in a number of statements. His professed goal was to correct mistaken interpretations of the Church's views. Not only are some unnamed sinful children of the Church responsible for misogyny, but prejudicial opponents were to blame. The "Church," as always, is innocent. In fact, it too is a victim.

In the *Mulieris Dignitatem*, the Pope offered a re-interpretation of the position of women attributed to St. Paul:

> The biblical description of original sin in the third chapter of *Genesis* in a certain way "distinguishes the roles" which the woman and the man had in it. This is also referred to later in certain passages of the Bible, for example, Paul's Letter to Timothy: "For Adam was formed first, then Eve; and Adam was not deceived, but the woman was deceived and became a transgressor" (*1 Timothy* 2:13-14). But there is no doubt that independent of this "distinction of roles" in the biblical description, that first sin is the sin of man, created by God as male and female. It is also the sin of the "first parents," to which is connected its hereditary character. In this sense, we call it "original sin" (9; Obtained online at http://www.vatican.va/holy_father/john_paul_ii/apost_letters/documents/hf_jp-ii_apl_15081988_mulieris-dignitatem_en.html).

With such a reworking of Timothy, the Pope seeks to drain the poison from what seems to be a misogynist statement. John Paul is able to assert a "distinction of roles" without appearing too misogynistic. Sin is due to our "first parents." Conveniently, the Pope ignores the literal details of the J Source. Adam is quite ready to scapegoat the female when he tells God that the woman gave him the fruit to eat. The woman is a quick learner for she in turn blames the serpent.

For a number of John Paul's defenders, the buck stops with Eve. Eve, they say, had an inflated self-image and believed that she deserved to share dominion with God.[2] And that is not all. The faithful hear the intimate details as if Eve herself were confessing her sins under torture to the good doctors of the inquisition. The woman's weakness lies in the fact *she desires power*, the *men of the Church* say. But (we say) such a desire appears paradoxical in light her passivity which fits God's original intention according to the Pope. It also seems to denote a corruption of feminine nature (masculinization).

But according to the story, this corruption of human nature has not yet occurred. Are these the flaws in her nature (which cannot be flawed since God created her according to His intention) that *motivate her to sin*? And by the way, is *not modern feminism* (not ancient) the source of *masculinization*? If it is free will, then *it* cannot be a corruption, only her power-hungry, inflated egotistical use of it. If the Fall has not yet brought God's curse upon her, how, then, is an inflated ego possible? Apparently Catholic thinkers feel the need (or are inspired) to psychoanalyze fictional characters and label the results history. But believers are forbidden to psychoanalyze real human beings. By some other miracle left unrecorded by sloppy scribes it appears that Eve has become a modern feminist, at least in the minds of certain apologists.

John Paul proceeded with yet another symbolic interpretation:

> The author of the Letter to the Ephesians sees no contradiction between an exhortation formulated in this way and the words: "Wives, be subject to your husbands, as to the Lord. For the husband is the head of the wife" (*Ephesians* 5:22-23). The author knows that this way of speaking, so profoundly rooted in the customs and religious tradition of the time, is to be understood and carried out in a new way: as a "mutual subjection out of reverence for Christ" (*Ephesians* 5:21). In relation to the "old" this is evidently something "new": it is an innovation of the Gospel. We find various passages in which the apostolic writings express this innovation, even though they also communicate what is "old": what is rooted in the religious tradition of Israel.... However, the awareness that in marriage, there is a mutual "subjection of the spouses out of reverence for Christ" and not just that of the wife to the husband must gradually establish itself in hearts, consciences, behaviors and customs. This is a call which from that time onward does not cease to challenge succeeding generations; it is a call which people have to accept ever anew..., All the suggestions in favor of the "subjection" of woman to man in marriage must be understood in the sense of a "mutual subjection" of both "out of reverence for Christ. (9; Obtained online at http://www.vatican.va/holy_father/john_paul_ii/apost_letters/documents/hf_jp-ii_apl_15081988_mulieris-dignitatem_en.html).

It has already been noted that this idea appears in *The Theology of the* Body. Here in the name of image restoration is a clever use of the hermeneutic. Spiritual reverence for Christ is inserted to soften the apparent misogyny. The strategy, in essence, is a reverse of the witchcraft theorist's proof: Empirical investigation of women's intercourse with

---

[2]Richard M. Hogan and John M. LeVoir, *Covenant of Love: Pope John Paul II on Sexuality, Marriage, and the Family in the Modern World*, (San Francisco, 1985), p. 52.

demons gives a measure of reality to the spiritual. In John Paul's case, the empirical possibility that scripture really is misogynist is buried beneath a spiritual reinterpretation of the Timothy passage. And the Pope discovers, thank God, it is not. Note, too, the contrast between the *old* and the *new*. The Pope must try to soften the implied anti-Semitism by saying that the apostles express the new while communicating the old. Here is a kind of Hegelian sublimation in the story of Reason's march through time.

The Pope expressed regret for the Church's contribution to misogynous acts in "Letter to Women," June, 1995:

> Equality between man and woman is in fact asserted from the first page of the Bible in the stupendous narrative of creation, The Book of *Genesis* says: "God created man in his own image; in the image of God he created him; male and female he created them" (*Genesis* 1:27).... This original biblical message is fully expressed in Jesus' words and deeds. In his time women were weighed down by an inherited mentality in which they were deeply discriminated. The Lord's attitude was a "consistent protest against whatever offends the dignity of women" (*Mulieris Dignitatem*, 15).... In the footprints of her divine Founder, the Church becomes the convinced bearer of this message. If down the centuries, some of her children have at times not lived it with the same consistency, this is a reason for deep regret. The Gospel message about women, however, has lost none of its timeliness (Sunday Angelus, June 25, 1995).[3]

The Pope expressed "deep regret" for occasions when children of the Church (unnamed of course) did not uphold the equality of women. Here he enacts mortification. Although the passage is vague, the impression it leaves is that these regrettable incidents have been few ("at times") and they are characterized as *inconsistent* with Church doctrine rather than as, say, *offenses* toward women. This is a form of minimization and it is simply not true. Misogyny, according to John Paul, is the exception to the rule. Again, the exception *is* the rule.

In 1995, the Pope acclaimed the gifts of women in the world and recognized that history has been written by men with patriarchal assumptions:

> In the message which, last May 26, I addressed to Mrs. Gertrude Mongella, Secretary General of the forth-coming Beijing Conference, I made the observation that because of a new appreciation of woman's role in society, it would be appropriate to rewrite history in a less one-sided way. Unfortunately, a certain way of writing history has paid greater attention to extraordinary and sensational events than to the daily rhythm of life, and the resulting history is almost only concerned with the achievements of men. This tendency should be reversed. How much still needs to be said and written about man's enormous debt to woman in every other realm of social and cultural progress! With the intention of helping to fill this gap, I would like to speak on behalf of the Church and to pay homage to the manifold, immense, although frequently silent, contribution of women in every area of human life (Sunday Angelus, July 30, 1995).[4]

---

[3]Obtained at http://www.va/holy_father/john_paul_ii/angelus/1995/documents/hf_jp-ii_ang_19950625_it.html.
[4]Obtained at http://www.va/holy_father/john_paul_ii/angelus/1995/documents/hf_jp-ii_ang_19950730_it.html.

The Pope acknowledged that throughout history, the Church contributed to unequal treatment of women by focusing most upon men. Also, he is prepared to expand the historical analysis, that has focused on forms of life, *he says*, that have been previously ignored (has he read Peter Gay's five volumes, *The Bourgeois Experience: Victoria to Freud*?). Does he hope that such studies would serve to verify the Church's image of women as mothers and caregivers (maids too)? Perhaps he has in mind the silent female proletariat who cleans the halls and domiciles of Vatican City and keep house for important men too busy to do their own laundry?

This acknowledgement also functions as minimization, as he suggested it was not the Church alone that was responsible. Then he bolstered: I want to "pay homage to the manifold... contributions of women in every area of human life." In actual fact, such manifold contributions come down to one, perhaps two: motherhood and being helpmates to men.

The pope also requested a pardon from women in a Letter to Women in June, 1995:

> Thank you, every woman, for the simple fact of being a woman! Through the insight which is so much a part of your womanhood you enrich the world's understanding and help to make human relations more honest and authentic. I know of course that simply saying thank you is not enough. Unfortunately, people are heirs to a history which has conditioned them to a remarkable extent. In every time and place this conditioning has been an obstacle to the progress of women. Women's dignity has often been unacknowledged and their prerogatives misrepresented; they have often been relegated to the margins of society and even reduced to servitude.... And if objective blame, especially in particular historical contexts, has belonged to not just a few members of the Church, for this I am truly sorry. May this regret be transformed, on the part of the whole Church, into a renewed commitment of fidelity to the Gospel vision?
>
> When it comes to setting women free from every kind of exploitation and domination, the Gospel contains an ever-relevant message which goes back to the attitude of Jesus Christ himself. Transcending the established norms of his own culture, Jesus treated women with openness, respect, acceptance and tenderness. In this way, he honored the dignity which women have always possessed, according to God's plan and in his love. As we look to Christ at the end of this second millennium, it is natural to ask ourselves how much of his message has been heard and acted upon. (Letter to Women, June 29, 1995).[5]

One might interpret this as a self-examination of the patriarchal tendencies within the Catholic Church and an implied request for forgiveness. In this letter, John Paul II bolstered (thanks women) then he tried defeasibility (They have been "conditioned by history," so they can't help themselves). Then he bolstered Jesus (certainly not in Fiorenza's way). He also enacted conditional mortification: "And if objective blame, especially in particular historical contexts, has belonged to not just a few members of the Church,

---

[5]Obtained at http://www.vatican.va/holy_father/john_paul_ii/letters/documents/hf_jp-ii_let_29061995_women_en.html.

for this I am truly sorry." John Paul also vaguely suggested that the Church can do better, a form of corrective action.

In 1996, the pope recognized the contribution of women to the Church and suggested they might play more important roles in the Church:

> It is equally important to point out that women's new self-awareness also helps men to reconsider their way of looking at things, the way they understand themselves, where they place themselves in history and how they interpret it and the way they organize social, political, economic, religious and ecclesial life.... In this context the consecrated woman, on the basis of her experience of the Church and as a woman in the Church, can help eliminate certain one-sided perspectives which do not fully recognize her dignity and her specific contribution to the Church's life and pastoral and missionary activity. Consecrated women therefore rightly aspire to have their identity, ability, mission and responsibility more clearly recognized, both in the awareness of the Church and in everyday life.... It is therefore urgently necessary to take certain concrete steps, beginning by providing room for women to participate in different fields and at all levels, including decision-making processes, above all in matters which concern women themselves (Apostolic Letter, *Vita Consecrata*, March, 1996).[6]

In this letter, John Paul II seems to support women's rights by acknowledging that women do good things that help men understand women. If this is so, might the Pope himself, after a good feminist education, change his mind about women in the priesthood? Given the pliability of scripture in the hands of his theologians, this ought not be too difficult a task. He does propose a goal of opening decision-making positions to women in the Church, although, as usual, he did not outline any concrete steps. If women cannot be priests, bishops, cardinals or popes, what real power is open to them?

The Pope has also used this opportunity to talk about expanding the role of women within the Church:

> Today I appeal to the whole Church community to be willing to foster feminine participation in every way in its internal life... The Church is increasingly aware of the need for enhancing their role.... The 1987 Synod on the laity expressed precisely this need and asked that "without discrimination women should be participants in the life of the Church and also in consultation and the process of coming to decisions" (*Propositio* 47; cf. *Christifideles Laici*, 51).[7]

This could function as a denial ("The Church is increasingly aware of the need for enhancing [women's] role"). It might also function as a very vague resolution of continuing corrective action. John Paul II seems to be asserting that since the Church convened a synod in 1987 during which the role of women in the Church was discussed, there is no problem. Apparently it counts as a major event when the Church merely discusses

---

[6]Obtained at http://www.vatican.va/holy_father/john_paul_ii/apost_exhortations/documents/hf_jp-ii_exh_25031996_vita-consecrata_en.html.
[7]Obtained at http://www.vatican.va/holy_father/john_paul_ii/apost_exhortations/documents/hf_jp-ii_exh_30121988_christifideles-laici_en.html.

women's issues, as if to simply acknowledge their presence is a theological revolution (or deeper reflection). He seems to be begging people to be nice. This hardly counts as a concrete instance of image restoration, but it is a step in that direction.

John Paul II expressed a similar sentiment at a Sunday Angelus in September of 1995:

> This is the way to be courageously taken. To a large extent, it is a question of making full use of the ample room for a lay and feminine presence recognized by the Church's law. I am thinking, for example, of theological teaching, the forms of the liturgical ministry permitted, including service at the altar, pastoral and administrative councils, diocesan synods and particular councils, various ecclesial institutions, Curias, and ecclesiastical tribunals, in many pastoral activities, including the new forms of participation in the care of parishes when there is a shortage of clergy, except for those tasks that belong properly to the priest. Who can imagine the great advantages to pastoral care and the new beauty that the Church's face will assume, when the feminine genius is fully involved in the various areas of her life? (Sunday Angelus, September 3, 1995).[8]

In this passage, the pope asserts that there is ample room for women already recognized in Church law. This sounds as if he is denying that there is a problem (Church law has *already recognized* this problem). Once again, if one carefully examines each specific instance, the reality seems to be that women remain servants, assistants to the males who provide leadership—what is "permitted."

In the *mea culpa* of March of 2000, the pope attempted to respond to accusations of discrimination against women in the Church. In response to the statement in the prayers of the faithful that recognized the persecution of women, John Paul II implored:

> Lord God, our Father, you created the human being, man and woman, in your image and likeness and you willed the diversity of peoples within the unity of the human family. At times, however, the equality of your sons and daughters has not been acknowledged, and Christians have been guilty of attitudes of rejection and exclusion, consenting to acts of discrimination on the basis of racial and ethnic differences. Forgive us and grant us the grace to heal the wounds still present in your community on account of sin, so that we will all feel ourselves to be your sons and daughters. (Obtained online at http://www.catholiclinks.org/sacramentodelperdonuniverpra.htm)

This statement may be part of a larger statement titled *mea culpa*, but there is little regret or mortification here, although he does acknowledge that "at times" equality has not been "acknowledged." This is not a strong statement acknowledging persecution or misogyny let alone apologizing for it. If one assumes that this as close to a genuine apology as John Paul II feels able to provide, he unwittingly returns to a pre-Church Christianity with its eschatological promise of sexual equality and spiritual community. Equality will arrive with the End of the World, in a completely unreal Kingdom in which

---

[8]http://www.va/holy_father/john_paul_ii/angelus/1995/documents/hf_jp-ii_ang_19950903_it.html.

there are no sexual differences—there are no women. The Pope then asked for forgiveness from God as well as grace to aid in future corrective action.

Throughout John Paul II's March 2000 *mea culpa*, he asked for God's aid in improving the altruistic capacities of members of the Catholic Church as if this were enough. Men ought to change their attitudes a bit. Changes in doctrine are forbidden. The question is if the male god YHWH can change his attitude? And that would lead into a frightful philosophical maze.

In this chapter, we examined John Paul's obsession with the Virgin Mary. We also examined and critiqued the tendency of the Church to leave people in "spiritual infantilism."

Chapter 13
Father Knows Best

We critique John Paul's claim that he was a feminist in this chapter. Personhood is manifested in human activity, according to Karol Wojtyla in *The Theology of the Body*, (p. 76). The body and its actions reveal what is invisible and therefore closed to scientific analysis. If this is, so then the actions of certain persons of the Catholic Church ought to "reveal" something of the invisible. Do they?

Females were allowed near the Catholic alter in 1992 when female altar servers were accepted by the church (a progressive break from the previous and the standing papal proclamation that women could not approach the altar). Such a step, however, could be construed as a feminine violation of priestly purity and was therefore opposed by conservatives. Therefore, John Paul II resolutely decreed that women could not exercise for the ritualistic priestly responsibilities of the sacraments. He repeatedly, consistently, and vehemently argued against even consideration or discussion of women clergy. Women are allowed out of the kitchen and are granted a peek at the main dining room, but they cannot become full-fledged waiters.

John Paul II codified the underlying differential treatment afforded males and females in the Church in November, 1995, when he ordered "Joseph Cardinal Ratzinger, Prefect of the Congregation for the Doctrine of the Faith, to declare as infallible the papal assertion that the Church cannot ordain women."[1] The Pope refused to allow Church leaders to even discuss actions that could be potentially truly correct. "Bishops will privately acknowledge that Pope John Paul II explicitly forbade them to discuss...'a married priesthood or women's ordination to the priesthood other than to defend the Church's official teaching.'"[2] This has included prohibition of discussion of female deacons. In a

---
[1] E. Kennedy, *The Unhealed Wound: The Church and Human Sexuality*, (New York, 2001), p. 32.
[2] D. B. Cozzens, *The Changing Face of the Priesthood*, (Collegeville, MN, 2000), p. 119.

review of his statements on the subject, Bernstein and Politi concluded: "His aim is to stop any discussion of the topic whatsoever."[3] Some feminists, such as Italian scholar Ida Magli, have argued that John Paul II's policies on women "betray a sort of unconscious hatred for the freedom of women."[4] These policies and prohibitions have and will continue to prevent real, effective corrective action. Do they reveal something about the person?

At a 1994 synod on Africa attended by John Paul II, German, Italian, and French bishops spoke in favor of a larger role for females in the Catholic Church. John Paul simply ignored them. In 1979, Sister Theresa Kane, president of the Leadership Council of Women Religious, implored the Pope "Your Holiness, the Church ought to respond to the suffering of women by considering the possibility of including them in all the sacred ministries."[5] The statement was featured in the mass media throughout the United States. Vatican authorities informally reprimanded Sister Kane. In 1980, during a visit by the Pope to Switzerland, Margrit Stucky-Schaller stated, "We regret that our work has so little importance for the faith and for the Church. We women have the impression that we are considered second class citizens".[6] Another woman openly challenged the pope in his presence in the Netherlands in 1985 when Hedwig Wasser asked John Paul II "How can we possibly have any credibility...when instead of making room for them, we exclude women?"[7]

John Paul's responses to such challenges have been paternal but courteous disregard. Like a good-natured father forced to say no to a child's demands, and who grows weary when the child keeps insisting, he firmly declares the discussion closed.

What exactly are these feminine "skills," he praised so highly? "Their deep sensitivity," and their "intellectual abilities?" They cannot be "made-masculine" as the Pope said elsewhere. Does not this "immense feminine tradition" derive ultimately from "motherhood," which is the giving of self, passive acceptance (the Virgin Mary), sensitivity toward the other coming from the closeness of having another being in her body? By praising women as he does, John Paul II reduces them finally to their biological status, but a status that is spiritualized to the point where he is able to deny biology in general. He then calls it a new, deeper, more humane feminism. As noted, many of these "talents" leave women open to intercourse with demons. Further, these prized female traits stand out in contrast to male traits: passive/active, self-giving/self-assertion, closeness/distance, and so on.[8] Consequently, they are defined in relation to men as they are defined by men. They remain incomplete men.

---

[3] Carl Bernstein and Marco Politi, *His Holiness: John Paul II and the Hidden History of Our Time*, (New York, 1996), p. 507.
[4] Quoted in Bernstein and Politi, p. 407.
[5] Quoted in Bernstein and Politi, p. 515.
[6] Quoted in Bernstein and Politi, p. 516.
[7] Quoted in Bernstein and Politi, p. 517.
[8] Here is where the Pope might have benefited from the empirical experience of married life. Near the end of pregnancy, many women behave somewhat differently than the Pope's romanticized version of child-bearing. Naturally the Pope has Scripture ready at hand: Eve's curse is to experience pain in childbirth. But let's be specific. By the third trimester, many women experience swollen feet and joints, muscle pain, fatigue, and a general discomfort at best, which for many is misery. The causes pose no mystery for medical science. Blaming original sin does introduce the spiritual element but this is

John Paul venerated and celebrated women, but refused to treat them as equals. His view of females seems to be that they are beautiful and generous gifts from God, but are existentially and spiritually different from men. The Church venerates Mother Mary although it denies that Jesus chose women to join his ministry. Women are not only holy because of their childbearing ability, but because they have an important and special gift which is the capacity to form men for the priesthood just as Mary is special because she bore Jesus, the priestly archetype. Like a muffled siren in the distance, one hears the irritating whine of ancient anthropology: women are "real" human persons as God intended only when they become men. Biology (at least the Aristotelian kind) is, contrary to papal denials of biological determinism, an adequate definition of women.

Women are equal (*imago Dei*) but inherently different, a position that reminds an American of the Jim Crow *modus operandi* of 'separate but equal.' Women have a special maternal gift. Presence unfortunately denotes absence: What women possess as mothers and molders of men, they lack in ability to perform the functions of priest, bishop, cardinal, or pope.

It has been noted several times, and it bears repeating, what the term "feminine genius" implies. The woman as the source of life, which establishes her intimate connection to God as Creator, expresses her unique genius in terms of her "vocation to love." The Virgin Mary is the ultimate expression of the feminine, the model of "true feminism:"

> While the dignity of woman witnesses to the love which she receives in order to love in return, the biblical 'exemplar' of the Woman also seems to reveal *the true order of love* which *constitutes woman's own vocation*. Vocation is meant here in its fundamental, and one may say universal significance, a significance which is then actualized and expressed in women's many different 'vocations' in the Church and the world." (*Mulieris Dignitatem*, 30, p. 36)

The biblical exemplar is of course the Virgin Mary, *theotokos*. The Vocation is Motherhood. All other special vocations actualize and express this universal significance of the feminine. According to Weigel, this apparent biological reductionism is not that at all, but a spiritual and moral significance as it signifies a "vocation of love." (p. 560) This is love rooted in the life of God, an inner dynamic of the Trinity, entrusted to women in a particular way.

Once again, Catholic authorities flee from the biological to the supernatural. Women are the spiritual dignified persons of *Love and Responsibility*, and yet everything about their uniqueness as women dovetails back to motherhood, of which the *Virgin* Mary is the archetype. The irony is that according to some scholars, the virgin birth, besides its possible connection to ancient mystery cults and the birth of heroes, and even Emperors, may simply be due to a misunderstanding of the Prophet Isaiah. The Hebrew word *almah* in Isaiah probably means young girl, maiden, but becomes *parthenon* in Luke's

---

hardly meaningful (or helpful) to most women. It does, however, produce feelings of guilt, martyrdom, and, once the baby is born, sainthood (perhaps). All of this has little or nothing to do with giving birth. Biology explains it all quite well, and evolutionary reasons (the narrowness of the birth canal in relation to a large primate brain) make far more sense than fairy tales. Besides, the addition of such "spiritual" meanings violates Occam's Razor.

Greek (1:27). In his *The Birth of the Messiah*, Raymond Brown gives an exhaustive discussion, trying to show that *almah* might indicate virginity, given most marriageable young women would be virgins (pp. 144–149). Nonetheless, he is forced to admit that one should not jump to any conclusions about the virginal birth of the messiah. It may well be an addition. After the birth stories, we hear nothing more about Jesus's virgin birth, although there may exist implications of something irregular about his legitimacy depending upon the reading.

Mistranslation or not, a virgin birth is surely what Luke's gospel proclaims. The fact that there exist countless other miraculous births in the ancient world should alert one the story has entered the realm of fable, not history. Naturally, apologists strive mightily to separate Hellenistic mystery cults from the Gospels. Anything can be made unique by sufficiently narrowing the definition until nothing but the specific phenomenon fits. It is like drawing the target around the arrow after it has been fired. All this seems special pleading and is really unnecessary. One does not require any sort of imperialistic metanarrative, imposed by the scholar, to suppose that any person writing in Greek would be aware of the common Mediterranean heritage. Chances are they learned their written Greek from classic examples beginning with Homer.[9]

Introducing the vertical also brings with it the demonic. The Pope is generally silent when it comes to demons and women. Yet, John Paul and his supporters constantly complained about the modern world's denial of the reality of evil. If one agrees with them for the moment and admits this reality, evil, then like sin, evil finds its visible expression in human actions. If this is true, evil must also find it visible expression in a visible cause of temptation, that is, in the visible form of the demons, to which women are especially susceptible. Is modern psychology, like biology, unable to grasp the full reality of the human because it refuses to include demonic possession? This is similar too to the idea that only women suffered from hysteria, thankfully buried by the papal nemesis, Sigmund Freud.

What if the modern skeptics of virgin birth turn out to be correct and the evidence is overwhelming, say like evidence for the heliocentric theory? There was no Virgin Mary. Jesus was simply a man, a Jewish Rabbi of the first century, teaching his own insights into the Torah. The Fall simply represents a human transition to an agricultural culture. What if love serves the evolutionary program and humans are animals, not created for their own or anyone's purpose? What if every miracle can be explained by ancient literary convention, or psychological wish-fulfillment, fraud, or what is more likely, delusion? What if angels and demons turn out to be chemicals and God exists only in our genes? In these and many other cases brought to the court of reason by the Enlightenment, the Church finds "herself" on the defensive. She scrambles to come up with counter-arguments, refutations, gaps in scientific knowledge, evidence from science itself like fine tuning, and even quantum theory (making the same mistake they did with Aristotle) until finally, cursing naturalism, she withdraws from the field into the supernatural. This creates a siege mentality. Siege mentalities create totalitarian attitudes.

---

[9]Dennis R. MacDonald, *The Homeric Epics and the Gospel of Mark*, (New Haven, 2000). Although this study focuses on Mark's Gospel which lacks a birth narrative, we believe the general principle applies to Matthew and Luke.

Perhaps John Paul II harbored such thoughts. The old myths no longer speak to modern people with the certainty they once possessed.

> "The presence of something beyond (what we call today) the "natural" is more palpable and immediate, one might say, physical, in an enchanted age. The sacred in the strong sense, which marks out certain people, times, places and actions, in distinction to all others as profane, is by its very nature localizable, and its place is clearly marked out in ritual and sacred geography. This is what we sense, and often regret the passing of, when we contemplate the medieval cathedral. God-forsakenness is an experience of those whose ancestral culture has been transformed and repressed by a relentless process of disenchantment, whose deprivations can still be keenly felt. But it has been part of a move from one religious life to another, long before it came to be (mistakenly) seen by some as a facet of the decline of religion altogether.

> ..... We have moved from an era in which religious life was more "embodied", where the presence of the sacred could be enacted in ritual, or seen, felt, touched, walked towards (in pilgrimage); into one which is more "in the mind", where the link with God passes more through our endorsing contested interpretations—for instance, of our political identity as religiously defined, or of God as the authority and moral source underpinning our ethical life.[10]

The struggle is not against the doubters outside the walls. Like the poor, they will always be here. The battle is with the doubters within, somewhat paradoxically, the spiritual doubters that like multiple personalities inhabit the soul of every modern person.

If the Church is committed to belief in angels and demons, miracle-working saints, and other supernatural entities, then this book has shown misogyny *must exist* in some form. No spiritual world, no misogyny. Since the Pope cannot give up the spiritual world (he cannot even exchange his version of it for something else)—indeed his very right to offer an apology derives from it—then he cannot in the end solve the problem of misogyny. It must continue. With Ratzinger as Pope, and later Pope emeritas, it has continued, and seems even worse, which illustrates our point.[11]

The very nature of John Paul II's own office, the entire magisterium and ecclesiastical authority, was a second to fifth century development, drifting away from egalitarian attitudes towards a hierarchical, patriarchal Church. The organization of bishops, priests, and dioceses reflected the organization of the pagan Roman Empire. Later, the Petrine doctrine, which held that the Pope was heir to St. Peter, the first bishop of Rome, the Rock of the Church and the holder of the Keys of Kingdom as given to him by Christ in the book of Matthew, bestowed upon the office an Imperial status likened to a Roman Emperor. These developments naturally brought along the old Roman patriarchal ideas, which, among other things, excluded women from high Church office.[12]

---

[10]Charles Taylor, *A Secular Age*, pp. 553–554.
[11]Matthew Fox's book, *The Pope's War*, reads like a cry of anguish.
[12]See D. F. Noble, *A World Without Women: The Christian Clerical Culture of Western Science*, (New York, 1992) on how such attitudes have carried on in Western history.

Many of the John Paul II's statements on women have been unprecedented. His words of praise for the female genius have seldom if ever been heard coming from the papal throne. He spoke with compassion, emotion, and sincere regret for past crimes against women. But was it sincere or an act, the performance of a masterful actor on the modern stage of the Areopagus?

Unfortunately, the reality is otherwise. Mother Mary is to be venerated and celebrated as a patron saint of mothers, but she had no place in the ministry of Jesus. Likewise, Mary of Magdala, who was a presence in the background of New Testament accounts of the ministry of Jesus, and the chief apostle of non-canonical gospels, was apocryphally reduced to a prostitute in the Catholic myth and liturgy. The continuing discussion of the basic inequality of women in the Church may offer a ray of hope, but John Paul II did not offer true corrective action in this area:

> Old prejudices and neuroses die hard, and having a good long look at them can be a step in the right direction of healing. As long as Christians continue to dance defensively around the problem of women, they will simply reproduce the system of double-think which has for so long bedeviled the matter.[13]

Pope John Paul II missed the opportunity to correct an important flaw in Catholicism. The Catholic Church in America faces a crisis in the lack of new priests. The reconsideration of a role for women in the Catholic priesthood may be one way that the Church can alleviate this crisis.[14] Unfortunately, in his rhetoric and in his actions, Pope John Paul II held onto patriarchal views. He asked for forgiveness (mortification), differentiated (only some members and representatives of the Catholic Church), and committed himself and the Church to corrective action. But the Catholic doctrine he defended prevents true corrective action.

The Pope, according to his most ardent supporters, revealed to the world the inherent barbarism of modernism and the culture of self-assertion. This barbarism is a defective humanism, similar to the defective humanism of his former, now vanquished foe Karl Marx. Its main defect is the understanding of freedom as the willfulness and not self-surrender, which is the source of all the evils of the present world (*Theology of the Body*, pp. 502–505). This false humanism results in the "culture of death."

What does this diagnosis say about human beings? The Pope claimed to have an exalted view of "man," that his views are far greater than what humanistic philosophy or psychology posits. Yet, without divine aid, men and women are *not able* to accomplish their own salvation.

As he lay dying, the Buddha admonished his followers to be lamps unto themselves. Following his dharma they could become their own saviors. Willfulness can also be the freedom to achieve one's own spiritual salvation. To become enlightened. To grow up.

---

[13] Karen Armstrong, *The Gospel According to Women: Christianity's Creation of the Sex War in the West*, (New York, 1987), p. xiv. She remains pessimistic that Christianity can totally rid itself of discrimination of women, which, she believes, is at heart Christianity's problem with the inherent sexuality of human beings, p. 345. The problem of human sexuality and Christianity will be the subject of Part IV.

[14] Cozzens, *The Changing Face of the Priesthood*, p. 119.

Warnings about the folly of pride, or Eve's so-called self-inflation, easily become excuses for spiritual laziness. They also hide religious self-righteousness—our community alone has the way and the truth. But true enlightenment, the Buddha said numerous times, is true humility.

Where it really counts, where a truly exalted view of the individual human being would fly against not only saviors from the higher archons, but against a savior-ridden culture of therapy (is not modern culture more a culture of therapy than of death?), John Paul II didn't think much of the human being at all. All talk about absolutes in human nature denies history. Once the contingencies of historical context are banished, the Church philosopher can prove anything (our Heisenberg Principle). Thus, the faithful remain children. Believers are locked in perpetual childhood. Rosemary Radford Ruether says that as long as one uses parent language for God—God's Fatherhood:

> God becomes a neurotic parent who does not want us to grow up.
> To become autonomous and responsible for our own lives is the gravest sin against God. Patriarchal theology uses the parent image for God to prolong spiritual infantilism as virtue and to make autonomy and assertion of free will a sin.[15]

In this chapter, we critiqued John Paul's claim that he was a feminist. He was not.

---

[15]Ruether, *Sexism and God-Talk*, p. 69.

PART III
Sex and Sex Scandals

"I absolutely renounce all higher harmony. It is not worth one little tear of even that one tormented child ..."

–Ivan Karamazov

Chapter 14

Sex in Heaven

In "Part III: Sex and Sex Scandals," we outline the causes of sexual abuse in the Catholic Church, explore the pervasiveness of the problem and shed light on the systematic, institutional conspiracy to cover-up these heinous crimes. In this chapter, we explore how John Paul's admirers claimed that he possessed unique insights into the psychology and theology of human sexuality. We find that his so-called insights, along with the Church's teachings on sex, create a climate of sexual abuse.

In the Kingdom of Heaven, the eschatological future of God's Imperial Rule, people will no longer marry (Matthew 22:30). In Catholic teaching, sex is permissible only in marriage. Its final cause, using Aristotelian language, is procreation in imitation of the deity's gift-giving act of creation. Its secondary cause, which flows from procreation, is the unity of persons in self-giving, also derived from God's gift of creation and His gift of Jesus. So it says in the *Catechism of the Catholic Church* (Part Three, Article 6, 2331–2400). In the Kingdom of Heaven, there is no marriage, and since sex *as humans know it on earth* is confined to marriage, this is another way of saying that there is no sex.

According to John Paul II—who, Weigel claims, despite his celibacy had a remarkable insight into sex (and he does not seem to be joking)—people will live in perfect "inter-subjectivity," which appears to be a philosophical version of the communion of the saints (p. 340).

All Christians will probably agree that Heaven is superior to the present fallen realm of earthly existence. The doctrine of an eschatological future introduces a linear sense of progress, life moving towards a goal that is clearly the opposite of earthly existence, as we noted in the Preface. Christians are on the way to something better, much better. Since this "much better" world exists without sex, a world with sex, as human beings know it, is "much inferior" to it. Life's ultimate goal of existence beyond the horizon of life must by necessity devalue sex.

Yet, sexuality in our earthly existence is not intrinsically evil or somehow especially corrupting. John Paul and the *Catechism* are at pains to make this clear. The sexual act, directed as it is towards reproduction, is rooted in the mystery of creation. In a sense, it "reproduces" God's great creative act, which is the freely bestowed gift of existence, says John Paul II in *The Theology of the Body* (p. 51). But since the Fall, sexuality has been inseparably joined to concupiscence, the inclination to evil. This is lust, the selfish and obsessive attachment to sex that uses the other as an object to serve one's own pleasure. The *Catechism* proclaims:

> *Lust* is disordered desire for or inordinate enjoyment of sexual pleasure. Sexual pleasure is morally disordered when sought for itself, isolated from its procreative and unitive purposes (Part Three, Article 6. 2351).

"Fallen sex" does not mean that sex in itself is intrinsically evil. Theoretically, it is good. But since the introduction of sin in the mythical garden during human "theological prehistory" (more on this later), it is in practical terms evil since it is always combined with concupiscence. And the inclination to sin (the old Hebrew *yester ha ra'*) is something humans cannot avoid because of our fallen nature. So, in theory sex is good as a procreative reenactment of God's creation. In practice it is evil, for who among humans other than a few saints (and one may doubt these stories) is able to resist the sheer pleasure of the physical act? Who has ever had sex for procreative reasons alone (and perhaps unitive purposes too) minus any sort of pleasurable self-gratification?

Catholic theology upends the old joke: A theoretical physicist and an engineer are trying to solve a construction problem. Here, says the engineer, is the solution. If they do this, and do that, and the problem is solved. Yes, replies the physicist, that and this may work in practice, but do they work in theory? In theory sex is holy and good. But not in practice. However, if no one practiced it, how could anyone ever theorize about it?

Too much rejection of the material could lead to Gnosticism (or something that now goes by that name) which completely rejects the world as bungled job. Similar dualistic heresies actually did erupt in medieval Europe as with the so-called Cathars in southern France. In contrast, martyrs often looked forward to the full physical resurrection of the body, having been deprived of the joys of the material world.

Bishop Irenaeus of Lyons (115-202) found a solution to the sexless after-life in the Millennium. During the thousand years of Christ's millennial reign, the fortunate saved would inhabit a New Eden with all its material amenities, including perfect physical bodies. Anticipating modern advertising, perfect physical bodies translated into perfect physical sex. Children would be born. Humans and the entire environment would be supremely fertile. No one grows old. No one dies.[1]

The later Church generally frowned on such visions, which were ultimately confined to mysticism. Mysticism was only grudgingly accepted. It sometimes opposed the way of the abstract intellect, say of St. Thomas, with the way of love. Female mystics of the Middle Ages—many were members of religious orders and Spouses of Christ—did write

---

[1] Irenaeus, *Against Heresies*, Book V, Chapter xxxiii, 3-4. www.columbia.edu/cu/augustine/arch/Ireneaus/

about their experiences in graphic erotic terms. Jesus himself, the divine bridegroom, is made to sound like an ardent knight in the tradition of Courtly Love.

Mechthild of Magdeburg (b. 1208) became a beguine in 1230 and towards the end of her life joined the community of Cistercian nuns at Helfta. In her mystic manual, *The Flowing Light,* the Trinity itself uses erotic language:

> I cannot be completely intimate with her unless she is willing to lay herself in utter repose and nakedness in my divine arms, so that I can play with her.[2]

Enough to make a celibate priest squirm.

Gertrude of Helfta (1256-1302) saw Christ appear to her as a handsome youth of sixteen. In erotic rapture—somewhat like Ratzinger's fear of plunging into the fertility current—she sighs:

> You are the delicate taste
>
> Of intimate sweetness.
>
> O most delicate caresser,
>
> Gentlest passion,
>
> Most ardent lover.
>
> Sweetest spouse,
>
> Most pure pursuer.[3]

Not only does the word *mysticism* contain in itself an unhealthy dose of erotic *mist,* but it also ends in *schism.* Mystic Marguerite Porete was executed as a heretic on June 1, 1310. Perhaps the first documented case in Western Christendom, the Dominican Inquisitor of Paris accused her of indifference to the Church as the only means of grace open to humans and their salvation.[4] Having experienced the deity *intimately,* she ignored the priesthood.

As many supernatural entities given actual form, heaven becomes rather concrete, like a building of infinite apartments with enough rooms for everybody. Heaven could be pictured as the New Jerusalem, the New Eden, the Swedenborgian city of spiritual progress, or some sort of computerized information process in which all events, our lives and everyone else's, are deposited in a kind of cosmic memory bank vault—or something. But *no sex* as human beings experience it here.

---

[2] Quoted in Bernard McGinn, *The Flowering of Mysticism: Men and Women in the New Mysticism-1200-1350, Vol. III of The Presence of God: A History of Christian Mysticism,* (New York, 1998), p. 236.
[3] Quoted in Colleen McDannell and Bernhard Lang, *Heaven: A History,* (New Haven, 1988), p. 102.
[4] McGinn, *The Flowering of Mysticism,* p. 245.

George Weigel believes that John Paul's *The Theology of the Body* was a kind of exorcism. It casts out of Catholic theology the Manichean demon that depreciated human sexuality and therefore caused untold mischief to the Church's image (p. 342). And this is not all. Weigel, with the spirit upon him, turns prophet. John Paul's profound insights into the human sexual condition may be a theological "time bomb," a crucial moment not only in Catholic moral theology but in the history of Western thought (p. 343).

Alas, history seems to show that historians make poor prophets. Theoretically, John Paul's teachings may be that time bomb, but it is set to go off in some unimaginable future ("perfect inter-subjectivity"?). Practically, however, it is a smoke screen behind which the Manichean demon still hides.

Not content with mere prophecy, Weigel issues a challenge. The burden of proof, he sternly declares, lies with those who argue that John Paul's theories on sexuality demean sexual love. And, as if to illustrate how well the problem is solved theoretically, he concludes that John Paul's exploration "of the nuptial character of God's relationship to the world would suggest the opposite" (p. 853).

What exactly is this "opposite?" Is God's creative love somehow embodied in the physical relations between men and women? If so, how? An answer immediately suggests itself: sex is restricted to marriage, which is a sacrament of the Church, and therefore within the province of the Church's ubiquitous authority. Is God's "nuptial" relationship with the world like a Platonic form (of what? Love? Sex?) that finds its partial realization in the natural world, in the cave of the Church's sacramental institution? Perhaps it does work theoretically—or theologically—but, how is it realized practically?

This is an appropriate spot for another old joke, this time from George Bernard Shaw: If the pope knows anything about sex, he has probably broken a vow. In John Paul's case, judged by his writings *about* sex, the joke actually flops. John Paul II's long-winded discussions and teachings on sexual love and human dignity are supposedly profound insights, especially, adds Weigel, from the perspective of women (p. 13). What they really are, however, are purely abstract and theoretical approaches to a "profoundly" physical and intimate relationship connected to love. Sexual love is an act of union, a merging with the beloved, that is intoxicating, frightening, ecstatic, painful and blissful, and overwhelming, all at once. It is an *act* that has generated the greatest poetry and music, art, literature, philosophy, and nowadays, scientific investigation. Love, says Erich Fromm, is the active concern for the life and flourishing of the beloved.[5] Sex is a fusion, not only a strong feeling, but also a judgment and a promise. Love arises from the essence of our existence as physical beings, and as we've noted earlier, may well be part of our evolutionary history. *But all the words ever written fail to fully capture the experience.* And much remains to be written. Sex and love exist across the border of theory. Theories are like reflections in a mirror.

This is not an argument for some sugary romanticized version of sexual love. It is far more complex and resistant to the ease of simplified absolutes. It can surely be abused

---

[5]Fromm, *The Art of Loving*, p. 25.

with devastating effects, as the Church well knows. Our point is simply that sex is an intensely physical act. One will never *know* sex by merely talking about it.

Everything reaches perfection in the Kingdom of Heaven, just as God intended. In the land beyond time and space, the redeemed are in perfect communion with God's love, an abstract (and therefore empty) inter-subjectivity which is superior to any sort of unitive physical (and transitory) experience here on earth. If this perfection, which grounds the Church's ethic, does not demean sexual love *as humans know it*, then Weigel's burden of proof is like asking one to specify the final number of an infinite series.

In theory, sexual love is the perfect self-dedication of persons to one another. *In theory*, sexual love recapitulates the creative love of God. *In theory*, sexual love without lust is a gift of God just as a person makes of "herself" a gift to another. It is a sanctification of married life; it is, unlike the animals, perhaps (and who really knows?), not simply an emotion but an act of judgment...*in theory*. But in fact? In earthly fact, sexual love is far more complex and complicated. The Pope seems to think in terms of one or the other. But in fact, sexual love may include *at the same time* what the Church finds objectionable and what the Church idealizes. Selfish pleasure and self-giving may exist within a single act. Furthermore, John Paul II and the Church betray a curious attitude towards pleasure. Being for pleasure apparently counts as sinful. Physical pleasures have no coordinates on the vertical plane. Why? Well, flesh and blood cannot inherit the Kingdom.

This is not idealizing sex. Nor is it saying that outside the Church is no sexual abuse. People are indeed treated as objects for selfish pleasure. People are abused. People suffer.

The problem for the Church, one requiring "profound apologies," is that despite all its theories about perfect love and communion, its priesthood lives and acts on the horizontal plane. On the x-axis, what works in theory hardly (if at all) works in practice. Therefore apologies are required if the Church wants to restore its horizontal image as the moral paragon of humanity.

There are those few, according to John Paul II, who are able, through a combination of personal choice and divine aid, to live in celibacy. This choice, the Pope taught in *The Theology of the Body*, is an orientation toward the "eschatological state" in which there is no marriage (p. 263). In other words, there are those few who with God's help practice love in this world as if they already lived in the Kingdom of Heaven. Theirs is not celibacy *in* the Kingdom, which is yet to come, but *for* the Kingdom. The only means by which a celibate is able to accomplish this feat, besides divinely aided choice, is renunciation and determined spiritual life (p. 267). Such is the priesthood.

Renunciation and spiritual effort—whatever this phrase means practically speaking (and apparently in the Pope's case the "effort" included flagellation, which is quite pleasurable for some)—are not one-time events. Self-discipline is a life-long struggle. And it is only possible with divine aid. But how does one measure that? In life, then, given the nature of the fallen horizontal plane, the celibate is in constant conflict with sexual love *as humans know it*. Physical sex is rejected for some sort of higher sex of the spirit. Despite all claims to the contrary, for example, that the human body makes visible what is invisible, or physical sex makes visible God's creative love (p. 76), this fateful dualism of so-called spiritual communion and real physical sexuality proves disastrous in practical life. The priesthood makes this disaster visible, and the burden of proof is met and surpassed by the on-going sex scandals in the Catholic Church.

A little fable is appropriate here. Our story comes from the gospel according to D. H. Lawrence. It is called: "The Man Who Died" (1929).

Lawrence tells us that there once was a man who died. A poor peasant living near Jerusalem had tied his spirited rooster to a post. At the exact moment the rooster broke free, the man who died awoke. Unlike the rooster in which the fire of life burned fiercely, the man longed to stay outside, at peace in the oblivion of cold inertia. But, like the animal, a compulsion drove him and so he returned to life.

He lived with the poor peasant for a time. He had risen, but without desire.

Little by little he came back to the living. Having died, he was now able to look "nakedly" on life. He saw "a vast resoluteness everywhere flinging itself up in stormy or subtle wave-crests, foam tips emerging out of the blue invisible, a black and orange cock or the green flame-tongues out of the extremes of the fig tree." Life appeared to him more compulsive than death, even those clods of earth like the peasant who seemed without fire. And the man who died realized that the clods of earth need to remain earthy, to serve the refreshment of life. In seeking to lift up what is of the earth, he concluded: "I was wrong to interfere."

And he was glad. He was glad that his mission was over and the day of his interference was done. The savior had died in him; death had saved him from his own salvation. He said these things in the garden, to one of his followers, Madeleine. And she knew he was not the Messiah. "The risen man was the death of her dream."

Still, he was not fully alive. He was yet a virgin, having rejected the little, greedy life of the body. But the man who died came to understand—John Paul II's heirs listen here—that celibacy is also greed. The taking and giving by making love serves the greater cause of life—the egoless, taking, the egoless giving, and unless human beings encompass the little life in the circle of the greater life, all is disaster. He refused the offered love of the peasant women whose soul was hard and greedy. Rather, he sought the woman who would heal his body and truly complete his rising, encompassing him in the greater circle, which was the real Kingdom of God.

He found that woman. She was a priestess of Isis.

The greater life is the sacredness of that very earthly instinct, the holiness of the compulsion, which the goddess represents. In being of the earth, the greater circle, this compulsion cannot be sinful, nor is it dehumanizing. But it dismantles the greedy small ego, which is the source of the virginity for the Kingdom and the origin of empty abstractions that reject the earth. As the man who died knew, giving is holy, and so is taking.

The priestess healed the man who died and his wounds no longer hurt. He was Osiris reborn. The great atonement was being in touch, in touch with life, in touch with the priestess and the feminine power she served. He never asked her name, nor she his (sacred sex is indiscriminate?). She was Isis, he was Osiris. Names reveal only the small self. But in the physical act of love, the small self is dissolved, swallowed up and merged with the great tide of life. It is personal and impersonal at once. Sex is a sacred act. At that indescribable moment of orgasm, which poets try to capture, but ultimately in vain, the hard, greedy ego is fused with the great ocean of life like salt dissolving in water.[6] One hears the song of the goddess, the poetry of the god.

Some people, however, fear this sort of fusion and loss of the ego. They see it as suffocating. Intimacy is dangerous since they become vulnerable to the beloved. They find it difficult to trust the other with their most valuable possession, their precious self. However, sexual fantasies, sexual perversions, preserve eroticism and yet dehumanize the person.[7] Once dehumanized, the sexual partner poses no threat to the ego. There is sex, but without human beings. Sex without intimacy is without risk. The man who died understood that this fear, the fear of the ego's demise, its nothingness, drove people mad.

What does all this mean for priestly celibacy? A person does not live in the future, not even priests. A person may choose to live, as John Paul said, for a certain vision of the future, revealed or otherwise. But one lives that vision in the present. In the revealed future, the world of the resurrection, there is no sex because—here John Paul quotes I Corinthians 15:28—God will be "everything to everyone" (*The Theology of the Body*, p. 267). But this future, like all futures, is nowhere present. It is a massive "no-thing."

---

[6]According to John Paul, sex (the conjugal act) is a giving of oneself to another and a profound expression of who I am. Male and female come to a new self-consciousness as father and mother, which is also a particular consciousness of their bodies (*The Theology of the Body*, p. 82). The emphasis here is upon the "I" function, the small self. The act itself only becomes religious in the context of the sacrament of marriage, which symbolizes God's creative act and which belongs (naturally) to the Church. In the sense of D. H. Lawrence's story, it is hardly spiritual at all when it is raised from the earth to airless realms of the heavens. The Pope says that sex decides "somatic individuality," the person's identity and concreteness (p. 79). But the man who died realized that this is precisely the gift (and the healing) one gives to and takes from the earth. One donates this "greedy ego." Ratzinger actually gives the whole thing away: The serpent in the garden is a symbol of the fertility in which human beings "plunge into the divine current of life and for a few moments experience themselves fused with its divine power" (*In the Beginning...*, 1986, p. 66). And this is a threat. It is the attraction of the fertility religions (with their goddesses) that threatened Israel and its God (male) of the Covenant. Today we might say that it is a case of worshiping the creation and not the creator. But the creator is something added to the creation as an abstract explanation based upon very human interpretations of ancient myths. It is also interesting to note Sigmund Freud's response to his friend Romain Rolland's talk about the "oceanic feeling." Rather than the fusion of the ego with the greater circle, the feeling arises from the ego's infantile need for protection from destruction at the hands of nature, "another way of disclaiming the danger the danger which the ego recognizes as threatening it from the external world" (*Civilization and Its Discontents*, 1939, 1961, p. 19). It is limitless narcissism, says Freud, patently infantile, like all religious feelings a series of "pitiful rearguard actions" (p. 21). Another form of narcissism would be an immortal ego living in perfect inter-subjectivity in a perfect Kingdom of Heaven. Mature religion may need to transcend both.
[7]Diane Ackerman, *A Natural History of Love*, pp.247-248.

This particular world is an abstract creation of hope and hermeneutics, trust in ancient texts and traditional interpretations. It is also the product of greed, the ego's desire for immortality. Real sex, not the perverted, dehumanizing kind, demolishes the "hard ego" in Lawrence's gospel. The self dies and lives at the same time, just as waves crash and break but the ocean remains. Celibacy as dedication to the Kingdom is, then, greed. It is a dehumanizing perversion of real sex and it leads real people to perverse, dehumanizing acts.

As in the Church faced with crimes of sexual abuse committed by its clergy.

In this chapter, we explored how John Paul's admirers claimed that he possessed unique insights into the psychology and theology of human sexuality. We found that his so-called insights, along with the Church's teachings on sex, have created a climate of sexual abuse.

Chapter 15
Clerical Sex

In this chapter, we postulate clerical abuse of children follows naturally from such attitudes on sex. Since the institution (the Holy Mother Church) stands above individual members, and since the institution is the last defense against moral disaster, it must be defended at all costs. Apologies become attacks on critics.

Pope John Paul II had to enact image restoration strategies in response to sexual abuse accusations against Catholic clergy, and charges that many church leaders failed to respond to these problems in a responsible fashion. The Catholic Church in the U.S. has been swamped with accusations concerning pedophilia, among other instances of sexual misconduct, by members of the clergy. The situation in Ireland may be worse, where out of a population of 4 million the Church has already paid about $4 Billion to 13,000 victims.[1] As of this writing, there is no sign that the problem will disappear any time soon. If celibacy is John Paul's ideal of self-dedication, then the burden of proof rests upon the Pope and his followers to explain its spectacular failure. And not only failure. The perversity of clerical sex cries out for an explanation. The Church's sinful children prey upon children.

Corresponding to actual abuse is institutional abuse in the form of cover-up. By various means—transfer to another parish is a prime example—Church officials around the world covered up cases in which priests were accused of sexual abuse. Cardinal Ratzinger might have been an accomplice in such a cover-up. For six years, after a canon law prosecution had been filed in 1998, he protected the powerful Fr. Marcial Maciel Degollado, founder of the Legionaries of Christ, and favorite of Pope John Paul II. Finally in May of 2006, as Pope Benedict XVI he ordered Maciel to a "life of prayer and penitence," for acts of sexual abuse that included 30 or more boys and young men.[2] Fr. Maciel, considered a saint by some, was a great fundraiser for the Church.

---
[1] Fox, *The Pope's War*, p. 157.
[2] Reported in the *National Catholic Reporter*, February 22, 2008, http://ncronline.org/node/332.

Pope John Paul's attempts to formulate apologies and excuses for such crimes differ from other forms of the apologia. He had to apologize not only for the sins of the past, but also the sins that appear to be ongoing. He had to find reasons for the Church's slow response to the crisis, or, in some cases, downright neglect and denial. The great theological sex therapist who spoke with such confidence and authority about human sexuality, seemed woefully unprepared if not perplexed by the rising tide of sexual abuse among those who supposedly are the paragons of self-dedication. As discussed in the previous chapter, his abstract theorizing, even if based as he claimed upon pastoral experience, seldom worked in practice. Therefore, he blamed modern culture, human autonomy, false ideas of freedom without responsibility, and selfish pleasure. It was all a kind of denial that diverted him from the real problems. Freud might have called it a pathetic and infantile attempt to escape repression. Probably it was more complex than that, a combination of many causes and conditions. This will be explored further.

Reading accounts of molestation done by priests is a revolting experience. It is like falling down the Malebolge into the evil ditches of Dante's Eighth Circle of the Inferno:

> Once there, I peered down; and I saw long lines of people in a river of excrement that seemed the overflow of the world's latrines.
>
> Canto 18

Many children suffered and yet priests were given repeated opportunities to victimize Catholic youths. Officials from dioceses throughout the world covered up accusations and shuffled priests around without sufficient regard for the damage they caused or potential damage they were prone to cause. For Catholics, the scandal has been a source of shame, humiliation, distrust, and even selective and decreased contributions. In this case, the sins of the children inflicted very real wounds upon the very real, material body of the Mother Church. Image restoration becomes not only a question of penance and mission but financial survival.

The U.S. Catholic Church has paid at least one billion dollars to settle cases of accusations of sexual abuse by clergy and cover-ups by Church officials. Potentially, a hundred thousand children had been molested by clergy members. Given members' real love for the Church and the powerful wish to believe in its purity, such statistics may exist on the conservative side of the scale. Many cases may well go unreported or simply denied.[3]

---

[3] See D. France, *Our Fathers: The Secret Life of the Catholic Church in an Age of Scandal*, (New York, 2004). Naturally this begs the question of clerical abuse of children in the past. If it is difficult to trust modern statistical studies, studies dealing with past instances of clerical abuse are highly suspect. We can cite apocryphal tales. There are plenty of stories that seem to indicate an ongoing problem. For example, Voltaire actually defended the Abbe Desfontaines who had been sent to prison for sodomizing little chimney-sweeps. Voltaire quipped that the Abbe must have mistaken them for Cupids (Mitford, *Voltaire in Love*, 1957, pp.33–34).

Priests have been arrested throughout the U.S. for molestation of youths. Here are a few examples. Rev. Paul Shanley was arrested in San Diego (Associated Press, 2002, May 4). In Baltimore, a young man shot a priest he accused of molesting him, although Church authorities and law enforcement had done nothing about the initial accusation (Associated Press, 2002, May 15). As many as 24 priests in St. Louis have been investigated for accusations of sexual abuse of youths (Associated Press, June 13, 2002). The St. Louis persecutor's office received 50 complaints of sexual abuse by priests in one week (Associated Press, 2002, March 29). Seminaries have also been implicated as centers for molestation, such as St. Thomas Aquinas Seminary in Hannibal, Missouri (Associated Press, 2002, March 10). One hundred and twenty-two cases were filed against priests in Kentucky (Associated Press, 2002, June 9). At least six New York priests were suspended after being accused of molesting youths, and the diocese turned more reports over to prosecutors (Associated Press, 2002, April, 8). In Lincoln Nebraska, a priest who was removed from diocese service was later court-martialed from the Navy for sexual acts with Navy personnel as a Navy chaplain (Associated Press, 2002, March 30). A Florida bishop acknowledged that he inappropriately touched teenagers and resigned his post (Associated Press, March 10). A California Cardinal was accused of sexual abuse, but denied the allegations (Associated Press, 2002, April 7). And on and on...

The case of Fr. Maciel is a paradigm. His Legion of Christ, founded in 1941, has twenty-one prep schools in America, a university, and three seminaries. He built schools, seminaries and universities in Spain, Italy and Chile. Pope Pius XII removed him as the Legion's director in 1956 for his morphine addiction, but he returned as a favorite of John Paul II who viewed him as a positive guide to youth.

Legionaries took a vow never to criticize Fr. Maciel or any other superiors, and in a fashion that recalls the Reign of Terror in the French Revolution, *denounce* anyone who did.[4] Meanwhile, Maciel pursued a secret life of sexual abuse and even violence. The Legion was a staunch defender of the Church against secularism. His defenders, therefore, attacked his accusers, which seems to be the modus operandi of the Church in almost every case examined here. It is all due to anti-Catholicism.

Again, to be fair, memories are frail and pliable, and it is easy to suddenly discover repressed facts of long ago especially when money is involved. Even one of the harshest critics of religion, Richard Dawkins, admits this.[5] The problem is that the Church inevitably tries to bury the whole thing. When it does acknowledge a problem, it instantly casts suspicion upon the accusers.

Yes, memories are easily manipulated. But not all. Yes, there is anti-Catholicism. But not every case is an example. The problem is similar to the objection against religious attempts to justify the existence of evil. In cases of sexual abuse: *Why are there so many cases in so many states and countries*?

If the Church on High, the City of God, is embodied in the Church on earth, battling the moral darkness of secularism, one would hope for fewer cases of abuse among its

---
[4]Fox, *The Pope's War*, p. 127.
[5]Richard Dawkins, *The God Delusion*, (New York, 2006), p. 316.

chosen, divinely inspired clergy. And given the power and reach of the earthly *and holy* institution, *there ought to be no cover-ups.*

As might be expected, there are plenty of explanations for the problem. Here are a few.

It has been argued that priests who abuse adolescent males may suffer from psychosexual immaturity. These priests did not have the opportunity to develop their sexuality, but were sexually smothered during their adolescent years under the over-protection of Catholic mothers and the stifling seminary atmosphere. Also, some of these priests may have been sexually abused themselves during their adolescent development.[6]

Also, it is claimed that boys require a separation from the mother in order to develop a self, and that this separation creates a self that views the world in terms of either/or. Girls, it is said, combine the opposites of identification and differentiation. Their construction of reality is both/and.[7]

Let one accept, for the moment, these distinctions as a kind of thought experiment. That is, this book makes no claims for or against them, but seeks to see where they might take believers. Could it be said that some priests never develop into mature men for this reason? They remain infantile, stuck in a limbo world of confused sexual identity. The Mother Church, the Virgin Mary, the Bride of Christ, and so on, mix incongruently with the male-only club of the priesthood and their Father. Priests therefore shun sexual passion (lust in evening clothes) with women because their only relationship with the female is infantile, she is a mother.

Combine this with their unique position. Priests are like ancient kings, the incarnation of god-on-earth. Symbols such as *in personae Christi* are all too easily reified into objective realities. Surrounded by lesser mortals who believe you a demigod, behold, you begin to think of yourself as one. Certainly this applies to anyone in a position of power, except the priest's power comes from the vertical dimension. God can do anything, so too His reified shadows. Victims are having sex with God.

These and other explanations may have relevance to the problem, but taken together they seem too easy. Why priests? Why mostly homosexual pedophilia in such numbers? If the Church possesses the true meaning of human sexuality with its true humanistic vision of self-donation, either in marriage or some eschatological future, why does its own celibate clergy, supposedly blessed with God's gift of grace, violate in such a perverse manner these so-called truths? Unless, as has already been hinted, these truths are rationalized abstractions built upon ancient myths combined with self-serving interpretations.

Or, approaching the problem from a different angle, it might be asked if there is something about the priesthood as a profession that attracts pedophiles? Is it the availability of children and power over them? The same might be said for teachers, coaches, Boy Scout leaders, and those professionals who interact with youth. Is it that the Church

---

[6] See D. France, *Our Fathers: The Secret Life of the Catholic Church in an Age of Scandal* for a summary of these speculations.
[7] Elizabeth A. Johnson, *She Who Is*, p. 69.

is an easy target for lawsuits that there seems to be a greater problem in the priesthood than among other professions?

In the name of fairness, therefore, one needs to know how pervasive such perversions are in the general population and in other professions. In other words, as seems to be the medical opinion, the sexual attraction to children *is not a choice*.[8] The problem is availability of victims in the institution. *So, priestly pedophilia may have little to do with Catholic doctrine per se, specifically the doctrine of celibacy.*

One of the most thorough studies—perhaps the only one of its kind—was done by Dr. Richard Sipe, who conducted about 1500 interviews from the period 1960–1985. His well-known report showed that about twenty percent of priests were homosexual, with about a two percent rate of pedophiles.[9] Since this may be comparable with the general population, one could agree with Philip Jenkins that the over-reporting of Catholic abuse is more the result of: "If you expect a group to be villainous, you will generally find ample confirmation of that view."[10]

Furthermore, Jenkins notes that it is easier to sue a centralized institution like the Catholic Church than, say, some independent Protestant Church, a scout troop, or even a school district, all of which report similar sexual abuses.[11] This assertion seems logical at first glance, but when one takes into account the nature of contemporary litigation, the sheer number of lawyers ready to pounce, and the awe and love Catholics feel for their Church—quite unlike anything one feels for a school district despite the old motto "be true to your school"—such excuses tend to whither on the branch. One can only hope that the Penn State case of an assistant coach's serial abuse of young men is the exception and not the rule in college football (more on this below).

Although most pedophilia involves adult males and female children, the pattern in the Catholic Church is predominately adult males and *male* children. Also, many of these cases are not strictly pedophilia in that they involve the priest and a teenage boy, or even a young male in his twenties.

Second, there is a clear pattern that emerges in most cases of sexual abuse: Usually there is a denial by the local bishop or some other authority. The parents themselves usually experience a similar denial, especially given the fact that they implicitly trust a *celibate* priest. Clergy are unquestioned moral authorities and completely entrusted with children, at least until recently.

Next comes a period of treatment and then reassigning the priest to another post. Most troubling is the new parish is not told about the priest's criminal past. The reason usually given is that the priest has been cured, has done penance, and is therefore forgiven.

---

[8]"What Is Pedophilia?" WebMD, http://www.com/mental-health/features/explaining-pedophilia.
[9]See his website, A. W. Richard Sipe, *Celibacy, Sex & Catholic Church*, http://www.richardsipe.com.
[10]Philip Jenkins, *The New Anti-Catholicism: The Last Acceptable Prejudice*, (New York, 2003), p. 145.
[11]Jenkins, p. 143.

Then, an attempt is made to discredit the accuser. There are appeals to loyalty and love of the Church, even to Jesus. Ironically, such appeals would seem to contradict John Paul's own philosophy of personhood. The accuser is no longer a wounded, suffering human being, but an object of ridicule and contempt. The accuser is labeled—anti-Catholic, delusional, angry Catholic, having an agenda—and is therefore an abstraction devoid of individuality.

Finally in some cases, a lawsuit results, usually out of frustration and deep feelings of betrayal.

Catholic sexual scandals revolve around two questions: 1) Why celibate priests? 2) Why homosexual sex with children? Even if the Church does not have a monopoly on pedophilia, this does still not explain the homosexual nature of abuse in the Church. Even if Jenkins has a point that the Church had been the victim of wildly exaggerated statistics and a media frenzy of anti-Catholicism (note the persistent tendency of Catholic defenders to claim victimization), this pattern of institutional response is troubling and seems to indicate a deeper problem.

In short, for all the psychosexual possibilities, *the real issue may be not sex but power.* In fact, the Penn State cover-up of sexual abuse shares on the surface a great deal in common with the Church. The institution, its moral image, the god-like status of its Head Coach, the abuse of power, are all very similar to the Church. So too is the availability of contact with young boys. The Church and the football society at Penn State (and perhaps elsewhere) share a male dominated culture in which women are not in positions of power. It might even be said that while misogyny in the Church reduces women to either virgins or evil temptresses, misogyny in the male-only football culture reduces women to sex-objects (The Dallas Cowboy Cheerleaders, for example). Plus or minus, it is still on the misogynistic x-axis.[12]

Is there a difference? Is the "power-not-sex" explanation also too easy? Does the institutional problem of power abuse somehow mesh with the Church's endemic misogyny? Further explication is necessary.

A previous chapter alluded to Pope John Paul II's obsession with the Virgin Mary. The motto of his papacy was *totus tuus*: "I am completely yours, O Mary." The Pope came to believe that the assassination attempt on him by Mehmet Ali Agca on May 13, 1981 failed

---

[12] On the night of August 23, 1980, sports journalist Christine Brennan stepped into the locker room of the Minnesota Vikings, the first female to do so. "As it was, as soon as I walked into the steamy, overcrowded room, I heard whoops and hollers from distant corners, from players I couldn't see...." Here for some cheap thrills?'" Brennan's memoir is about sports journalism, but one can sense the underlying misogyny in the culture. Christine Brennan, *Best Seat in The House: A Father, A Daughter, A Journey Through Sports*, (New York, 2006), p. 121. For college football see Jeff Benedict and Armen Keteryian, *The System: The Glory and Scandal of Big-Time College Football*, (New York, 2013), especially Chapter 12 subtitled "Friends with Benefits," also Chapter 2, subtitled "The Life of a College Football hostess."

because of a miraculous intervention of the Virgin Mary. The evidence for this belief comes from the fact that it was on that very day that the Virgin first appeared at Fatima.[13]

The Virgin Mary is the Church's idealized view of women as virgins and mothers (an irony if there ever was one). She was the *Theotokos* (God bearer), the mediatrix between Christ and man; in 1854 Pope Pius IX declared the dogma of her own immaculate birth (free from sin in the first instance of her conception), and in the twentieth century the Church declared her heavenly assumption. John Paul calls her "the new Eve, placed by God in close relation to Christ, the new Adam...the Mother of the Church" in his popular book *Crossing the Threshold of Hope*, (p. 213). The ideal woman, the woman before the Fall, is a virgin, but also—keeping with the Pope's ideal of motherhood as the specified feminine identity—a virgin *mother*.

Complicating matters is the general view of women as dangerously tempting, corrupting, and inferior to men. If the idealized woman is an asexual being, and given the fear of real sexual women, in the all-male world of the priest the female can never truly be the object of sexual desire. In a sense, the devotion to the Virgin Mary contributes to a kind of sexual (if not spiritual) infantilism.[14] The only permissible sexual object, then, is infantile and male.

Like the whiptail lizard in the Western United States, the Catholic priesthood reproduces asexually. As previously noted, the sacraments, especially the Eucharist, transmit a patriarchal succession that reaches back to the all-male apostles and their male Son of God—and beyond this to the male celibate YHWH. Because priestly reproduction is accomplished mainly through ritual, the emphasis is upon ritual purity as distinct from moral purity. The priest could be ritually pure and yet at the same time morally deficient. Such is the recipe for infinite mischief. Ritual purity was Augustine's answer to the Donatists who insisted that the validity of the sacraments was tied to the moral purity of the priesthood. If the sacraments belonged to the Church and operated by simply following a recipe, like a mathematical proof, ritual purity is what counts. Before officiating the Eucharist, the priest must have confessed all his sins. Although it may be argued that such confession is a sign of moral purity, it is also another ritualized sacrament that belongs to the Church. Therefore, confession, too, implies ritual purity.

In the days before priestly celibacy became a rule of the Church (more on this below), the priest was to refrain from sexual relations with his wife before officiating the sacrament. Celibacy itself, either in marriage or later as a rule of the priesthood, could be separated from moral purity. This might mean that the celibate priest preserved his ritual purity by avoiding female pollution (which was also morally polluting). On the other hand, homosexuality, while sinful, *was not ritually polluting since ritual pollution comes from the rule.* True enough, it was a *moral pollution*. Leviticus calls homosexuality

---

[13] As we also speculated earlier, the Pope, perhaps unconsciously, continually looked for evidence of spiritual causation in seemingly unexplained events. The bullet could not have missed his aorta by chance. Chance is not an explanation. Thus a gap opens and the Pope, like his followers, is prepared to throw God (in this case the Virgin Mary) into it. Weigel quotes him as saying: "in the designs of Providence there are no mere coincidences" (p. 4). Weigel seems to believe this himself. Read between the lines, his biography is the myth of the great man sent by God to rescue modernity from itself.

[14] Gary Wills, *Papal Sin: Structures of Deceit*, (New York, 2000), p. 205.

an abomination (*to'evah*). In Judaism, moral pollution led to degradation of the sinner and Israel itself. As moral pollution, homosexuality seems far more serious than ritual pollution.[15] It is different in the Catholic Church.

Ritual pollution was a major concern of the priesthood in preserving its lineage from Christ and his apostles. Moral lapses can always be forgiven. Ritual lapses break the patriliny and threaten the very existence of the priesthood as well as the institution itself. The Church's tendency, then, is to forgive (and sometimes ignore) sexual abuse, a moral stain, in order to preserve institutional integrity, a tendency that reverses the relative severity of moral and ritual pollution in Rabbinic Judaism. Why?

The lineage stands in for the land of Israel. It cannot pass through the female. Priests must give birth to priests by means of the sacrament of Ordination. In *Love's Body*, Norman Brown calls such initiation, rebirth. The man, born of woman, is reborn of the Mother Church. "Birth from the mother is nullified, and a new spiritual mother found" (p. 33). In a crude, perverse way, homosexual sex could be seen as a sign of apostolic succession, just as John Paul II claims that the "unity" of male and female is a sign of the sacrament of marriage in which two persons become one (*The Theology of the Body*, p. 163).[16] There appears to be no shortage of spiritual signs.

Once more, all of this remains speculation. On a more mundane level, textbook pedophilia is the result of four possible states:

1. Genetics: A person's biological inheritance.
2. Psychodynamic: The condition is due to causal factors in early relationships, say sexually abused children become abusers.
3. Desire: One simply desires sex with minors.
4. Social/Situational: The condition is due to the social/ideological environment (the male power structure of the Church).

It is this fourth category that may contribute to child abuse in the Church, arising from the cult of Mary, the tradition of patriliny as outlined above, as well as the obvious problems connected to priestly celibacy, especially in the modern sexually soaked

---

[15] Jonathan Klawans, "Moral and Ritual Purity," in *The Historical Jesus in Context*, pp. 268-269.

[16] It is fairly obvious that Hogan and LeVoir do not know what to do with homosexuality (*Covenant of Love*). They lump it together with premarital sex, adultery, contraception, and everything else they find objectionable. The cause, according to them, is the mistaken equation of freedom with *selfish* independence (p. 84). This seems to be an attack on the Kantian declaration of autonomy in the Enlightenment and Voltaire's *Ecrasez l'infame*, which was not aimed against religion but against the tyranny of the Church over men's minds (Cassirer, *The Philosophy of the Enlightenment*, Chapter iv). We think that we are masters of nature, they declare, so we may govern our bodies. But we are not masters of nature, for the order of existence depends upon God. Biology, a product of the human mind, abstracts its version of nature from a higher reality. Here again, repeated *ad nauseam*, is to the appeal to the vertical dimension. This causes problems for medical science that require all sorts of parsing: some treatments apparently do not arbitrate nature, others do (like stem cell research, organ transplant, etc.).

Homosexuality, it appears, seems to be a natural inclination as the Church itself readily admits. How it is caused by runaway freedom is a mystery. And why the priesthood, and why children, are greater mysteries. Theology, it seems, when it ascends to the vertical dimension, has a way of ending in mystery. And, it is plain silly to blame any of these sins upon modern culture. A glance at the Bible is enough to show how long "selfish independence", abuse, and adultery have perverted human life.

culture. The ideal woman is a virgin and mother, and therefore off limits. If one understands celibacy as forbidden sex with a woman (with Mary doubly forbidden—and horrifying), then homosexual pedophilia may be the only alternative. God's gift of celibacy may be no match for the daily gifts of the sexuality obsessed media industry which inflates a normal human need. So, here at least, the Church may have a point. Like the ancient areopagus in Athens, the modern communications industry is quite slippery.

In the face of it, one might still maintain with Jenkins that "the linkage between clerical misdeeds and celibacy is dubious" (p.150). However, the tendency to deny, to cover up, to abuse the laity's love for the Church (and Jesus, of whom the priest is the image), does seem to illustrate a deeper problem that ties together the infantile sexuality of the priest, the Mary obsession of the present Pope, institutional purity and patriliny, and the *kind* (not necessarily quantity) of sexual abuse. As in similar institutions where women are kept from power (would a woman head coach knowingly allowed a pedophile to continue his abuse of children?), and where children are readily available, pedophiles tend to find a safe house. Sexual abuse is institutionalized as is misogyny. In this way *they are interdependent.* Cover-ups demonstrate a "blind instinct" for preserving the aura of the priesthood even at the expense of people who love the Church, which is a crime as horrible as the abuse itself.[17]

These allegations presented a severe public relations crisis for John Paul II, a pope celebrated for his "profound" insights into human sexuality. In the end, despite all the speculation, sexual abuse may be no more (or less) that proverbial abuse of the power of the strong over the weak and trusting. The problem may not be unique to the Catholic Church. But the sins of its children against children have gravely wounded the Holy "Mother" Church.

We postulated the idea, in this chapter, that clerical abuse of children follows naturally from institutionalized Catholic attitudes on sex. Since the institution (the Holy Mother Church) stands above individual members, and since the institution is the last defense against moral disaster, it must be defended at all costs. Apologies became attacks on critics.

---
[17] Gary Wills, *Papal Sin*, p. 202.

Chapter 16

Suffer the Children: John Paul II's Response to Child Abuse

In this chapter, we examine the sexual abuse of children by some members of the clergy and the Church's response.

The pope issued an acknowledgement of sexual abuse on the Internet on November 22, 2001. In section 49, his *Post-Synodal Apostolic Exhortation* to the clergy and "peoples of Oceana" admitted that: "In certain parts of Oceania, sexual abuse by some clergy and religious has caused great suffering and spiritual harm to the victims." As usual, the Pope implicitly distinguished between those who commit such crimes and the central body of the Catholic Church:

> It has been very damaging in the life of the Church and has become an obstacle to the proclamation of the Gospel. The Synod Fathers condemned all sexual abuse and all forms of abuse of power, both within the Church and in society as a whole. Sexual abuse within the Church is a profound contradiction of the teaching and witness of Jesus Christ. (Obtained online at http://www.vatican.va/holy_father/john_paul_ii/apost_exhortations/documents/hf_jp-ii_exh_20011122_ecclesia-in-oceania_en.html)

This is yet another instance of shifting the blame, similar to the strategy identified by Brinson and Benoit as blaming (limiting the guilty to) a few bad apples in the barrel. This statement makes it clear that the Church as a whole does not condone these abuses; in fact, the offensive acts supposedly *contradict* the teachings of the Church. There is also an element of bolstering in this statement, as the Pope explained that the church stands for positive things. This bolstering refers, too, to his writings on the sacred nature of sexuality as the attraction of one person to the total value of the other, which is nothing less than the image of God shining through human personhood. As if people needed to be told that sexual abuse in a profound contradiction to personhood.

The Pope then engaged in mortification: "The Synod Fathers wished to apologize unreservedly to the victims for the pain and disillusionment caused to them." However, it is worth noting that the previous statement absolved the Synod Fathers of wrong-doing. This is an example of what might be called a "third party" apology: One group (who did no harm) apologizes for the actions of another group. It is another version of the Holy Mother Church apologizing for the sinful acts of Her children. It is also a means of co-opting victimhood.

The Pope also pledged corrective action in the message, reporting a desire to respond to complaints:

> The Church in Oceania is seeking open and just procedures to respond to complaints in this area, and is unequivocally committed to compassionate and effective care for the victims, their families, the whole community, and the offenders themselves. (Obtained online at http://www.vatican.va/holy_father/john_paul_ii/apost_exhortations/documents/hf_jp-ii_exh_20011122_ecclesia-in-oceania_en.html)

Note that these procedures had not yet been devised or implemented (the Church is "seeking" such procedures), so this is more of an announcement of a goal of corrective action rather than implementation of any actual redress. Thus, in this discourse over the internet, the pope enacted shifting the blame (denial), mortification, bolstering, and corrective action. It is important to note this was a relatively brief response buried in section 49 of the document.

Pope John Paul also addressed the sexual scandal on March 17, 2002, St. Patrick's Day. In this instance, the Pope referred to sexual abuse accusations against some clergy. The letter addressed priests of the Catholic Church, which no doubt influenced its tone, but the Pope and his advisers were savvy enough to realize that the press and the public would be secondary audience. The Pope identified the root cause of these failings as man's mysterious capacity for evil:

> At this time too, as priests we are personally and profoundly afflicted by the sins of some of our brothers who have betrayed the grace of Ordination in succumbing even to the most grievous forms of the *mysterium iniquitatis* at work in the world. (Obtained online at http://www.vatican.va/holy_father/john_paul_ii/letters/2002/documents/hf_jp-ii_let_20020321_priests-holy-thursday_en.html)

Here again, the Pope shifts the blame or limits the scope of guilt. The *Church as a whole* has not sinned, only "*some* of our brothers." Further, he offers an excuse based on human frailty: Things like this happen because there is a capacity for evil in human hearts. As the *Catechism* says, Baptism imparts God's grace and erases original sin, but "human nature" weakened and inclined to evil is inalterable (Part I, 404, 405). These utterances employ the strategy of defeasibility: these priests could not help themselves because they are imperfect human beings. Can the same be said for cover-ups by a holy institution?

When it suits the Church's purposes, the priesthood suddenly becomes a democracy—in this case a democracy of sinners.

John Paul also bolstered the Church and committed it to a course of corrective action:

> As the Church shows her concern for the victims and strives to respond in truth and justice to each of these painful situations, all of us – conscious of human weakness, but trusting in the healing power of divine grace – are called *to embrace the "mysterium Crucis"* and to commit ourselves more fully to the search for holiness. (Obtained online at http://www.vatican.va/holy_father/john_paul_ii/letters/2002/documents/hf_jp-ii_let_20020321_priests-holy-thursday_en.html)

His statement stresses the Church's "concern for the victims" and its desire for "truth and justice," bolstering the Catholic Church. Again, no specific corrective action was announced, only a general desire to do the right thing.

The Pope prayed to God for the strength to engage in authentic corrective action: "We must beg God in his Providence to prompt a whole-hearted reawakening of those ideals of total self-giving to Christ, which are the very foundation of the priestly ministry." In this way John Paul sought to communicate that the church members and leaders would vigilantly guard against such crimes.

He took the opportunity to explain that true dedication to the precepts of the church is the only way to avoid such evil in the future:

> It is precisely our faith in Christ which gives us the strength to look trustingly to the future. We know that the human heart has always been attracted to evil, and that man will be able to radiate peace and love to those around him only if he meets Christ and allows himself to be "overtaken" by him. As ministers of the Eucharist and of sacramental Reconciliation, we in particular have the task of communicating hope, goodness and peace to the world. (Obtained online at http://www.vatican.va/holy_father/john_paul_ii/letters/2002/documents/hf_jp-ii_let_20020321_priests-holy-thursday_en.html)

Here the Pope enacted bolstering by identifying the good done by most clergy members. In this passage, John Paul also referenced a commitment to reconciliation, a concept that would play a key role in his negotiations with U.S. bishops over reform policies designed to address this problem. It is also interesting because the sexual abuse crisis had led some Church members to waiver in their faith: He explicitly declares that Catholic believers must strengthen their faith to deal with this crisis. In sum, in the letter to the priests on Holy Thursday, 2002, the Pope shifted the blame, alluded to a form of accidents, promised corrective action, and bolstered the image of the church.

John Paul again addressed the sexual abuse scandal at the World Youth Convention, Toronto, Downsview Park, on Sunday July 28, 2002. The pope asked the attendees to keep faith in the church despite the scandal and admitted a "sense of shame" from the abuse on some children:

Even a tiny flame lifts the heavy lid of night. How much more light will you make, all together, if you bond as one in the communion of the Church! *If you love Jesus, love the Church!* Do not be discouraged by the sins and failings of some of her members. The harm done by some priests and religious to the young and vulnerable *fills us all with a deep sense of sadness and shame.* (Obtained online at http://www.vatican.va/holy_father/john_paul_ii/homilies/2002/documents/hf_jp-ii_hom_20020728_xvii-wyd_en.html)

The recognition of "sadness and shame" was an implicit form of mortification.

Ironically, the statement, "If you love Jesus, love the Church" is often the very argument the Church uses to silence the families of the abused.[1] Here again the Church should be understood in Augustinian terms. The visible, the pilgrim Church navigating the City of Man is certain to have sinful members. The invisible, spiritual Church in the City of God is the true Church of the elect founded by the sinless redeemer. Nevertheless, the visible apostolic Church remains the gateway between the two worlds, the only aperture for the flow of grace through the sacraments. One must not confuse the two; the visible Church is a vague shadow of the brilliantly shining spiritual Church outside our cave. It is the heavenly cathedral in which he seeks sanctuary, the ultimate transcendent safe-house. No critical barbs, no logical assaults, no empirical evidence can breach its infinite vertical walls. John Paul II's entire apologia plays upon this theme. Equating the love of Jesus with the love of the Church is a yet another example.

The Pope again distinguished between the few who have committed such acts and the most that have not: "But think of the vast majority of dedicated and generous priests and religious whose only wish is to serve and do good! There are many priests, seminarians and consecrated persons here today; be close to them and support them!" This was another instance of shifting the blame intermingled with some bolstering of the good priests who are the majority.

To be fair, there can be little doubt that the popular press tends to exaggerate the problem. Every priest becomes suspect. The Church begins to look hypocritical with its teachings on such things as contraception, marriage, women priests, gays and celibacy. In a *Chicago Tribune* cartoon, a bishop is lecturing a couple lying in bed about sex and sin when the man holds up a newspaper article about pedophile priests. The bishop retorts: "We'll do the lecturing about sex around here!"[2] It is surely this sort of image the Pope wishes to correct with his emphasis upon the "vast majority of the good."

The Pope's statements on this occasion received more international mass media attention than his other statements on the scandal. The *New York Times* reported, "Speaking to a public audience about the child sexual abuse crisis for the first time since it engulfed the Roman Catholic Church this year, Pope John Paul II called the crimes and misdeeds of some priests a source of shame today and urged young Catholics not to lose faith."[3] Although the pope had addressed the issue indirectly earlier in the year, the coverage amplified the pope's message. The mere fact that the pope discussed the

---
[1] Gary Wills, *Papal Sin*, p. 175.
[2] Jenkins, *The New Anti-Catholicism*, p. 152.
[3] F. Buni, "Pope Tells Crowd of 'Shame' Caused By Abusive Priests," *New York Times*, (July 28, 2002), A1.

scandal at all seemed to be perceived by the international press as notable. Nonetheless, shifting the blame to a few rotten apples or a generalized human nature are forms of denial.

The Pope was also involved in the discussion about new policies with which to deal with such issues in the future. Initially, he rejected a policy that did not allow for the reconciliation of erring priests. This could have served as further grounds for criticism against Rome, but the idea was not prominently articulated in the mass media. The eventual policy adopted by the U.S. bishops is much more open and strict, and was a notable improvement over the secretive policies of the past. Settlement funds have also been distributed by the Catholic Church in the United States, another form of corrective action, although there is scant public connection between the Pope and these diocesan settlements.

The strategies of shifting the blame (to a few malfeasants), mortification and corrective action are of particular importance. As noted earlier, shifting the blame is a form of denial in which the accused claims that another is responsible for a transgression. Corrective action was also an important strategy enacted by the Pope: He would remedy the problem by promising not to repeat this error. These are the two most prominent strategies in the pope's *mea culpa*. These two strategies can be particularly useful when used together.

Nevertheless, corrective action is very vague and represented nothing more than a goal (no particular policy had been enacted—or even *formulated*).

One change did help. The openness of the new policy in the United States is a viable corrective action in response to accusations of cover-ups. This is significant given the history of a powerful church hierarchy. Most likely, however, is the possibility that an outraged public outcry forced this supposed openness. The Church had to make the best of a bad situation.

The Pope's demand that forgiveness continues to be a part of the church's response to the pedophilia by its priests could easily undermine the attempt at corrective action. It might be perceived as an admission that more abuse is sure to follow. But of course. With that evil spirit of secularism haunting the minds of the Pope and his Grand Inquisitor, one must expect such things.

John Paul II cannot ignore a central tenant of the Catholic response to sin: penance rectifies. But where are the sanctions that rectify the sin of institutional abuse, a sin shared by the Pope and his male-only club?

There may other problems the Pope wishes to ignore. In this chapter we examined the sexual abuse of children by some members of the clergy and the Church's response.

Chapter 17

A Thoroughly Incomplete History of Sex in Religion

We identify conceptions of human sexuality change over time in this chapter. We will conclude this abuse will continue as long as the Church sees sex as a moral problem tied to cosmological presuppositions.

There is a deeper theological meaning of the term *mysterium iniquitatis*, especially in regard to sexuality. And it is not so mysterious. Sexual desire and its actualization in sexual union is a fact of nature (obviously). In the cultures of pagan Greece and Rome, reproduction was the life's answer to the ever-present specter of death. In a certain sense this was also true of the ancient Hebrews, probably ancient people in general. The promise to Abraham is not realized in some future sexless realm of saintly communion, but in the production of children and the passing of the promise to future generations. In an age when few lived beyond fifty, children were humanity's tenuous hold on the future; future generations were the only real resurrection of the dead.[1]

The human body was part of the natural world. The person was fully immersed in the visible world and understood fully in that context. The same living spirit that ignited human sexuality burned in stars as well as in all earthly creatures. A deep and essential bond existed between humans and the cosmos, between animals and humans.

Sex is a fact of nature, humanity's tenuous hold on the future. It is, however, the locus of possible problems, says Foucault in something of an understatement. As a fact of nature sexual union cannot be harmful in itself, yet it can have harmful effects

---
[1] Peter Brown, *The Body and Society: Men, Women, and Sexual Renunciation in Early Christianity*, (New York, 1988), p. 7

such as a wasting of the life-force.[2] Sex was seen as the outward flow of energy in the male; ejaculation meant a diminution of power. In Aristotelian science, as we've seen, sperm provided the "form" that organized the passive, unorganized matter supplied by the female. Among the ancients, passivity and disorganization meant inferiority. Women could be considered dangerous as well as inferior in that they were like sexual vampires. Galen advised Olympic athletes to practice celibacy in order to remain strong.[3] Orgasm, too, was dangerous in that it resembled epilepsy. Like that disease, it was divine madness.

One could easily become enslaved to desire. In societies obsessed with domination, the loss of control illustrated a weak character, even in the strongest like Samson. In a later Roman society manliness was often equated with self-control.[4] To be free of desire's authority was to practice the supreme virtue of self-discipline, as Socrates shows in the *Symposium* by mastering his desire for Alcibiades, or the later Stoics, who sought *apatheia*, a non-attachment to things which brought them peace of mind.

The pagan paradise of unrepressed sexuality is largely a myth. Sex was not evil in itself, it was like a strong wine. Used properly, it brought pleasure and the prospect of immortality through the future generations. Abused, it could become addicting and potentially dangerous to one's health. It also belonged to economics. As the desire for food can be brought under human control through the discipline of fasting, thus separating humans from the animals, chastity was honored as an expression of self-mastery as well as the source of exceptional power.[5] As an economic category, it was governed by social rules.

In ancient Judaism, the human being was a unity of flesh and living spirit (*ruah*), defined by the heart, an inner principle that could respond to the will of God. The heart was subject to the good inclination and bad inclination, both sent by God, as when He sends the evil inclination upon King Saul (1 Samuel 19:9: "An evil spirit from the Lord

---

[2] M Foucault, *The History of Sexuality: The Care of the Self*, Vol. III, trans. Robert Hurley, (New York, 1988), pp. 112–113, and p. 142.

[3] Peter Brown, *The Body and Society*, p.19.

[4] Kyle Harper, *From Shame to Sin*, p. 56. Women were passive, males active, continuing Aristotle's division. A man (not necessarily a boy) who allowed himself to be penetrated was socially inferior, such as a slave. If adultery was theft and therefore a social-economic question, slaves were social non-entities, another form of property. One could do with his property what he saw fit. Harper portrays the vast sex industry of the late empire in terms of social-economic categories, not the cosmological-moral categories of Christianity.

[5] Mahatma Gandhi took the brahmacharya vow, the vow of chastity, in 1906. His political strength was based upon this sort of supreme self-discipline. In Hinduism, the brahmacharin has accomplished self-mastery and hence freedom. It usually belongs to the later stage of life when the person becomes a forest dweller seeking liberation (*moksha*) from world. It recognizes the allure of sex but does not pronounce it evil or fallen. The vow is like fasting. Fasting does not say that hunger is good or bad. Hunger is a natural inclination of life. Like all appetites, it can enslave a person, causing problems like obesity, disease, and so on. For Gandhi, chastity was as aspect of the inner strength for his great political struggle against the British. Sex was not immoral; he gave up sexual intimacy, says Erik Erikson, for communal intimacy (*Gandhi's Truth*, 1969, p. 192). Gandhi devoted celibacy to strength and freedom *in the world* based upon his own self-discipline. It was not devoted to or living in some transcendental future state; it was devoted to living in the future state of a free India. In Left-handed Tantra, on the other hand, the conquest of sex may be achieved by indulging in intercourse without the enslaving desire that gives rise to it, indulging without being attached to sex. But sex in itself is not considered evil. See Wendy Doniger O'Flaherty, *Shiva: The Erotic Ascetic*, 166–7. The title aptly expresses the idea.

came upon Saul."). Failing to respond to God's will with a singleness of heart could easily come about due to sensual distractions. Overwhelmed by lust, the human being might ignore God completely.[6] This was a hardening of the heart.

For the ancient Hebrews, then, there is nothing intrinsically evil about sex, nor is it condemned in the garden after the Fall. Eve is made to suffer labor pains and told that her desire will be for her husband and he will rule over her. What this does establish is a patriarchal family system and may reflect the ancient transition (if there was one) from matrilineal to a patrilineal society, which does seem to be a major concern in the stories of the patriarchs in Genesis.[7] Sex is hardly mentioned (one wonders if the celibate YHWH is even fully aware of it—or perhaps he has forgotten). On the other hand, God had ordered humans to be fruitful and multiply, thereby blessing procreation. Augustine's interpretation, as this book shall show, makes all the difference.

As mentioned earlier, one could perceive the creation of the woman as a rival to God in that she distracts Adam's attention, twisting it away from the Lord and thus dividing Adam's loyalty.

Nonetheless, Eve is a guarantee of the future, through her the generations are born. Like paganism, children are the source of humans' tenuous hold upon life. Sex as a relationship between people is also the origin of human society, for as God Himself acknowledged it was not good for man to be alone. Sex is still intrinsically necessary and good.

On the other hand, the overwhelming power of sex, its tendency to swallow the person whole, could pose a challenge to God's own jealous addiction to exclusive praise and worship. Having never participated in divine sex, God is in some ways ignorant of its pull on the human heart. Or, keeping with the archaeological plot, perhaps he still has dreams of the goddess Asherah which cause him some embarrassment.

To his credit, John Paul tried to meet the problem with his claim that in sexual reproduction humans recapture the creative act of the deity, "the original unity and mystery of creation" (*The Theology of the Body*, p.49). From this rather strained comparison, the Pope is able to introduce his celebration of love (humanizing the animal instinct) as the self-giving of the entire person, a gift of persons, as God's creation was a freely given gift of love—the will of God "who is the omnipotence of love" (p. 59).

This hopeful blessing of sexuality might work better if God actually participated in divine sex with a goddess and personally experienced what self-donation really meant. The fact is, however, that neither the P Source nor the J Source understands creation in any form of cosmic sex. The idea was probably repugnant to them, it is primitive anthropomorphism of folk religion. Later, the prophets will use the language of sexual promiscuity as a symbol for Israel's infidelity to monotheism. Israel is like a whore, polytheism is adultery, over and over again. Israel could be seen as a stand-in for Asherah. Yet it is all symbolic. The real issue is idolatry, spiritual promiscuity one might say.

---

[6] In the Qur'an human sin results from the forgetfulness of Allah, the failure to remember and celebrate Allah's oneness.
[7] In the Homeric epics, Menelaus was King of Sparta by virtue of his marriage to Helen the daughter of Tyndareus, the former King. Rejecting him for Paris, Helen places him in danger of losing the throne. Pomeroy, *Goddesses, Whores, Wives, and Slaves*, p. 20–21.

An abstract spiritualized god, our friendly supernatural agent, lives in a sexless universe. Sex is an act. Acting in this world implies a body. Spiritual beings do not have physical bodies. Spiritual beings can know nothing about the sexual experience much as pronouncing the word medicine cannot result in a cure.

In the John Paul school of hermeneutics, the two sources in Genesis become objective and subjective: P tells of the creation of male and female in God's image (objective) while J talks about their subjective feelings like shame, fear, and so on (p. 30). But such superficial interpretations ignore centuries of scholarly analysis, if not, what Hebrew text actually says. They are another instance of the Uncertainty Principle at work.[8]

In the Priestly account, the cosmic God (*'elohim*) creates (*bara'*) by separation. Like the Babylonian god Marduk in the *Enuma Elish*, he pulls things apart, sets them in place, not by battle but by the command of his voice as if pronouncing a set of laws, "let there be..." He is a kind of divine engineer, manipulating resistant matter, establishing the laws of nature, and setting everything in its natural place. His final act is to create human beings.[9] The earlier J writer (or writers) begins his creation with man (*adama'* is a noun not a proper name) and like a potter working in a desert clay medium, he "forms" (the Hebrew is *yatzar*) the man from the dirt (*adamah*). The opening scene in J is hardly cosmic at all; it is a desert, a waste land, and God causes water to flow in order to fertilize the place. Like any Mesopotamian King, he establishes life by irrigating the fields and settling humans in a fertile dwelling, say in the garden of Ur. As He is a divine architect or engineer in P, He is a divine gardener in J. *But in neither myth does he engage in divine sex. The world is not born through the sexual union of god and goddess.*

John Paul is somehow able to intuit God's unspoken intentions. God (but which one?) intends to grant existence as a freely given gift, an overflow of His divine love, and create sex as a sign of that love, thus rooting procreation in creation.

As an aside, there is in fact an invisible narrator in both stories, watching God act and hearing Him speak. We, the readers, are privy to God's acts, speeches and even thoughts through the eyes of this narrator. *The narrator cannot be God, for He would then be making himself an object of His own subject.* Who is this seer behind seeing, asked the Upanishads?

Other interpretations of the myth are possible. Hermeneutics is a game that can played by multiple players. The psychology of literary characters (God is, among other things, as Jack Miles taught us, a literary character) is open to endless speculation.

For example, God's main concern may simply be narcissistic self-love. His self-giving love is really self-receiving, it is meant for Him alone. Creating a world that sings His praises on cue inflates His divine ego. In His awful loneliness, consumed by His unrelenting need to know His own subjectivity, He requires infinite devotion and infinite love. Later, when

---

[8] Attempts to unify the two creation stories include actually changing the Hebrew verb tense. The Hebrew verb *yatzar* in verse 7 means "formed" and is in the simple past tense. It is mistranslated as "had formed" which is meant to infer the earlier story. Hector Avalos, *The End of Biblical Studies*, (Amherst, New York, 2007), pp. 46–47.

[9] He creates them male (*'ish*) and female (*'issah*) at the same time. This need not be two individuals but a whole population of people. In other words, humanity in general becomes God's earthly satraps, as in any ancient Mid-eastern empire (see Kugel, 2007, p. 52).

poor Job questions His justice, He lets go a barrage of boasting—where were you when I created the world, etc.—indicating a certain lack of insight into His own character (for a psychoanalysis of God's repressions see C. G. Jung, *Answer to Job*, 1952).

Perhaps He secretly envies humans their ability to truly love, which includes experiencing disappointment, loss, heartache and pain. Having never experienced sex, or perhaps having forgotten the experience after Asherah left town, He cannot know the vulnerability of real intimacy. He cannot know the vulnerability of trusting another. Beginning with Abraham, He takes from men their foreskin, which on the surface is a sign of the Covenant but is really a symbol of His jealously.

Human sexuality is a challenge to God, a challenge He cannot really comprehend. His "be fruitful and multiply" actually backfired. It created an experience He cannot understand with any real empathy. Somewhat like the science of complexity in which simple mathematical rules may produce incredibly complex and unanticipated effects (the Mandelbrot set, for example), God surprised Himself with a wholly unanticipated creation.

The depersonalization of sex John Paul believed he had uncovered in so-called modern hedonism, the exploitation of women as mere objects of pleasure, selfish gratification at the expense of others, the impoverishment of human relations, contraception, abortion, all of this and more come from modernity's decision to live independently without God (*The Theology of the Body*, pp. 510–511).

As if such things did not exist for all those centuries that God was around.

From another hermeneutical perspective, such problems may result from the "de-divinization" of sexuality. For the Church, fully passionate sexuality is not a joy—perhaps it is actually one of the greatest joys we poor humans are able to experience—but a moral problem. Women are exploited when their main "personhood" is understood as "reproductive technology." Selfish gratification is the human "sign" of God's jealously. Objectification and exploitation of people for one's own pleasure comes from the fear of intimacy, the fear of a real sharing of the self and non-attachment in the service of the other, the greater circle, as Lawrence has it. It is a sign of unhealthy sexual development, of infantilism. Hedonism may also be religious intoxication and not merely an addiction to materialism (it can be both too), the ecstasy of merging with divine nature that Ratzinger found in pagan threats to the mysterious God of the Covenant. How well he knew.

The Pope stands against this kind of divinization (a specific belief immediately negates another). He adamantly believes that it is a misunderstanding of nature's dependence upon the Creator's plan (p. 510). His objection betrays the weakness of his hermeneutics. His god is a planner, an architect, designer, sculptor and craftsman. God treats all nature as an object, a thing to be subdued and used to fulfill His own need for love and praise. He loves the world only as far as it worships and loves Him back. He loves the world for payment in the currency of the self. He cannot allow His creatures to develop their own purpose and meaning of life (to grow up). If my purpose in life comes from another being then I am a slave. Whatever dignity I potentially possess is taken from me. Again, I remain a child.

The Pope accuses modern human autonomy of this sin; it arises from our mistaken idea of independence. In his own sort of unconscious self-disclosure, as Jung saw in God's response to Job, John Paul II attempts a bit of cleverness: Nature, from being "mater" (mother) is reduced to "matter" (509). But even if this bit of wit is symbolic, nature could never have been "mater." God did not know the goddess Asherah, unlike the man who died. Real communion with the world (an artifact that receives its value from the outside) is impossible. If the Pope really does want to symbolize nature as "mater," he would require a priest *and a priestess*. All he has is a virgin mother who like his father god remains immaculately ignorant of the real sexual experience.

The earthly method of procreation, not in theory, but in practice, is directly opposed to the biblical myths of creation. Procreation cannot be found in biblical creation any more than sexual desire in a rock. Compare these two creation stories from Genesis with the creation myth that appears in the *Brihaharanyaka Upanishad*:

1. In the beginning this was Self alone, the shape of a person (*purusha*). He looking round saw nothing but his Self. He first said, 'This is I;' therefore he became I by name...
2. But he felt no delight. Therefore a man who is lonely feels no delight. He wished for a second. He was so large as man and wife together. He then made this his Self to fall in two (*pat*), and therefore arose husband (*pati*) and wife (*Patni*). ...He embraced her and men were born.
3. She thought, 'How can he embrace me, after having produced me from himself? I shall hide myself.'
   She then became a cow, the other a bull and embraced her, and hence cows were born. The one became a mare, the other a stallion; the one a male ass, the other a female ass. He embraced her, and hence one-hoofed animals were born. The one became a she-goat, the other a he-goat; the one became a ewe, the other a ram. He embraced her, and hence goats and sheep were born. And he created everything that exists in pairs, down to the ants.
4. He knew, "I indeed am this creation, for I created all this. (Part II, pp. 85–86).

At Qumran near the Dead Sea, celibacy was apparently an important practice of the community. The Jews of Qumran were the remnant of the true Israel, purified and prepared for the final war against the Sons of Darkness. They, too, dedicated themselves to the future Kingdom:

> ...they kept the laws of purity laid down in Scripture for soldiers in Holy Warfare, an ascetic regimen which at the same time anticipated life with the holy angels before the throne of God, a situation requiring similar ritual purity.[10]

---

[10]Frank Moore Cross, *Canaanite Myth and Hebrew Epic: Essays in the History of the Religion of Israel*, (Cambridge, MA, 1973), p. 334.

Sounding a bit like John Paul, the Stoics, as we've noted, rejected the attachment to pleasure, especially sexual pleasure which was inferior because it was common to the animals. Sex also implied privation. Logically, desire indicates a need, which means that something is lacking. Since the female was a misbegotten male, whatever a man lacked surely could not be found in her embrace. Sexual desire was like an illness. That women were its cause and object, the illness and its cure, demonstrated its danger.

As discussed earlier, the canonical gospels are silent on the subject of Jesus' sexual life. Silence in scripture is like a highway without a speed limit. Critics often complain loudly about the argument from silence, such as Paul's silence on the life of Jesus. When it suits them, however, silence is an open invitation to self-serving interpretation, which has a way of becoming fact.

It is inferred that he was unmarried and therefore celibate (a rather large assumption since it does not always follow that the unmarried are celibate—obviously). If he were celibate, this condition might have arisen from his prophetic office, the prophet who is completely dedicated to God to the exclusion of all else—but not all prophets are celibate. Celibacy may derive from connections to Qumran or even the possibility that he was a "Nazarite," an ascetic, like his brother James. Yet, Jesus certainly associated with women, even women who were counted among the "lost sheep of Israel."

It is evident from recent books and movies, and sensationalized archaeological "discoveries," that the Catholic Church lives in mortal fear of the unexpected discovery of some empirical evidence for his wife and children. Never fear, all historical facts, like evidence for evolution, may be "refuted" given the time and resources. The largely misunderstood pliability of historical possibilities and plausible arguments (high probabilities can be computed with some accuracy) makes for endless speculation. But once again such things have a way of becoming doctrine when they support previously held beliefs.

As previously noted, the Catholic Church has never disputed the inclusion of married priests for the first thousand years of Church history. Married priests were banned between 1073 and 1139. As Spoto explained:

> As for the clergy, since early Christian times, ministerial celibacy had been an honored option but had not been required. It was mandated only a century before Francis, during the papacy of Gregory VII (1073-1085), who went so far as to urge the laity to revolt against married clergy and who called for priests' wives to be hunted down and banished (or worse). By the time of the Second Lateran Council, in 1139, the wives of priests were proclaimed to be disreputable concubines, and their children were kidnapped to become Church slaves. There was massive resistance against this ruling, but Rome prevailed, at least legally. As a tactic for restricting ecclesiastical solely by the clergy and for disenfranchising the laity, it was brilliantly successful. But compulsory celibacy also severed the ministerial life of the people, who became completely subordinate to a priestly caste, themselves considered lower than the lordly pope. p. 8

What worked for the first thousand years in the Catholic Church will work for the third millennium. While it may extend enfranchisement to the laity, decrease the subordination to the patriarchal authoritarianism of Catholic leadership, and it will also help alleviate an atmosphere in which pedophilia can occur and be covered-up.

Paul is another matter. The human being according to Paul is basically composed of spirit, mind, and flesh. Although they form a unity, which the Pope reformulates in his doctrine of personhood, this unity is more like a fissionable uranium atom. There may be an echo in Paul of the dualistic antagonism between the Neo-platonic mind (*nous*) and matter. As noted elsewhere, the Law, the Torah, is righteousness itself, given by God to humanity. It calls out to the heart and the will. But the flesh is infused with an opposing principle that resists the good. The flesh is possessed by an evil power that resists holiness and prevents the human being from fulfilling the Law. Thus, the flesh is not merely unspiritual or weak, but it possessed of an *active demonic power* that is hostile to God, and therefore to be of the flesh is sold under sin.[11] The end result is death. Paul wrote in Romans:

> I discover this principle, then: that when I want to do the right, only the wrong is within my reach. In my inmost self I delight in the law of God, but I perceive that there is in my bodily members a different law, fighting against the law that my reason approves and making me a prisoner under the law that is in my members, the law of sin. Miserable creature that I am, who is there to rescue me out of this body doomed to death? (7:21–24)

The body, composed of demonic flesh, is in rebellion against God. Sex is the form (but not the exclusive form) of that rebellion. Death is the result. As reproduction, sex is the precondition of death. Who is there to rescue me? Only Christ, free from sin, was able to fulfill the old Law.

> Paul believes that the world has been given over to evil powers (archons), the rulers of this age. Some may argue that these powers are temporal, the Romans, but it is clear in Paul's overall corpus that he is speaking of supernatural powers that infuse the visible world. By implication, then, natural inclinations actually harden the heart to an unheard of degree.[12]

John Paul's culture of life and his rescue of sex from Manichean dualism have other meanings. Sex brings the body into the world. Bodies are doomed to suffer and die. Death, like concupiscence, is beyond human control in this fallen world. It is truly a bleak picture. Norman Brown puts it this way: "Life and death, equated. Every coitus repeats the fall; brings death, birth into the world" (*Love's Body*, p. 48).

The world, once deemed good, ruled by such powers is evil. In the grip of those *archons,* many natural desires are twisted into rebellion against God. Strictly speaking,

---
[11]Otto Pfleider, *Primitive Christianity: Its Writings and Teachings in Their Historical Connections*, Vol. I., trans. W. Montgomery, (New Jersey, 1965), p. 277.
[12]Peter Brown, *The Body and Society*, pp. 46–47.

the claim that the physical world is good because God pronounced it so occurs in the context of a lost, non-recoverable past. Calling it intrinsically good (like sex) may work in theory, but not in practice. Why else would any sane person look forward to the end of the world in an orgy of destruction?

Christ's incarnation and resurrection have shattered the natural order. In Paul's lifetime the evil world will come to its apocalyptic conclusion. It is in this context that Paul speaks of a universal leveling in Galatians 3:27-28; believers are no longer Jew or Greek, male or female. Equality occurs within the context of the apocalyptic. Did Paul expect the world to last another two thousand years?

Under these circumstances, human continuity in the coming Kingdom of Heaven is no longer tied to marriage and reproduction, which means no sex, good or bad, as noted earlier. Immortality, the conquest of death, is made possible by Christ's overcoming of sin and the fallen natural world; it is his victory over the grave. There will be a new "spiritual body" that is no longer slave to the flesh and the evil principle that lodges in it. The old biblical idea that human immortality is guaranteed in the survival of future generations is overturned. A kind of non-personal life after death is exchanged for personal immortality of the self. *I* will live eternally. Eternal life is *mine*. God has a plan for *me*. *I-mine-me* forever. Is this not monumental selfishness? Compared to modern hedonism, it is like choosing between Las Vegas and a hayride (Buridan's ass would hardly suffer the slightest hesitation). Furthermore, the flourishing of future generations implies a healthy and fertile environment *on this earth*. The Kingdom of God does not.

Implicit in Paul's theology of the evil-possessed flesh is a negative valuation of sex. As Brown suggested, procreation only serves to provide death with further prey. It is bondage from which no human is able to escape. Platonism with its emphasis upon the ideal and the good is now grafted to a religious anthropology in which instincts that humans share with nature are under the sway of evil powers. Unlike the pagans and even the Jews, *sexuality in our world is intrinsically evil*, hence a moral problem due to cosmological fantasies.

For early Christians, however, humans did have free will, the fault was not totally in their stars. How else could a person be held responsible and punished? A person could remain unmarried like Paul himself. Humans still possessed the moral agency. In fact, the sexual disorder of Roman society (as perceived by Christians) was a sign of the world domination by the evil archons. Moral autonomy was also a cosmological postulate.[13] This optimism would come crashing down.

St. Augustine drew out the implications of Paul with the theory of original sin. Adam in Eden had the ability not to sin (*posse non peccare*). He possessed completely rational control over his members (unlike, apparently, poor Paul in Romans). In his body there was no corruption, no fear, no death, and no inclination that opposed the law of God. If God commanded Adam and Eve to be fruitful and multiply, they had sexual intercourse free from lust, pure of heart, the organs of reproduction subject to calm reason

---

[13]Harper, *From Shame to Sin*, p. 83.

and will. They lacked the same lust for carnal pleasure as these bodies of ours do now, writes Augustine in *The Literal Meaning of Genesis* (p. 384).

For Augustine, the Fall was a major historical event (the *Catechism* calls it a "primeval event" Part I, 390) in order to avoid challenges from paleontology. "Primeval" reads like "in a time before time..." Afterwards, the human condition became *non posse non peccare*, human beings are "not able not to sin." Obedience of the lower members was lost by disobedience to God. The proof, says Augustine, can be seen in the following:

> Sometimes the impulse [sexual arousal] is an unwanted intruder, sometimes it abandons the eager lover, and the desire cools off in the body while it is at boiling heat in the mind. Thus strangely does lust refuse to be a servant not only to the will to beget but even to the lust for lascivious indulgence; and although on the whole it is totally opposed to the mind control, it is quite often divided against itself. It arouses the mind, but does not follow its own lead by arousing the body (The City of God, p.577).14

The evidence is open to observation. Again Augustine:

> We do in fact find among human beings some individuals with natural abilities very different from the rest of mankind and remarkable by their very rarity. Such people can do some things with their body which are for others utterly impossible and well-nigh incredible when they are reported. Some people can move their ears, either one at a time or both together...There are others who imitate the cries of birds and beasts and the voices of other men, reproducing them so accurately as to be quite indistinguishable from the originals, unless they are seen. A number of people produce at will such musical sounds from their behind (without any stink) that they seem to be singing from that region (p. 588).

Males may be able to fart like an opera singer, but men are unable to control their erections. John Paul updates this weird comparison when he says in *The Theology of the Body*:

> The natural and somatic substratum of human sexuality was manifested as an almost autogenous force. It is marked by a certain 'coercion of the body,' operating according to its own dynamics, which limits the expression of the spirit and the experience of the exchange of the gift of person (p. 126).

Few people who live a healthy sexual life would find anything limiting in the intimate exchange of the great gift of self in love. There is little need to quibble with profound insights on human sexuality by the celibate Pope. Where a man cannot master his lust, the Pope goes on, a woman is overwhelmed by her desire for her husband, and thus he

---

[14] Modern chemistry solves this problem with products like Viagra. Given that chemistry is rational, it may not be a stretch to say that sex is once again under control of the rational mind: the organs of reproduction are aroused at will. More seriously, the ancient disciplines of Yoga and other forms of meditation may prove, after further studies, to alter the nervous system itself. The enlightened brain undergoes substantial changes, according to James H. Austin, M. D., *Zen and the Brain*(1998). Zen, says Austin, does not diminish the pragmatic ego, leaving us with an identity crisis. Rather Zen training is targeted at the distorted self, the "selfish I" (p. 35). Zen therefore goes beyond narcissism and depersonalization. So much for Ratzinger's silly idea that meditation is "mental masturbation".

rules over her (quoting Genesis 3:15). This is high comedy indeed, an upside down version of the women of Sparta and Athens who in Aristophanes' play, *Lysistrata*, decide to abstain from sex in order to get the men to stop fighting. The Greek women are able to rule the men by actively controlling their so-called uncontrollable desire for their husbands. It contradicts the Pope's view of the "passive" woman. In *Lysistrata,* the men seem helpless, at the mercy of the active women. Interestingly, the cause is peace.

The British ascetic and heretic Pelagius taught that all human beings were born in a state of innocence as Adam before the Fall (although they could be easily corrupted by society). With the proper discipline, men and women were able to fulfill the Law. For Augustine, and the Catholic Church, this is foolishly optimistic and dangerous. Original sin has corrupted the body and will beyond repair. Who can control the lower members that create the bodies doomed to the grave? Who can prevent the body from dying? The natural world is fallen, and with it all natural inclinations. By creating corrupted bodies enslaved by death, the sexual act bears in itself the curse.

It is like a kind of Lamarckian inherited, acquired characteristic. And despite all arguments to the contrary, again taking the Pope and his supporters on their word, it still sets up a dualism: The way God intended humanity as opposed to the way human beings actually are *in the present world*. And it all rests, like a dying person's hope that a desert mirage of a lake is really a deep lake, on ancient myths and "official" interpretations.

And there's more.

We identified conceptions of human sexuality change over time in this chapter. We conclude this abuse will continue as long as the Church sees sex as a moral problem.

Chapter 18
Archaeology of Theological Prehistory

George Weigel refers to the opening chapters of Genesis as mythical stories about human origins. At the same time they are, in his reading, "profound reflections on enduring truths about the human condition" (p. 336). He would probably agree, then, that the accounts in Genesis cannot be taken as literal history. One need not believe that there was a real physical garden somewhere in the Mideast, inhabited by Augustine's superhuman twosome, complete with talking snakes and a god who strolls in the garden during the cool time of the day. In comparison, scholars have today a fairly good scientific understanding of human origins, the diffusion of human populations on the globe, the beginning of language, and maybe even art and religion. Biblical Literalism seems oddly quaint and outdated.

The Genesis myth is *a story about something*. It is also a reflection *of truth* according to Christian defenders. *It does not establish the truth, it reflects it* as, say, a mirror reflects an object but does not create or contain it. It is not history, but ancient people telling stories *about history*. These distinctions must be kept in mind.

What are these "enduring truths" reflected in Genesis? Historical "man" and modern "man," John Paul II insists, participate in the history of human sinfulness (*The Theology of the Body*, p. 33). This history includes the grace of original human innocence, the free will of choice, and the ability to rationally judge and decide. Human beings are images of God in their choosing, judging and especially their self-donation to the other. Such are the "profound truths" of human nature to which the myths refer. John Paul dubs this original state of innocence "theological prehistory" and asserts that all humanity shares its inheritance (p. 32).

As the Pope proceeds with his "time bomb" (Weigel) theology of human sexuality and love, the ancient methods of expressing truth begin to shed their mythical magical cloaks and stand out as naked historical events. The Pope begins to sound as if he is reciting from some medieval chronicle; this event followed that event and this was the result. Neither he nor his followers explain exactly *how* human history is rooted in theological prehistory (which seems to be another updated term for myth and one that lacks the negative connotations of the word). Merely using the word "prehistory," even if qualified by "theological," introduces the sense of factual realism. The story *about* origins becomes the story *of* origins. Thus his followers speculate on Eve's inflated self-image as if she existed as a real person with certain psychological issues, and not what she probably is in the context of the Hebrew word itself, a symbol of life.

Notice too how divine mystery takes a back seat. It is suddenly quite clear what God "intended" (that *man* can have erections at will?).

Mythos in the Greek meant "to narrate," to tell a story. Stories include a particular perspective on an event, human feelings about the phenomena, how the event affects the human being. In turn, events and things assume human qualities. History means "to inquire," to search for the causes and reasons of events. Thus does Herodotus inquire into the causes of the Persian Wars. In order for the human propensity to sin to be a profound truth about the human condition, the cause must be the Fall in the garden as portrayed in Genesis. But how do myths yield "enduring truths" about human nature, which, extending through the generations, seem to be our *historical* inheritance?

At most, the story reveals that some writers perceived human beings to be sinful creatures, and that sometimes as sinful creatures they make bad choices for selfish reasons. What *causes* them to do so is an aspect of the *particular* story dynamic itself (the serpent challenging God's authority and His truthfulness). There are plenty of other myths that give plenty of other reasons. Without some historical anchor, one is as good as another. They do not reflect "enduring truths," but certain historically placed individuals' perception and understanding. The bible is literature, it invites the reader to share a certain perspective on the world of contingent historical experience. To call that anchor "theological prehistory" is a way of turning myth into history. It is like saying that because the weather god is angry today because it is storming.

Modern research is accumulating more and more evidence indicating that so-called human nature evolved from earlier forms. While humans are certainly distinct from the animals, they are not separate, as John Paul II adamantly maintained. Many of those prized human traits that define human "nature," especially such unique possessions as morality, reason, and judgment (God's image), human beings share with the animals, where they appear in very primitive but identifiable rudimentary form.[1]

---

[1]There are many traits that are still thought to be uniquely human: theory of mind, inhibitory control, abstract moral systems and so on. But little remains unchallenged. And Marc Hauser warns that reports of human uniqueness are often shot down before they have had much of a shelf life (*Moral Minds*, 2006, p. 413). Without thorough studies of animals, such claims are more like wishful thinking.

Let us for the moment take the Church at its word. If sin is a kind of selfishness, then those creatures that evolved a sense of enduring personal identity and selfishly guarded this identity as well as its possessions, their young, for example, would probably survive and reproduce, as opposed to those creatures who did not. At most, conscious continuity may suggest identity, but is not itself enduring and unchanging.[2] In Buddhist thought, the person is a process (the doctrine of *anatman*) and rises with the causes and conditions that make this specific personhood possible at this specific place and time. The so-called enduring self, the soul, is an illusion, but a useful one. Selfishness, then, is built upon a false sense of self, and original sin in this telling turns out to be the illusion of a soul, or an atman (the impersonal immortal Self), as the Buddhists have it.

Rational moral codes would be required to curb the self-centered tendency, delusional though it is, if humans required cooperation and some sort of empathy to survive in a larger society beyond the nuclear family. Such codes would require knowledge of good and evil (using the biblical language), which could be seen as working out through *human* reason a sense of "objective" good. Naturally, empathy and sympathy work much better in small bands in which no one is a total stranger, an object. After a life-time studying primates, Frans De Waal concluded that early humans were pretty moral while roaming the savannah, that empathy is easier in small bands. Only when societies begin to expand and the primate rules of reciprocity and reputation falter did we require moral instruction from on high.[3]

Again, Genesis *may be* (or may not) a mythical reflection of the human transition to an urbanized social life. It is about humans growing up. Cain, don't forget, the first murderer founds the first city.

The *Catechism* tries to blur the distinction between myth and history. The account of the Fall in Genesis uses "figurative language" say the authors of the Commission (led by Cardinal Ratzinger), yet it affirms a "primeval event, a deed that took place *at the beginning of the history of man*" (italics in the text, Part I, 390). Does this "beginning" stand outside history or within? Wherever it is located, the primeval event—the myth—cannot be *about* an enduring truth (as defined by the Church), but the *establishment of* an enduring truth, no matter how and in what language it is stated. Where is the historical evidence for this enduring truth except in the myth? The myth establishes the history. It explains the cause of human selfishness (rebellion against God inspired by the snake-philosopher) and is not merely a literary reflection on selfishness. The mirror creates the object.

After a brief and a grudging nod to modern sensitivities, the Pope and his *Catechism* proceed to update Augustine as if nothing new has been learned about human origins in two thousand years.

---

[2] Owen Flanagan, *The Bodhisattva's Brain: Buddhism Naturalized*, (Cambridge, MA, 2011), p. 97.
[3] Frans De Waal, *The Bonobo and the Atheist: In Search of Humanism Among the Primates*, (New York, 2013), p. 220.

Now, it can be argued that language creates experience. Theories yield facts. Observation creates history in a way similar to John Wheeler's participatory universe, that present observers have a hand in somehow contributing to the actuality of the past.[4] This gives new meaning to Collingwood's old dictum that all history is contemporary. In this way, history is indeterminate, the Uncertainty Principle with a vengeance.

Whatever one thinks of such speculations, or of their nearly infinite (and subtle) variations, one could make the same argument as does the *Catechism,* but instead of arguments for the Genesis myth, for the great Freudian myth of origins in *Totem and Taboo.* The father tyrant, possessing all the females in the "primeval" horde, is murdered by the sons, the brother band. Later he is promoted to heaven, so-to-speak, he becomes a totem, because the brothers feel a lasting guilt over the murder. The same "primeval" event occurs in *Moses and Monotheism* when the Hebrews in the wilderness murder their father Moses, an Egyptian. The atonement of the Son rescues them from their Jewish guilt. Those who do not accept the Son religion remain Jews, murders, and hence the world has anti-Semitism.

Although Freud may have felt otherwise (yet he did call *Moses and Monotheism* fiction), the historical reality of these primal crimes is by no means essential to the mythical reflections on enduring truths (oedipal fantasies). *The myth does not cause oedipal rivalries. Family relationships do.*[5] The causal evidence stands apart from the myth that reflects upon it. Unlike Genesis, Freud's myths need not be seen as historical explanations at all. Freud, like the Pope, did tend to blur the lines. Without some basis in history, some evidence outside the myth, how is one to judge the "truths" the myths supposedly convey? Why prefer the Genesis myth? Why not Freud? Original sin and Freudian primal murders are both myths about the evolution of historical people. They are how certain writers perceive and try to explain that evolution.

The Church must claim that *its myth is the true myth*. Tellingly, the results are the same as they were during those many centuries in which the myth was taken as history. Humans are selfish, sinful creatures, weakened by the Fall. Without God's grace imparted through the Church and its sacraments (in the case of sex it is marriage), humans are unable to control their lust. We treat each other as objects, violating the dignity of the person (derived from the image of God in human beings). The story is its own evidence.

Weigel makes these "built-in" truths into natural laws—truths, he says, that do not rest upon God's unilateral and arbitrary declarations, but are built into human beings as male and female (p. 338). Created in God's image, human nature reveals something about God (how about this for intelligent design: human complexity not only points to a designer, but actually illustrates many the designer's own qualities, that is, the designer's own design). But then without some historical evidence, why not turn the statement around and argue like Ludwig Feuerbach that the myth relates how humans created God in our image? It is about the ideal human. In religion, humans contemplate their own nature, projecting it outside themselves, calling it God, the sum of all human perfections,

---

[4] See John D. Barrow, Paul C. W. Davies, and Charles L. Harper Jr. eds., *Science and Ultimate Reality: Quantum Theory, Cosmology, and Complexity*, (Cambridge, UK, 2004).
[5] Peter Gay, *Freud: A Life For Our Time*, (New York, 1988), p. 333.

and worshiping it. In loving God as a being standing over humans, we alienate ourselves from what is best in us. It is "the disuniting of man from himself."[6]

Further, if God creates from nothing and chose to create humans in his own image (hence the built-in truths), *He really does choose arbitrarily.* By His "absolute power" (William of Occam) He might have chosen to create worlds one could hardly imagine. He might have chosen to save humanity in ways that appear blasphemous; for example, not-believing-in-God is necessary for salvation. But then, how can a necessary being make a choice that is not necessary?

In the end, the myth of God creating humans in His own image must contain at least a kernel (probably a whole bushel) of historical reference. That humans sinned and corrupted the divine image must somehow be a real primal event. The myth creates the truth of which it is supposed to be a reflection. One ends up seriously discussing Adam and Eve, the Garden, and the philosopher snake (who teaches the transformational virtue of knowledge) *as if* they are more than characters in fiction. That any of this speaks to modern issues in a world the P and J writers could never have possibly imagined in their most fantastic dreams, or darkest nightmares, is highly questionable, to say the least.

When myths become beliefs they do have historical repercussions. The benevolent chain of life had snapped, writes Peter Brown (p. 437). Sex was no longer the cosmic energy that linked humans to the natural world. It became a prime example of lost innocence, the rebellion of sin that infests bodies headed for the grave. Norman Brown again: "Every coitus repeats the Fall." If the Catholic Church is still the primary source of Western culture, and this may be debatable, then a culturally inherited distrust of sex is woven into our lives and should still be detectable.

It would seem at first glance that this is no longer true. Our culture is soaked in sex. And here is where John Paul's critique of materialist hedonism and the dehumanization of sex may have some relevance. The cause, however, may not entirely be the cultural disappearance of God's ancient incarnation as the Christ, but the appearance of a new incarnation of the deity.

Modern economics manipulates sex, turning it into a sales pitch. In this way, the advertising adopts a "natural inclination" and uses it to bend, if not control, the will to consume. Sex in advertising means that the product becomes a natural inclination, a need. Like the old cosmic energy of the stars it burns irresistibly in the "heart" of the consumer. The product is in a sense substituted for the act. Capitalism is the new rebellion of the lower members.

The Pope was most concerned with the problem of depersonalization. Being used as a mere object for the gratification of another's selfish pleasure, the sexual partner is no longer a person. The sexual act is not a communion of persons, which entails the giving of the gift of self (*Theology of the Body*, p. 127). Real freedom expressed in the giving of

---

[6]Ludwig Feuerbach, *The Essence of Christianity*, trans. George Eliot, (New York, 1841/1957), p. 33.

this gift was lost because of original sin. If the freedom of the spirit and self-mastery are expressed and made visible by the body, then the surrender of the body to lust is a visible manifestation of lost spiritual freedom.

Sex is not the communion of persons as it was meant to be. John Paul II builds this interpretation on the foundations of Christ's critique of divorce—that the Law allowed it—against the Pharisees. Moses allowed divorce because of your hardness of heart, says Christ in Matthew 19:3. But in the beginning it was not so. Abandoning history completely—Were these words addressed to some early Christian community? Placed in the mouth of Jesus? Was Jesus a Jew building a fence around the Torah?—John Paul takes the literary scene and rockets into the heavens of hermeneutical bliss where God's intentions are written in the stars. Apparently these stars are seen only by Catholic astronomers (unlike the supernova of 1054 which somehow they didn't see although it was seen elsewhere).

The Pope arrives, then, at his predetermined conclusion: The person becomes an object to be used. The gift of the other is consumed for the purpose of self-gratification. In other words, the person becomes an object, a commodity.

Capitalism requires people who are obsessive consumers. Such people need to be free of conscience, that is, not subject to any authority or discipline other than the appetite to consume. Self-discipline, the kind that might restrict or even abandon the urge to consume, is the enemy of capitalism. Happiness means consumption; the goal of life is "having fun." Eric Fromm says: The world is one great object for our appetite, a big apple, a big bottle, a big breast; we are the sucklers, the eternally expectant ones, the hopeful ones—and the eternally disappointed ones. Our character is geared to exchange and to receive, to barter and to consume; everything, spiritual as well as material objects, becomes an object of exchange and consumption.[7]

Humans are commodities. As commodities, they become depersonalized objects meant for the gratification of others, *for having fun*. The unitive and spiritual experience of sex, which as the man who died learned was the medicine that cured his suffering and loneliness, is abstracted and made into an object of exchange. Finally, it is transformed into advertisement. It sells products, some of which have only a tenuous connection to it. Like humans and sex, God, too, becomes, at last, a commodity. In some countries He is transformed into an advertisement for patriotism.

The selfish use of persons by others is hardly news. Depersonalization is hardly a great discovery. John Paul II did not exorcise the demon of dualism, Manichaean or otherwise, from the Church. He may have recognized, however, the challenge of another demon more powerful than any yet encountered. Under capitalism, the reduction of the person to an object becomes a sacrament. The supposed absence of God has little to do with it. In fact, God has become just another commodity in the ever-expanding cosmos of commodities. Or better, God has accomplished a new incarnation. In the very process of exchanging products, including ourselves, *'immanu-el*, God with us.

---

[7]Erich Fromm, *The Art of Loving*, (London, 1957), p. 64.

Chapter 19
Once Again, Celibacy

Pope John Paul II firmly believed that celibacy was not the cause of abuses in the Catholic Church. Celibacy in fact is the answer to them. Celibacy is a gift from God. It is living towards the eschatological future in which sex as human know it does not exist. In the fallen world, human beings find it exceedingly difficult to control themselves. Like death, concupiscence is inevitable. Herein exists the problem. For the old pagans, for brahmacharyns like Gandhi, celibacy is the supreme act of self-discipline. As such, it is liberation (*moksha*) from the small, infantile self, the I-me-mine.

The heretic Pelagius, like the great *rishis* and *yogins* of ancient India, believed that humans can, with discipline, free themselves from the impurity and prison of uncontrolled desire. Priestly celibacy, on the other hand, assumes a theology of human powerlessness (as with Paul) and the uncontrollable demands of sexuality (as with Augustine). Without God's help, vows of celibacy are bound to fail.

But celibacy is more than this. As it has been shown, it is also a question of institutional authority.

Mandatory celibacy did not actually become a Church dogma until the Second Lateran Council of 1139. Up till then, most priests were married. However, Catholic doctrine demanded that before officiating the Eucharist—transforming the elements was a power denied the highest angels—the priest had to be in a state of purity. This book has already touched upon the sociological theories that may explain the preservation of the male-only sacrificial lineage. Examination of the practical outcomes is appropriate.

Since sex with a woman was impure, the priest had to refrain from intercourse with his wife. Beginning with the eleventh century reforms connected to the monastery of Cluny, and Pope Gregory VII's emphasis upon papal power, the Pope became the voice of Christ on earth and his priesthood an earthly corps of angels. The creation of a caste-like priestly elite had begun. The priesthood becomes a male only sacred band of spiritual soldiers.

Monastic asceticism has been a powerful subculture in Christianity since the days of the desert fathers who, like St. Anthony, challenged the worldly Church with their ascetic practices. In fact, many of these early monasteries were dual houses, comprised of men and women. Justin Martyr had compared chastity to martyrdom.[1] Women, too, by such feats of abstinence could achieve a strength that made them equal to men, as did the female martyrs of the early Church. But the strength of martyrdom, like celibacy, is also a gift from God. So, if women martyrs become the equal of men based on the strength of their own determination and God's gift, might they, too, become pure enough for the priesthood? That is, might they become men?

Medieval heretics often used feats of asceticism to attack a lax clergy. While it is true that some heretics attacked the Catholic ideal of celibacy, many exalted sexual abstinence as an aspect of the ideal of Christian poverty.[2] In order to combat these criticisms, to meet the challenge of women, and to preserve its inheritance, the Church instituted clerical celibacy.

Clerical celibacy brought an economic bonus, the Church inherited individual priestly wealth. However, the rhetoric of chastity as poverty seems to fly against such material gain, unless one claims that the inheritance of property is "the visible sign" of priestly descent, of succession, which does not contradict "spiritual" poverty (Matthew's "poor in spirit") Theology can be made to pay handsomely.

But all this begs a simple question: How can the Pope demand celibacy of priests when it seems to be beyond their personal power (without God's help)? The inclination to sin resides in the heart of Everyman. The sacrament of ordination may partially answer the question. As all the sacraments, ordination is the means by which God's grace enters the world and makes celibacy possible. It flows from the transcendental world through the exclusive gates of the Church. The sacraments replace the power of reason, the autonomous freedom to discipline themselves, which ancient Christians opposed to pagan fate.[3] But after Augustine the now- impossible freedom of will is replaced by the sacraments.

Only the Church holds the keys to that eschatological future towards which the priest lives. The sacraments are the guarantee. They are a healing medicine as well. If this is so and God keeps His tradition-interpreted promises, *there should be a mere few, if any priests who violate the rule, not to mention ones that become abusers of children.*

The fact that there are exceptions, and exceptions in significant numbers, might cause one to question the Church's claims. The Church may just another human institution in which men in authority are tempted, beyond any deity's aid, to abuse the innocent. Enforced celibacy simply compounds the situation.

---

[1] D. F. Noble, *A World Without Women: The Christian Clerical Culture of Western Science*, (New York, 1992), p. 13.
[2] Jaroslav Pelikan, *The Christian Tradition: A History of the Development of Doctrine. The Growth of Medieval Theology* (600-1300), Vol. 3, (Chicago, 1988), p. 232.
[3] Harper, *From Shame to Sin*, p. 180.

Does priestly celibacy contribute to sexual abuse? Practically speaking, the casual connection remains questionable, as we've already noted. In theory at least, it is impossible to ignore the traditional disdain for women and the possible sociological meanings of ritual pollution. Yet, the nagging suspicion that some deeper reason exists, especially given the general objects of abuse (male children), keeps buzzing about the dome of St Peters.[4]

Using the language of Aristotle, the Church maintains that the Final Cause of sex is reproduction. All other aspects—like pleasure, intimacy, sharing of self—are secondary, if recognized at all. Again, in sex, according to the saintly expert on the subject, John Paul II, male and female are given a new self-consciousness as mother and father. When practiced for anything other than procreation, and secondarily the union of marriage (a sacrament owned by the Church, naturally) the sexual act becomes sinful, the use of another for selfish pleasure.[5]

Contraception and homosexuality fall under this rubric. It remains a matter of biblical exegesis exactly how scripture understands homosexuality (generally it is seen as a moral impurity according to Leviticus). Homosexuality is obviously sinful in the eyes of the Catholic Church. It is a grave depravity. Further, the Church teaches that homosexuality violates "natural law" (*Catechism*, Part III, 2357).

Beginning in the 1970s, it became apparent to psychologists that homosexuality was intrinsic to the person. In 1973, the American Psychiatric Association removed it from its list of illnesses. The Vatican's response was to proclaim a difference between

---

[4]We have refrained from Freudian analysis of the problem simply because that would take another volume (or two or three). "Normal" sex, however, is hard to define and according to Freud is an achievement of a long process. Neither have we *fully* examined the results of evolutionary science. Love and its sexual expression may be a biological imperative. Those creatures that developed the drive would be favored to produce and care for more young than those, for example, that are born with the ability to fart in tune. Or, as we've already speculated, it may arise from the parental care of young. But the Pope and his followers sternly reject biological explanations and wish to maintain a high wall between humans and animals. They declare the scientific description of the body inadequate without having ever studied it. Their flimsy excuse is that it cannot grasp humans in their entirety, apparently ignoring the fact that science has a way of explaining things it was previously declared unable to explain. In order to get around this problem, they introduce the so-called "spiritual" element. This sets personhood beyond what science could ever describe. Well sure. Others call this the scientific ideological bias of naturalism, meaning science declares the spiritual world non-existent. But methodological naturalism does no such thing. Rather, it recognizes the limits of its methods. There is no instrument or laboratory experiment we know of at the present time that is able to measure the "spiritual." Also, should we develop instruments that do measure the spiritual, the data would be processed through bodily eyes, ears, fingers, noses, and human brains. To do that, the spiritual would have to become spatial and temporal in order to interact with our senses. Having a body, it is no longer spiritual, Michael Martin, *Atheism, Morality, and Meaning*, (Amherst, New York, 2002), p. 129. What is it? The spiritual turns out to be what the Church says it is. In the laboratory of the spiritual, the instruments are ancient texts distilled through self-serving hermeneutics. But what if despite everything we've just said, modern biology is able someday to detect the spiritual aspect of human beings? Scientists would be overjoyed; what a vast new world of discovery would await them. *What if the scientific discovery did not match, say, John Paul's specimen of human sinfulness*? The Church ought to fervently hope that science does remain tied to naturalism.

[5]Here the Church is quick to establish the excluded middle: selfish pleasure or procreation. But sex need not be imprisoned by such a dichotomy. We have already noted its religious possibilities. Another interesting example comes from primate studies. Among bonobos, sex is not just for procreation but it is a social tool. When faced with a crisis, say a battle over food, the bonobos make peace by having sex. Sex solves many social tensions. Instead of war, the bonobos really do make love (Carl Zimmer, *Evolution: The Triumph of An Idea*, (New York, 2001), p. 255). Sex is used among other things to prevent war. John Paul does have a point. We are indeed distinct from the beasts.

tendencies and acts (there must be something amiss with a discipline that keeps having to make distinctions in order to avoid contradictions). If being gay was a natural sexual orientation and could hardly be considered a willful sin, indulging in homosexual acts was not. As acts, homosexual relations were sinful, a moral evil. The essential Final Cause is absent. So, despite the APA, homosexual acts are unnatural. Gays, then, are called to chastity (*Catechism*, Part III, 2359).

A number of questions "naturally" arise. If Gays are called to chastity and chastity is God's gift, must the faithful believe that God bestows this gift upon every single gay person? Yet, if God's grace flows only through the Church, and not every person is lucky enough to be a priest, then how can they fulfill the Church's teachings? Does this mean that gay Catholic men are attracted to the priesthood? What about lesbians who cannot become priests? Perhaps it is not a question of doctrine creating homosexual activity, but homosexuals are drawn to the priesthood for numerous reasons, say feelings of guilt, religious beliefs, and so on. Further, if homosexuality is "a strong tendency ordered toward an intrinsic moral evil," as Cardinal Joseph Ratzinger said in 1986, one must ask if God deliberately created people with an intrinsically sinful inclination? Or, was this too a consequence of the mythical garden scene (which by now is becoming over-burdened)? What parent would give a child a task that child could not by his or her intrinsic nature accomplish? Maybe it is God's morality that requires an apology.

Assume homosexuality is intrinsic to the person. A person by nature seeks unity with another of the same sex. If he or she decides to act on this "natural" inclination, the act cannot be procreative. By the Church's own logic, the homosexual act cannot be an expression of self-donation. It is selfish hedonism, the use of another for one's own selfish ends. Again the extremes. Would it not be more fair to say that homosexual sex, like heterosexual, is an expression of love, of drawing closer, tenderness, a deep sharing and bonding, a selfless act of giving to the other? And why not a bit of hedonism? Is it really physical pleasure or one's obsession—craving, attachment—for physical pleasure, to the point of domination, that does the harm?

Nature, warned John Paul, has its origin in the Creator and should not be altered by human beings (p. 509). Now, "biological nature" is a human abstraction from "Nature" and human authority is valid only within this realm. But scientists must not meddle with human nature. They must not try to recreate humans *in their image*.[6]

Following this line of argument, if homosexuality is an aspect of "Nature," not simply a cultural artifact (in our image), a *tendency,* to use the Church's own language, then does it not belong to God's plan? Or, is it a perversion of sex due to the Fall? If so, it is a sinful corruption of a *natural tendency already created by God*. Did God decide to create some humans as homosexuals? Ultimately, *God must be responsible for homosexuality*.

The homosexual *urge to act* must come from the loss of self-control and hence the Fall. But this loss of human innocence is the result of the disobedience of our first parents (unless one interprets the P Source as meaning a whole population of people. But then this conflicts with sin originating with Adam and Eve. Maybe another population

---

[6]Richard M. Hogan and John M LeVoir, *Covenant of Love*, pp. 59-60.

related to bonobos did not commit sin?). The *Catechism* declares it a primeval event. However the garden myth is twisted and tortured to yield orthodoxy, a cursory reading of Genesis reveals that there were no homosexuals in the garden. (Again, we, too, can use the argument from scriptural silence) So how does the corruption of heterosexual sex pass to homosexual sex?

If the answer is that it is cursed because it is fruitless, then God must have created a form of sex that was corrupted from the beginning, without any help from the two heterosexual gardeners. The same thing applies to loss of self-control. Even if homosexuals could rationally practice intercourse as Augustine taught, the act even without lust would be a grave sin with or without the Fall. If sex is defined as an act, then God created a form of sex that is not sex. God sure is a mystery, maybe even to Himself.

Recall that Augustine included Eve in the garden only for the purpose of reproduction. Therefore, it must be God's intention from the beginning that homosexuals *never* practice intercourse. But if this is so, why create them at all? If they are not implicated in the corruption of heterosexual sex, why should God burden them with a desire that is intrinsically sinful *before sin entered the world*? If homosexual sex is intrinsically evil because it does not result in procreation, then why did God create it as part of "Nature"?

After the death of Pope John XXIII in June of 1963, Pope Paul VI removed the issues of priestly celibacy and birth control from the table of Vatican II. These issues belonged to the Magisterium, the Pope claimed. The Church had to wait until 1968 before the Pope pronounced on contraception. When the pronouncement came in the form of the encyclical *Humanae Vitae*, many members felt a sharp disappointment: Paul VI upheld the ban on birth control.

Paul VI said that while it is true that the conjugal act expresses love (all love, however, ultimately derives from divine love) and mutual support, and while it is also true that causes independent of the couple's intentions mean that not every act is followed by new life..."the Church, calling men back to the observance of the norms of natural law, as interpreted by their constant doctrine, teaches that each and every marriage act (*quilibet matrimonii usus*) must remain open to the transmission of life" (*Humanae Vitae*, par.11). The human sexual act derives from the creative act of God, as marital love derives from the love of God, which makes marriage a sacrament. To interfere with sex as procreation is a violation of the natural result in children. No matter what—incest, rape, illness—contraception and abortion are evil.[7]

---

[7]Biblical support for the opposition to birth control is problematic. Sometimes people refer to the sin of Onan in Genesis 38:8-9 who when he slept with his deceased brother's wife spilled his seed on the ground rather than bringing forth children not legally his. This act was wicked in the eyes of the Lord who took his life. Onan's wasting of his seed is a condemnation of contraception and masturbation. But in ancient Israel, the crime is failing to uphold his dead brother's line of descendants and has nothing to do with sex per se. Onan was guilty of violating his tribal duty. Neither is scripture clear on abortion. Exodus 21:22-25 discussed the penalties incurred when striking a pregnant woman and causing her to miscarry. The passage seems to make a distinction between a viable or fully formed fetus and one that cannot survive

In 1960, the birth control pill was approved in the United States. Developed by a Catholic, John Rock, the "father of the pill," this form of contraception used the body's natural chemistry to prevent ovulation. It could be easily maintained that this method was not in violation of natural law. Yet, the pill was still condemned.

Jesus taught the moral significance of intentions behind acts (the famous lusting in the heart). Therefore, it is the intention of the conjugal act that has moral significance. If one indulges in sex without the intention of creating new life then one is guilty of sin. If this is true, then it could happen that one may commit sin with one's own wife or husband.[8]

On the other hand, Pope Paul VI taught that given "psychological conditions" or "external controls" (population pressures for example), it is licit to take into account the natural rhythms of the female reproductive system (*Humanae Vitae*, par. 16). Even if this answers the problem of "natural law," how does it address the problem of sinful intentions? Natural contraception is based upon natural rhythms of the female. The purpose of contraception is sexual relations without the burden of children. John Paul II condemned the "contraception mentality," which is rooted in hedonism and views procreation as an obstacle to personal fulfillment, and "responsible parenthood" (*The Theology of the Body*, p. 502). However, the desire for a large family may arise from selfish pride and not be in the best interests of the family or the community. It, too, is sinful.

Contraception that is not lived in respect for the "truth" of the conjugal act (as defined earlier), but practiced out of a self-centered ideas of freedom is sinful. It comes from the same seed as abortion, which directly violates the divine commandment of killing (which, historically speaking, probably referred only to one's fellow Jews). Instead of "birth control," the Church favors "fertility regulation" says Weigel, who ought to be doing stand-up (p. 34). So, without the proper intent, one may still sin with the rhythm method even when the Church says it is legal.

Science cannot help human beings decide these thorny issues, according to John Paul II. The interior dimension of the human being eludes biology just as it eludes history. Having banished science by a priori fiat, John Paul may proceed without having to wrestle with any objections from that quarter. But science has a way of breaking down

---

outside the womb. Over the years Church leaders never reached a verdict. "Quickening for some signified a separate life and made abortion murder. But even Augustine was unclear. In the *Enchiridion* he writes: "Now who is there that is not rather disposed to think that unformed abortions perish, like seeds that have never fructified" (Chapter 85). It was only in the nineteenth century that the Church finally came to reject all abortion. For John Paul, of course, it is part of the modern "conspiracy against life" (*The Theology of the Body*, p. 505). In actual fact, fertilization of an egg is the beginning of individual life but certainly not the beginning of life per se since the egg and sperm are already alive (Gazzaniga, *The Ethical Brain*, 2005, p. 3). Adopting the Pope's own principle, a purely biological definition of individual life does not describe the complete human person. If this is so, then the question really becomes: When does the mass of tissue become a "person," that is, when is it infused with a spiritual soul? But this is a metaphysical principle and hardly open to measurement (as of yet). It must therefore be an arbitrary decision (since scripture is unclear) made by the Church. The Pope cannot say that God in the Bible forbids abortion. Nor can he rely upon tradition since tradition never spoke with a single voice until the nineteenth century. The issue is further complicated by spontaneous abortions. If nothing happens by chance, then spontaneous abortions in which something goes wrong in the natural process must be by the will of God. Given the frequency, God becomes the greatest abortionist of all.

[8]Gary Wills, *Papal Sin*, p. 101.

barriers. The history of science owns an immense vault of forgotten and obsolete currency that goes by the domination: "never can."

The application of scientific reasoning to an understanding and healing of the human body (and perhaps the human spirit) has done much to relieve a vast amount of suffering in the world. Reason and the freedom to make moral choices are usually what theologians mean when they discuss the image of God. In the beginning was the *logos*, and the *logos was God*. Many scholars wish to see Western science as somehow dependent upon Christian civilization. They should take great pride when science relieves human suffering.

Human reasoning, the desire to relive suffering, and moral intent, the desire to remain within the Church's doctrines, gave rise to the pill which adopts the body's "natural" chemistry in order to prevent fertilization. Yet, this is dehumanizing says the Church. How many other "artificial" or "natural" medical marvels could be labeled the same? What about a heart valve? A hip replacement? Plastic lens? Organ transplants? Fertility therapy? Each must pass the Church's test of dehumanization. In the end, the Church assumes the ultimate authority over medical science—and over everything else.

Sex is one of the most powerful adaptive forces of evolution. It is also a threat to all authority, especially to God's and that of His Church. This may be the real profound and enduring truth that concerns the myth of the garden. An organization of self-reproducing celibate men must feel this deeply. Each has declared personal war against what is most natural in their physical being. They have declared this war in the name of an abstract and unreal magic kingdom. In this war, they are truly sons of their Father (or His scribes) who carried on the same struggle against Asherah. Without a divine goddess and without divine sex, the true energy of creation in all of its beauty, joy, intimacy, and, yes, religious sensitivity, remains the Church's eternal foe.

Illness of its members can only be the result. And so, too, the constant need for apologies. Today the Church may be less anti-Semitic, less misogynist, less exclusivist and more open to dialogue. Or, as Matthew Fox seems to think, conditions may be worse under Benedict XVI (since retired). But after every apology is made, and every theological tome is composed, the sexual abuse of children continues and shows no sign of fading away. In our opinion, this crime eclipses all the others.[9]

As in other cases of John Paul's apologies, promises of corrective action ring hollow when the root causes of transgressions remain part of church doctrine. The church compels priests to repress their sexuality, which can lead to the perverted manifestation of this most basic aspect of human beings and life itself. E. Kennedy has argued that John

---

[9]Ivan's rebellion in *The Brothers Karamazov* puts the question to God. Why create a world a world in which children suffer? They are the innocent; they cannot even comprehend the tortures done to them. The little girl locked in a freezing and filthy outhouse after she has been beaten, crying with gentle and meek tears for "dear God;" the little boy torn about by vicious dogs for the amusement of a general; the babies blown apart by Turkish soldiers, who, by the way, like sweets-and we might add the uncomprehending child abused by some perverted pedophile priest and told that he is having sex with God-all of these crimes and more cry out in their "meek" voices for an accounting. Shifting the blame to the media, to opponents, to a few bad apples, to the culture, will not do. Crimes against children exist on another plane all together, as Ivan protested. And as he also concluded, nothing is worth the price; "And therefore I hasten to return my ticket."

Paul has been "ever restless because his wound is the result of thinking one way about persons as sexual beings and acting in a quite different way when dealing with them".[10] It as if John Paul II has refused to acknowledge the existence of sexuality in all its complexity. He believes that somehow sexuality can be simply suppressed—that is, dedicated to a future existence—with no negative psychological repercussions.

While still a priest, John Paul II counseled couples on how marriage was a vocation, like that of the priesthood. This example by itself reveals a man who is completely ignorant of intimacy, sharing, and everything else discussed in this book that make sex and love greater mysteries than God.

John Paul II failed to see the damage sexual repression has done to the Catholic Church, as Kennedy asserted:

> For, as what is of nature is slain, so an emptiness overtakes the surviving but separated spirit that is now sexual restive, sexually damaged, sexually impotent because humanly no longer whole—in short, the contemporary West and the guardian of its spiritual tradition, the papacy, the sexual wound a crimson seam that runs through them all.[11]

John Paul II held to the idea that the sexuality of priests could be simply suppressed. In this he opposed the physical drive for life, the burning fire humans share with the beasts and the stars. Dare he even speak of the culture of death?

John Paul II refused to allow Church leaders to even discuss actions that could be potentially corrective. "Bishops will privately acknowledge that Pope John Paul II explicitly forbade them to discuss 'contraception, abortion, homosexuality, masturbation, a married priesthood or women's ordination to the priesthood other than to defend the Church's official teaching.'"[12] As with misogyny, true corrective action, in our opinion, would entail allowing priests to marry, and to a lesser extent, allowing females to become priests. The Church as a whole requires the healing of Isis.

Cardinal Bernard Law resigned from the Boston arch-diocese in the deluge of accusations that he had covered-up sexual abuse by Catholic priests and did not remove suspected priests from positions in which they had access to young Catholics. At the death of John Paul, the Vatican selected Cardinal Law to preside over the Pope's funeral. The Church, apparently, still has some things to learn about the modern areopagus.

---

[10] E. Kennedy, *the Unhealed Wound: The Church and Human Sexuality*, (New York, 2001), p. 31.
[11] Kennedy, p. 33.
[12] D. B. Cozzens, *The Changing Face of the Priesthood*, p. 119.

Chapter 20

A Fable: The Mother Who Died

Many centuries after the Man Who Died joined with the Priestess of Isis, an eight year old boy from a distant land far to the north lost his mother. She was young and beautiful, and her love for him was unconditional. She was there for him always; when he came from school, when he suddenly awoke from a nightmare, when he had an accident. Her embrace was warm and comforting. It healed the day's bruises. No matter what he had done, what mischief he had caused, how good or bad he had been that day, her love never wavered. It was bliss, peace, protection. He was loved because he was her child, because he simply existed. Her love was selfless; she wanted nothing in return, only that he simply *be*. Her love taught him to trust life, for life itself loved him. Because he was loved, he loved in return.

Then one day, and no one knew the precise day it started, her kidneys began to fail. The toxins began to accumulate in her blood. Her energy slowly drained away and her world became colder. She felt the chill of renal failure. Everyone around her felt it too, including the boy. A pall settled upon his once joyful home. Finally, her heart failed. Then came the dark day he returned from school and discovered that his mother had died.

He was a sensitive, intelligent boy, at times he could become moody, even morose. His father's love was military strict. His father's love made demands, set principles and standards to be met. But he was a dutiful boy, blessed with powerful self-discipline. The precise rules, the strict laws and codes, helped him forget. Yet, his father's love never replaced the intimacy and warmth he knew when his dear mother was alive. His father's love was like ice applied to a deep bruise, it numbed the pain but did not heal the wound. And his world, too, became colder.

From a very early age, the boy had learned the ancient legends of The Man Who Died. He learned how the Man had awakened in his grave and how he had conquered death. In later years, he came to understand that the Man Who Died had perfectly fulfilled his own father's rules and regulations. In later years the boy came to believe that life itself arose from a Father's love, for he had forgotten his mother's touch, her face, her smell and warmth, even the sound of her voice. He had forgotten because the pain was too great when he remembered. But his dreams remembered.

His father (and many other fathers) explained to him that his dear mother now lived eternally in the presence of the Man Who Died and his Father. The boy found it difficult trying to picture that eternal world. It could be reached only by means of frail words. His yearning for that world became a dull ache, like another arrow in his flesh, but not as deep as the dart of his mother's death.

In that eternal world beyond was life that would never fail, the love that would never die. But this was the sort of love that never touched him, never cuddled him, kissed his tears, tasted soft and sweet. It was more like his father's love, hard and cold, severe, like frigid stone buildings and bodiless words. He never felt it as he had his mother's embrace. He thought it. It was love inscribed on hard stone tablets, a love of prohibitions and demands—but mostly prohibitions. It was not the love that envelops every living creature, that burns in the stars, the here and now love of joy and life.

And slowly his trust of life grew cold, for his love became abstract and intellectual.

The boy became an adolescent and then a man. He learned all there was to know about the Man Who Died. His dreams flowed along other paths. He found solace in the theatre. There, too, either on stage or in the company of the rules governing the stage, he was able to ignore his ache and pain. There, too, he could be someone else, living another life in which Mothers Who Died did not die. But such moments were all too brief. The deep memories rose like a sour aftertaste. And the theatre was an illusion. The legends of the Man Who Died were true.

At age twelve he lost his beloved brother. At twenty his father. Life appeared so frail. How could he trust it? It seemed to him that with every birth came the heartbreak of death. The Risen Man promised a different life, one he could trust. The Risen Man was the death of his old trust. Soon after his father's death, he pledged himself to the Risen Man.

He found little difficulty renouncing the tenuous joys of earthly life. Yes, he knew many young women in his small town. He found himself drawn to them. They glowed with beauty and promise, and for a while they occupied his dreams. Sometimes he even felt in those dreams the joy and warmth and bliss he knew as a small child. He experienced a different sort of ache, one his habitual words failed to grasp. But fear invaded desire. What if he really did give himself again? What if he offered his trust and placed his fierce love on their altars? Would they love back? Would they give in return?

He heard weeping. It came from a place he did not know. It brought memories to the surface, feelings really, of loving because he was loved. But there it stopped. He never took the next step into maturity. He never realized that mature love says: "I am loved because I love." Not being able to fully give and fully take, he refused their love in the end. Total dedication to the Man Who Died was his reason and excuse.

In later years, after he achieved great things in the service of the Man Who Died, he came to love and worship women from a distance. His worship and love were things of words, though it is said the words caused him to sweat and gasp for air, often leaving him limp afterwards. It is said that he punished his rebellious flesh.

But these women were ideal forms, and their collective name was "Mother." He came to love abstractly with all the formidable power of his intellect. He gave himself freely to this "Mother." For she did not die and her love never failed. Like the Man Who Died, and who was said to be her son, she lived only in the legends. Like him, she was perfect. Like him, she was eternal.

In later years he did not understand why many real women refused his abstract love. The old memories were dead, although in those rare, uncanny moments when his guard was down, he heard *her* voice, caught *her* scent, felt *her* touch. Once she even rescued him, deflecting an assassin's bullet from his heart. Yet, it made no sense to him when the real women spoke of love in terms of touch, sight, taste, smell, and sound. It confused him when they talked about sacred compulsions and blissful joy. Long ago, he had rejected these earthly clods of mud. Rather, he tried to raise them up as he believed the Man Who Died had done.

Alas, he knew not all the legends. Or, if he knew he rejected and ended up in the same place. He never learned that the Man Who Died had come to regret his interference with sacred nature, even with the noblest mud to which human beings return. This most profound mystery had never risen in the disciple's heart. And the disciple never knew of how the Man Who Died came to the Priestess of Isis.

Like his fabled master, like men and women in all times, the Man Who Followed died. Everywhere, the fearful ones sang his praises. Everywhere, the betrayed ones, the selfish ones, the wounded and those who cause wounds, and especially those who loved deeply only to see their love abused, by others or by life itself, everywhere they celebrated his cold and hard love. Like the man who followed, pure and eternal love fulfilled the great aching need in them. They wished to be loved unconditionally for simply being. And so they always remained children.

Among the sages who lived isolated in caves high in the snow-capped mountains, the story is told that the Follower Who Died not have a particularly happy rebirth. He was quickly taken on the wheel and his life re-woven. The sages smiled knowingly. Much remained to be learned. They smiled but without malice or disdain. The Way is an ancient path covered by forest growth. It takes many lifetimes to discover.

And so the Follower Who Died felt new life stirring within him. He wished to remain outside, in that place where even memory is dead. He felt a deep nausea. But he was on the wheel.

He felt new life, life wildly different than the old, yet oddly similar. He opened his eyes to many shades of green, to warm moist brown and brilliant yellow. Others might call this new life primitive, lesser being, but the wise sages knew better. It was the life of the pure and innocent, before the garden, before the giving of names. It was a life of pure, naked experience in which sensations ruled. Here was no conflict, no war. All disputes were settled through love.

Before he received once again the great gift of humanity, he had to relearn trust and the sacred compulsion of giving and taking. And she was there to teach him, for the great goddess Isis exists in many, many forms.

PART IV
Preaching the Kingdom

"Go then, preach the good news about the kingdom. Do not lay down any rule beyond what I determined for you, nor promulgate law like the lawgiver, or else you might be dominated by it."

The Gospel of Mary from Nag Hammadi.

Chapter 21
Ecclesia in Europa

Many Christians would like to think that the Enlightenment proved a poor age for prophecy. The moral progress of human beings and human society, so confidently predicted by the great *philosophes*, suffered a serious wound in the trenches of the First World War. The genocidal twentieth century may have buried it.[1] The "heavenly city of the eighteenth century philosophers" (Carl Becker) did not "crush the infamous thing" (Voltaire). The Church, like the state, did not wither away (Marx), and the faithful have yet to encounter the last Pope (Nietzsche). Christianity in its older institutionalized incarnation, the Universal Church, has weathered the storms of skeptical philosophy, science, and secularism. It has yet to succumb to the assaults of the higher criticism or New Age spiritualism. At the dawn of the Third Millennium, the Church stands prepared to renew its mission to the nations. Many in the Church would like to think this reading is true.

Others do not. Despite the failure of its original vision, and the "shakiness" of its assumptions, the Enlightenment still stands as the rational foundation for Western culture, says E. O. Wilson in *Consilience* (p. 22). This is worth preserving, for there is still much to praise, especially the Enlightenment idea that our destiny is in our hands. "The denial of the dream leads back to barbarism" (p. 23). Such praise, of course, comes from a scientist. As noted, Steven Pinker chronicles the lurching rise from barbarism in *The Better Angels of Our Nature*. The debate is sure to continue and given its tendency to

---

[1] David Berlinski provides a two and a half page list of "excess deaths" due to war and genocide since 1914 in *The Devil's Delusion: Atheism and Its Scientific Pretensions*, (New York, 2009), pp. 22-24. Without God, the monstrous becomes possible is his conclusion, p. 25. However, from a much wider perspective (in time and areas of study) Steven Pinker argues just the opposite in *The Better Angels of Our Nature: Why Violence Has Declined*, (New York, 2011). He writes: "For all the violence that remains in the world, we are living in an extraordinary age. Perhaps it is a snapshot in a progression to an even greater peace." p. 480.

simplification (atheism is a precondition of state-sponsored genocide), easily slides into rhetoric (strange that *we* should make this criticism, eh?).

The thirst to generalize may not work so well in the study of religion. The Enlightenment drive to conceptualize religion, to globally define those characteristics that make a *religion*, uproots the object of study from its own unique cultural soil. Ancient religions, the religions of non-Western peoples, even the historical variations of Christianity, are altered and deformed when viewed through the prisms of the generalized concepts, which are themselves historically created. They are just that: *ways of looking at the world*. But they are hardly features of unique historical cultures.

Is not the Church's conceptualization of modernity simply another one of these ways? From the beginning, Christianity claimed for itself a globally exclusive outlook, a universal right of judgment. The "Old Testament" must be understood in the light of the "New." Other religions are partially true only insofar as they bear the seeds of the gospel. Science must not violate certain predetermined boundaries. And so the battle is joined between too universalizing tendencies.

There is a third contestant, the modern consumer culture of Western capitalism. In place of an enlightenment utopia, people live in a thoroughly commodity-driven cosmos of images and signs, an all-encompassing universe of objects of desire. These objects, or better, their rootless images, are replaced so rapidly by other images that the consumer hardly has the time to get bored with the previous ones.[2] At last, desire becomes globalized. The desire to desire is a universal value. A never-ending desire for happiness through a never-ending consumption of objects is the real outcome of Teilhard de Chardin's "spiritual" evolution of the "noospehere" as outlined in *The Phenomenon of Man* (1959).

In such a cosmos, the abstraction of religion becomes a series of spectacles created as a means of seduction. While the secular consumer is on a quest for material fulfillment, the "religious" consumer is on a quest for spiritual meaning. Drained of demands, discipline, community, and especially history, religion at last appears on the global market as nothing more than empty spectacle. The Catholic Church, given its inherited tendency to imperial Roman spectacles, is most suited for this new media culture.[3]

The former actor John Paul II understood the power of gesture and imagery. He became the darling of a spectacle driven media. On stage, doctrine, theology, discipline, and admonishment count for little. Spiritual consumers engage religion on only the most superficial level. And so the Church evolved during the pontificate of John Paul II. He became a spectacle, a superstar, an image, a celebrity. But within the old Christendom, the Church's European homeland, the importance of religion in people's lives steadily declined. Most people discovered meaning in possessions, career, success, and status. Personality, infinitely pliable, replaces person and character, and commodities become sacraments. Today shopping is a ritual.

---

[2]Vincent J. Miller, *Consuming Religion: Christian Faith and Practice in Consumer Culture*, (New York, 2004), p. 118.
[3]Miller, *Consuming Religion*, p. 80.

One of Pope John Paul II's last Apostolic Exhortations, *Ecclesia In Europa* (28 June 2003), brings the audience full circle. A kind of Papal farewell, the Exhortation summarizes the great apology without mentioning it.

Ecclesia In Europa opens with a diagnosis. The Christian homeland has lost sight of its historical foundations, says the physician-Pope. Deaf to the Church's message of hope, the Europe of today shows signs of "existential anguish" (paragraph 8). The symptoms of the illness are such things as divorce, diminishing number of births (read contraception and abortion), the decline of the priesthood, drugs, loneliness, scientism, conflict, weakening of the family, the attraction of "Oriental" philosophy and other esoteric but false forms of spirituality and religious deviance (paragraphs 8-10). Further on, the Pope adds stem cell research, abortion, even prenatal diagnostic techniques (leading to selective abortions, paragraph 95). Untreated, the disease is fatal. Western culture is the "culture of death."

Change a few words and it is easy to hear echoes of former ages of disaster: the year 1000 for example, the Mongol onslaught in Europe during the 1240s, the terrible fourteenth century in which it seemed the world was coming to an end in the anarchy of the Hundred Years War and the Great Plague. If there ever truly was a culture of death, it was in that calamitous century, the time of the dance macabre in which the figure of Death haunted the works of artists and writers. For the sake of argument, however, let us grant John Paul his premise and see what he prescribes.

Christ is the cure, naturally. The Church remains the only hospital, which administers the medicine of grace, *which is available nowhere else.* Only in Jesus does all history find its meaning, direction and fulfillment. The prescription reads: "In him and with him, in his death and resurrection, everything has already been said" (paragraph 6).

And yet, John Paul II can hardly avoid the paradox at the heart of this atonement theology. If the ultimate meaning of Christianity is the sacrifice of Christ for our sins, the most significant aspect of his life is his death. His life is meaningful only in terms of his death (leading to his resurrection, which is a kind of receipt for his suffering). If his death pays our debts, what need believers worry about his many protests against injustice? Why should the faithful overly concern themselves with his inclusion of the destitute, the sick, the outcastes, *abused children and women in his kingdom*? He opposed the patriarchal Roman Empire, and by extension, all unjust and oppressive imperial ambitions. Jesus scholar Stephen Patterson labels the atonement "credit card theology," the faithful need not work "Daddy always pays the bill."[4]

Jesus was killed by the Empire. *This historical fact is the historical meaning of his death.* All empires, all institutions that claim power over people's lives—be that power physical, dogmatic, beliefs, or even based on love (the kind that reduces the "person" to an object of manipulation)—are in such a way opposed to Jesus and his teachings.

The Enlightenment failed to see (but how could it?) that Christianity with its version of credit card theology might gain new life in a credit card culture.

---

[4]Stephen J. Patterson, *Beyond the Passion: Rethinking the Death and Life of Jesus*, (Minneapolis, 2004), p. 114.

The Church, however, did experience a steady decline of *institutional power*. Those long years of cultural and social domination came to an end as the Western world evolved into a secularized cosmos. Pure physical power passed into the eager hands of the state. As did loyalty. In many places, religion became just another servant of the nation, another office or section in its vast bureaucracy.

Like the state, it too became intertwined with the market, which was the source of national power. Ultimately, the consumer culture of modern capitalism replaced religion itself, or better, swallowed it up and digested its internal organs, leaving only a fossilized image. Bereft of its former power, the Church sought to revive itself by creating a spectacle designed for consumers. It was well suited for this task. Like all products, the new image required a facelift. It was repackaged with new symbolism, not the old imagery of inquisitions, crusades, and trials of scientists, but a new, humble image. It also appropriated the image of the rebel, of an outcaste, of the moral rock of "truth" amid a raging flood of oppressive relativism. In the new environment, apology became indispensable. In such a way did the Church evolve.

The cure, however, must be administered within the context of pluralism, which is dictated by the new global market. Therefore the "truth of Christ" must be proclaimed in peace and love. No more declarations of crusade (that is, military invasions), no more inquisitions (that is, physical torture and burning), no more anti-Semitism (that is, ghettoes and distinctive clothing), no more misogyny (that is, the torture and burning of women), and no more sexual abuse of *children* (that is...?). Like the early-modern physician who finally gave up his Galen for Harvey, the Church was forced to adopt modern methods of mission, the new areopagus.

So John Paul II encouraged the Church to engage in dialogue to meet the needs of image restoration. In so doing, he faced yet another paradox. An authoritarian institution is not in the habit of conducing dialogues with equals. In religious terms, equality translates as indifference. He sternly warned that such engagement must not yield to religious indifference; religious indifference arises from an erroneous and dangerous relativism, which falsely teaches that one religion is as good as another (paragraph 55).

One need not be a relativist to realize the preconceived notion that one already has the Truth and other religions, if they are worthy of consideration, point in some way to our Truth, makes real dialogue impossible. John Paul II and his Inquisitor-successor wish to *appear as if they engage other religions in friendly discussion*. They wish to *appear sympathetic to women*.[5] But such discussion, after all the exchanges of pleasantries and statements of beliefs, comes to a halt before the sealed gate of exclusiveness above which hangs the sign "religious indifference." Feminism means abortion, contraception, lesbianism.

Such claims create resistance. Resistance leads to defense as the other feels the need to defend herself or her religion. The supposed dialogue is in danger of becoming less peaceful. Serving the gospel of hope, John Paul II added, means following

---

[5]According to Matthew Fox (*The Pope's War*), Benedict XVI believes that freedom of conscience leads to loss of faith. Freedom of speech leads to demagogy, mental confusion, and pornography, p. iii.

the path of love (paragraph 83). "In truth," the Pope's kind of love is not between two consenting adults (which is beyond the limits of his experience), but between a teacher and a student, at best a parent and a child. The other is an infant, sitting at the feet of the priest, the "Father," who patiently but sternly instructs the erring youngster. The patriarchal Church "shares Christ" with the dull children whomever they may be: women, secularists, Muslims, Buddhists—"Orientals"—even the Jews. Indeed, John Paul II stated explicitly the Church's traditional teaching that while the Jewish Covenant remains irrevocable it has attained "definitive fullness" in Christ (paragraph 56).

In the same paragraph on the Jews, John Paul states that forgiveness for anti-Semitism must be sought from God. The real question is—and we are certainly not the first to ask—can the Jews forgive God for the Shoah? That, however, is another book.

It is evident throughout the Exhortation that the apology plays an important role in the new evangelization. That role is to restore the Church's image in order to grease the new engine of mission. The apology in reality is not about the victims, but about the Church. John Paul II stated this fact explicitly when he said:

> In order to respond to the Gospel's call to conversion, "we must join in making a humble and courageous *examination of conscience*...Far from fostering an attitude of hopelessness and discouragement, the evangelical acknowledgement of one's sins will surely awaken within the community the experience of each one of the baptized: the joy of profound liberation and the grace of a new beginning which will enable it to set out with greater vigor upon the path of evangelization (paragraph 29).

The apology is self-serving. It is evangelization by other means. Having purified conscience and experienced the forgiveness of God, Christians are filled with new hope and energy. It is somewhat difficult to "evangelize" when one is burdened with regrets or assailed by doubts. Armed with personal forgiveness, granted by God and guaranteed by the Pope, the new crusading knight is equipped to recapture Europe from the armies of modern religious indifferentism, secularists and feminists. Less an attempt to amend behavior and thus affect real change, the apology is more a therapy session. It frees the Church to go to the nations with confidence and certainty. It allows the faithful to feel better about themselves and their past.

The apology that is no apology provides the Church with an advertising advantage in the global market. No other religion, it can now claim, is as honest and forthcoming as the Catholic Church. It alone has shown the humility and courage to admit its crimes and seek penance. The spectacle of apology is like a many-sided prism, splitting and reflecting light in many directions. Like any sign, it incorporates a multitude of meanings, appealing to as wide an audience as possible. The Church, too, is a victim. The faithful are all Semites. The Church has recognized scientific autonomy. Has science followed? No, evolution presumes to persecute the spiritual. The Church has apologized for misogyny, but to ordain a woman is a grave sin. The Church stands like Galileo and stamps its foot—but it does *not* move.

Meanwhile, John Paul II played the role of cultural physician. Everyone, he claims, requires the Sacrament of Reconciliation. Everyone needs to acknowledge that they are sinners and throw themselves upon the mercy of the Heavenly Father (paragraph 76). The inability to admit that they are sinners is the root of modern people's hopelessness. Without God, there is "no one from whom they can seek forgiveness' (paragraph 76).

Now, where in his countless journeys did a modern crowd shout out this bit of news? Apparently seeking and receiving forgiveness *from those you have harmed* does not count. Only after Penance and Reconciliation *within the Church* does one experience the joy of true liberation. Otherwise, according to the Pope, humans are trapped in their misery, which is the cause of our hopelessness.

That modern people suffer from hopelessness is a belief shared by the Pope with many other writers, religious or not. As noted earlier, after the period 1914–1950, it is difficult for some people to share the optimism of the Enlightenment. And as we've seen, Christian apologists have made a cottage industry of blaming "atheistic regimes" for the blood-soaked twentieth century. A serious assessment would have to go beyond the body counts, especially in the case of Ant-Semitism. Again, that would take another book.

At most, it may be said that people *hope* some possible future scenarios will not come to pass—that is, they hope for the negative.[6]

But is this the sort of devastating hopelessness that can only be solved in the Church, as John Paul II seems to believe? Is it rather that John Paul II hopes modern people suffer from hopelessness? Or is it more personal? Naturally Weigel immediately intercedes on the Pope's behalf, warning investigators against the temptation to psychoanalyze John Paul II by examining his personal past.

Why not? Perhaps John Paul II generalized from his own experience, just as Freud is accused of doing. Perhaps his diagnosis of hopelessness was experienced in his native Poland under the tyranny of the Nazis? Or in his beloved Church beneath the heel of the communists? Predisposed by his personal sufferings, perhaps he heard, during many of his mass gatherings, especially his youth day rallies, excited voices crying out for the medicine he prescribed? Thus he criticized the hopelessness of hedonism and materialism as paths to self-fulfillment. Thus he condemned secularism and its culture of death. Did he believe that the frenzied response of the crowd was proof of the critique? Did he believe that modernity stood condemned by the twentieth century?

Was it not the opposite?

In fact, the second half of the twentieth century, despite its wars and genocides, has been in sheer numbers considerably less violent than the period 1914–1950, says Ian

---

[6]Daniel Johnson, *The Future of Hope: Christian Tradition Amid Modernity and Post-Modernity*, (Grand Rapids, MI, 2004), pp. 43–44.

Kershaw in agreement with Pinker.[7] It is no coincidence, then, that this blood-soaked era should serve as John Paul's reference point. Technology, a child of science, was certainly one of the contributing factors to the horrendous death toll. It might be said too that applied scientific knowledge, especially in the medical field, has saved just as many from certain death sentences, John Paul included. Surely mass killing is nothing new in history, be it in the name of absolute religious truth or ideological "partial truth" made absolute. Technology and modern bureaucratic methods certainly raised its efficiency. But, to reverse the equation, the pathology of a disease does not change when modern science discovers a cure.[8]

Frenzied crowds do not prove a doctrine. The modern culture of consumerism turned John Paul himself into a commodity. As Marx so famously wrote in *Capital* (1867), as soon as an everyday thing steps forth as a "commodity" it becomes a very queer creature, as if it descended from the heavens dressed in all sorts of "metaphysical subtleties and theological niceties" (p. 71). It is stripped of all its former meanings, removed from its natural context, packaged and brought to market as something of unique value, concealing, one might say, the very materials and activities that went into its original production. But as also noted earlier, the commodity is further reduced to a sign, ultimately a brightly wrapped box containing nothing.

John Paul became a media commodity, loved, cheered, admired, but hardly identified with Church dogma and the long history that gave rise to his claim of papal infallibility.[9] Most likely he sincerely believed that the crowds responded to his version of hope, Christ, and the Church, which he surmised they most desperately craved. Focusing his critique on the culture of consumerism, another ally of the culture of death, he failed to perceive how the monster had swallowed him. He had become the show.

Weigel desperately tried to come to the rescue. The Pope was not just another celebrity, he howled, but the youth took to him because he took to them. He treated them seriously, as persons (p. 494). Poor Weigel. Could he not see—or maybe he saw too well—how the Pope tried to cynically manipulate youth culture? Like a good advertising agency, the Pope and his minions scouted the "generational niche" and inserted a prepackaged, finely crafted image.

He was cynical and naïve at the same time. Yes, the youth responded. But did they respond to his doctrinal positions, especially his admonishments against contraception, abortion, divorce, pre-marital sex? Did they respond to his critique of materialism, as

---

[7] Ian Kershaw, *Hitler, the Germans, and the Final Solution*, (New Haven, 2008), p. 374.
[8] The so-called atheistic regimes sounded strangely religious at times. Hitler's "providence" and the Nazi's mystical notion of the *volk gemeinenschaften* incarnate the deity in race. Stalin's eulogy at Lenin's funeral—"We pledge to thee, Comrade Lenin...this thy commandment too" sounds like an Orthodox Sunday sermon. Because someone rejects your version of god does not mean they have none at all. On the contrary, it might be so strange you are unable to recognize it as a god, just as we humans may not be able to recognize alien forms of life in the universe even if they danced on the head of a pin. Apologists have apparently forgotten Eric Hoffer. Again, that is another book.
[9] Vincent Miller, *Consuming Religion*, p. 7.

when in 1999 he called it "selfish satisfaction"?[10] Rather, the market system absorbed his denunciation by turning it into a spectacle.

Spirituality is sold in the market as the commodity "cultural critique."[11] Being opposed to shallow materialism becomes a new cultural symbol, an image, a style, shorn of meaning except as a thing to be consumed. Thus are products packaged in green wrappings and labeled "environmentally friendly." Oil companies loudly advertise their devotion to the discovery of new sources of energy as well as their environmental responsibility. The physically vast and wealthy Church opposes materialism. It too is concerned with environmentalism and lays claim to the legacy of St. Francis—in historical fact, it persecuted the Spirituals who wished to remain true to the original rule of the order and live the way of a humble founder who preached to the birds (according to pious legend).

Like a tragic hero in some modern epic, John Paul fought valiantly against the forces of consumerism, the newest and most insidious religion of the West. Cynically, he tried to manipulate these forces. But he was overwhelmed. Or, better, he was transformed. He became the thing against which he battled. The tragedy is that he might not have even known. Or perhaps he paid the price willingly, something like the Grand Inquisitor in Dostoevsky's great novel.

Pope John Paul II died Saturday, April 2, 2005. From that day until his funeral on April 8, over one million people, some waiting for twenty-four hours, filed past his corpse in St. Peters. Network interviews with pilgrims were revealing. They *had to come*, they said. Many were unable to give a clear reason. They were not Catholics, not overly religious—if religious at all—but this was a great pope, even a saint, he loved people, he truly cared, he was compassionate. Some wanted to share the experience of the sacred, as if somehow the viewing of the corpse brought them closer to God. They were all consumers. The sacred had become a commodity, the Pope a spectacle, even in death—especially in death. The amount of time given by the networks to this event proved it. Sponsors, no doubt, were ecstatic.

So John Paul II was a celebrity, even in death. As a celebrity he became an abstract commodity, a transcendental commodity, at last an empty sign. People mourned him, called him great, a saint; they went on pilgrimage to his burial. They purchased a commodity labeled the sacred. At the same time they ignored the Pope's doctrines. Unlike the wilderness two thousand years ago, the modern consumer wilderness is inhabited by *many* dark spirits. They are far more crafty. They do not tempt, they infuse. One breathes them in with the air.

---

[10] Vincent Miller, *Consuming Religion*, p. 133.
[11] Jeremy Carrette and Richard King, *Selling Spirituality: The Silent Takeover of Religion*, (New York, 2005), p. 135. During the Jubilee of 2000, thousands of young people came to Rome to hear the Pope. Besides their prayers, they left 300,000 used condoms in the area where they spent the night. Gianni Vattimo, "A Prayer for Silence," in *After the Death of God*, ed. Jeffrey W. Robbins, (New York, 2007), p. 96.

Chapter 22
Apology without Reform

Jesus said, "Let one who has become wealthy reign, and let one who has power renounce it."

The Gospel of Thomas from Nag Hammadi, 81.

Despite his talk about human dignity and freedom of conscience, John Paul II oversaw a resurgence of Roman centralization. Historically, the issues for which John Paul enacted image restoration discourse arose as a result of the authoritarian character of the patriarchal structure of the Catholic Church. John Paul II supported democracy in national governments during his opposition to communism and, particularly, his support of Solidarity in Poland. Not in Church governance. The Catholic Church's organization is not egalitarian. The Vatican is intolerant of free dissent within the institution.

In this way the Church is faithful to the biblical model. Elite males are the *imago Dei*, and like a mirror, God is the reflection of their words.[1] Excavating the many layers of fossilized biblical history, the prime artifact, the lost treasure, is the ancient god-king of the Near East. Women are barely worthy of attention. They are property.

Now, one might protest that the triune God tempers the ambitions of the Father God, in that the Trinity forms a kind of divine society, a community.[2] Ah, but what a mystery this is. Is it not easier to paint your Christ with the face of the Emperor? Mysteries, sacred or profane, have had little effect on *realpolitik*. Absolute monarchs, be they Emperors or Popes, have lived quite comfortably with the Trinity.

The pope's power is not derived from a democratic mandate but from his place at the apex of an ancient authoritarian patriarchy.

---
[1] Carole. R. Fontaine, *With Eyes of Flesh: The Bible, Gender and Human Rights*, p. 158.
[2] Elizabeth A. Johnson, *She Who Is: The Mystery of God in Feminist Theological Discourse*, p. 208-209.

John Paul never enacted image restoration discourse for these dictatorial tendencies. He did not apologize for his own absolute power and never promised the corrective action of reforming the Catholic Church in a democratic direction.

The European spiritual and cultural situation, he said in *Ecclesia In Europa*, suffers from "horizontalism" (paragraph 34). Modern culture is closed to the vertical, the transcendent. Does one not hear echoes of the young Polish philosopher protesting modern philosophy's turn to subjectivity? Is John Paul II not Plato reborn, engaging in his eternal struggle with Protagoras? No, he shouts, man is not the measure of all things.

If the vertical is a monopoly of the Catholic Church, and if Europe suffers the disease of "horizontalism" and is bereft the vertical, then this explains why the Church has become irrelevant in the lives of many people, except as spectacle. The Church for most Europeans is ironically similar to some aspects of the later Roman Imperium as drawn by Edward Gibbon (another possible narrative). No one was especially loyal to its teachings or its Emperors, especially after Marcus Aurelius. It commanded people's attention as entertainment, spectacle, circus. The difference is that the Roman Imperium still commanded physical power. But this too would pass. John Paul's pontificate was a campaign to re-conquer *Europa* by other means. Like the Roman Emperors, he was not about to return power to the Senate. The apology was actually one of his new legions.

The secularization of society was one of the causes of horizontalism. And this followed, as John Paul repeated *ad nauseam*, from the subjectivist philosophy of modernity. The modern rejection of God means freedom and autonomy of the self. Things outside the subject follow natural laws, but carry within themselves no moral meaning, only what they are assigned by the experiencing subject. According to John Paul, the disasters of the modern world do in fact bear testimony to meaning outside the self: *that human beings cannot live without God, that rejecting God is not an option.*

Is this not yet another interpretation that assigns meanings to things?

It does reveal something about the Church itself. The so-called vertical dimension is the Church's Augustinian mask, frowning in mistrust of the world. Engaging the world is its Thomism mask, smiling sweetly. The apology fails because the Church is Janus. To be blunt, two-faced.

Meaning, agency, and values may be emergent properties. Stuart Kauffman points out that a simple bacterium swimming up a glucose gradient illustrates the evolutionary onset of choice. The bacterium's glucose receptors detect the presence of glucose; the bacterium alters its direction and swims up the gradient. It interprets the sign and changes behavior. Glucose has value for the bacterium. Acquiring food is purpose, and the bacterium *acts*.[3] All of this is done without attributing consciousness to the bacterium. Nonetheless, value, purpose, and agency have entered the universe; they have emerged for selective reasons. Meaning, then, is an emergent property, *and can be*

---
[3] Stuart Kauffman, *Reinventing the Sacred: A New View of Science, Reason, and Religion*, (New York, 2008), p. 87.

explained without the god option. What was once the jealously guarded province of the vertical now appears to be a natural attribute of the horizontal.

For John Paul II, on the other hand, the meaning, the moral of modern history, exists *within* objective events, placed in them by God's creative act. These impact and shape the self. With this sort of mentality, John Paul once again betrays himself an inhabitant of Charles Taylor's "enchanted world." And as we've noted, such a world is no longer available to modern people. The more "enchanted people" shout and stamp their feet for belief, the more that still small voice of modern skepticism whispers sour nothings in their ears.

The enchanted world is filled with meanings, minds, powers and spirits, good and bad. The enchanted self is porous to such powers. According to the true believers, a radical human autonomy that refuses to acknowledge the enchanted world of spirits opens itself to the invasion of evil, especially with women as witnessed in *The Malleus Maleficarum.* The devil is very much alive. The world, as Christianity teaches and modern history proves (according to John Paul), is possessed.

Modernity's false promise of human autonomy, and the disasters that flowed from it, proved to the Pope that human beings are not able to cultivate their own gardens without the Master gardener. Humans are flawed creatures. Human nature may be malleable but only up to a point. Neither is the state capable of radically improving the human condition. Governments are simply violence on a grander scale—criminal gangs writ large—and are useful insofar as greater power is needed to restrain lesser powers. For without such restraint, society would shatter into unlivable chaos. Liberal democracies may be an improvement on totalitarian dictatorships, but up to a point. Democracies betray their own inherent violence and sin when they sponsor such things as contraception and abortion—John Paul's culture of death. Some progress in making a better world is possible, but only under the tutelage of the Church.

This ultimately negative view of the human person is the operating article of Christian belief. Opposed to Enlightenment optimism that begins with the liberation of human beings from their own self-tutelage, it reveals a deep pessimism as to the prospects and possibilities of the human agent in this world. It freezes human nature, so to speak, and casts it in the worst possible moral light. It is why Catholic dogma requires an ontological rupture separating human beings from the natural evolutionary process.

In the glittering market place of the modern, pessimism usually does not sell. Therefore John Paul talked about human dignity and hope, praising personhood and God's love for humanity. He taught a reformed humanism, which was in fact the ancient doctrine of *imago Dei* after a bit of cosmetic surgery. But all the surgery in the world does not alter the essentially distorted image marred by the mythical sin in the mythical garden.

Uprooted and repackaged, the doctrine still betrays an extreme moral skepticism, a deep, almost paranoid distrust of human abilities to reform the world and rationally work out a code of ethics that preserves the Pope's highly valued human dignity *for everyone.*

Such moral skepticism, wrote Karl Popper in *The Open Society and Its Enemies*, calling it "ethical nihilism," finds its expression in authoritarianism.[4] John Paul II acted quite consistently. Beneath the smile, the outward expressions of love, compassion and caring, he harbored a deep suspicion of human abilities. Weigel grudgingly admits that having spent a great deal of his youth under totalitarian regimes, he greatly mistrusted the human capacity to build a just and peaceful society upon the foundations of enlightened humanism with its false promises of human freedom (p. 8). Without Christ, Weigel eagerly adds, showing himself yet another citizen of the "enchanted world," man succumbs to the reality of evil (p. 8).

Weigel bragged about understanding John Paul from the inside in order to demystify and correct wild misconceptions, such as his intolerance and authoritarianism (p. 9). But he never once probed deeper than John Paul's Augustinian critique of modernity. Thus he failed to detect the Pope's own "ethical nihilism," developed under those totalitarian regimes. How beautifully it fits the ancient Augustinian interpretation of the two disobedient children, as well as the "credit card" theology of St. Anselm. The rest follows. Only the vertical Christ, the god-man, is able to pay the infinite credit balance, cultivate and restore the garden. In Christ everything has been said—said John Paul II.

Only Christ. Not Muhammad, not Krishna, not Buddha, not Gandhi—or Marx, or Lenin, or Thomas Jefferson. *And especially no women*, except for virgin mothers. Only Christ and his Church. And if only his Church, then only the appearance of his Church on earth as told by the story in Matthew 16. And the rock upon which the Church is built according to that text is Peter, the Bishop of Rome, the Pope, the Holy Father. The result can be none other than authoritarianism and patriarchy. Authoritarianism by its very nature does not tolerate serious discussion and dissent. Intolerance is its disease. The cure for this disease does not exist within the institution and teachings that award power.

The Church may apologize for the *symptoms* of the disease, but it cannot accept modifications of its basic dogma, not to mention a searching historical critique of its basic texts from which the dogma originates. By such refusal, the Church opens itself to accusations of being inflexible, backwards, and reactionary. Image restoration without theological and institutional reform is like prescribing aspirin for cancer.

Human beings are all children in the eyes of the Magisterium. John Paul's love for people was probably sincere, but it was like the love of an authoritarian father who never learns to trust the child since his trust has been betrayed in the past. By not taking *the risk of trust, faith,* the father never allows the child the freedom to mature. He never gives the child the free space to err, to learn from mistakes, to change. John Paul's love reduces people to infants. Indeed, his admirers exhibit such infantilism. It is strangely naïve and simple-minded to imagine that his mother's early death, the sudden death of a beloved brother, or the suffering of his country and his church did not contribute to his ethical nihilism. There is much work to be done on the influence of what are perhaps unconscious forces in his adult life. His real biography is yet to be written. The mind is

---

[4] Karl R. Popper, *The Open Society and Its Enemies: The Spell of Plato*, (Princeton, N J, 1962), p. 72.

a part of a living organism, writes Jonathan Lear, "over which the mind has incomplete control."[5] One ignores this fact at one's own risk.

The authoritarian nature of the Catholic Church precludes real corrective action. But this was never the purpose of the apology. As this book has demonstrated—and John Paul stated in *Ecclesia In Europa*—penance and atonement were aimed at a new wave of evangelization. Complete with a new advertising campaign and a shiny new image, the Church's message was reclaimed from the antiquities shop and displayed anew amid lights and fanfare in the modern global market. At the same time, feeling cleansed and re-energized, the new crusaders are off to conquer the Holy Land once known as Christendom.

---

[5] Jonathan Lear, *Open Minded: Working Out the Logic of the Soul,* (Cambridge, MA, 1998), p. 85.

Chapter 23

Analysis of Image Restoration Strategies

> I was afraid, and look, I saw within the light someone standing by me. As I was looking, it seemed to be an elderly person. Again it changed its appearance to be a youth. Not that there were several figures before me. Rather, there was a figure with several forms within the light. These forms were visible through each other, and the figure had three forms.
>
> *The Secret Book of John*, from Nag Hammadi.

John Paul used several image restoration strategies in the *apologia*. These include: pledging corrective action; asking for forgiveness (mortification); attempting to reduce the offensiveness of some transgressions by bolstering his image and that of the Catholic Church, sharing blame, and evoking a form of transcendence; and attempts to evade responsibility through charges of provocation.

He offered promises of corrective action in every area of image restoration, but these promises amount to little more than vague statements of intention to do better. However, to apologize for the symptoms of intolerant doctrines without treating the cause of the disease is not unprecedented transformation. It is merely public relations. The Pope's apologia was a noble gesture, but only a gesture.

Mortification was a consistent feature of John Paul II's image restoration strategies as he articulated the Catholic Church's request for pardon. In all of these cases, he apologized for the actions of nameless Catholics who were involved in transgressions. Again, it is important to note that the mortification is not to the victims of the transgression or their descendants, but to God. In this plea for forgiveness to God lurks the strategy of transcendence.

Only God, not humans or human history, may judge us. The sinners remain faceless, empty symbols of over-zealous Catholics carried away by the spirit of times long past. But not exclusively past. Sexual predators within the priesthood remained anonymous, even in their own parishes. The paragon of morality cannot itself be immoral. John Paul's lifelong critique of modernity's "defective anthropology" collapses beneath the weight of continuing scandal. John Paul II demonstrated real talent in his ability to manipulate the media. His use of mortification with commitments to corrective action was a strong strategy. As argued throughout, the combination of these two strategies creates *apologia* synergy that elevates them to worth greater than the individual strategies on their own. For example, asking for forgiveness while not promising change in the future can ring hollow in many contexts. John Paul employed a solid strategy when he asked for forgiveness (albeit from God) and pledged to promote corrective action (which, of course, he never intended, or simply could not do without undermining his own authority to ask for forgiveness—from God).

The strength of an expressed commitment to corrective action can depend on the level to which this reform is enacted and implemented. In the long run, it is healthier for the institution to enact the reforms they themselves feel necessary. But in the case of the Catholic Church, a healthy lifestyle seems impossible. The addictions are too many, too ancient, and too powerful.

John Paul II also attempted to reduce the offensiveness of the deeds of some Catholics in the past when he enacted *bolstering*, or the attempt to make himself and the Mother Church exempt from bad behavior. Offering himself as a new feminist served to answer charges of misogyny. He emphasized provocation, a strategy in which he argued all parties were responsible for conflicts. In many instances, John Paul II attempted to share the blame with others. He also found ways to co-opt the victims: the Church suffered alongside the Jews in the camps; it too is a victim of religious intolerance under the Nazis and later the communists. It is a victim of the modern inquisition in which scientists replace cardinal inquisitors. It is the victim of radical feminists and lesbians. It stands for the culture of life against the culture of death. To oppose such positions is akin to moral degeneration, if not plain insanity.

The appeal to the other-worldly Mother Church—whatever one wishes to call it—along with the propensity to create all sorts of fine theological distinctions, refinements, and qualifications, serve to deflect responsibility away from the earthly Church in Rome. This is not to say that the Church refuses all responsibility. Otherwise what would be the use of Penance? Rather, this Church on earth shelters both the saved and the damned (Augustine's double predestination) and it is sometimes impossible to separate the two. *Memory and Reconciliation* is even prepared to consider the "uncomfortable question" of believers' responsibility for certain forms of atheism. But this consideration hardly goes beyond a short, very general paragraph (5.5) in which it is implied that Catholic bad behavior drives some people to unbelief—hardly a momentous discovery.

Once the apology makes the distinction between the Church as the transcendent Bride of Christ and "the weakness of her members," the mischief has begun. That intolerance, misogyny, anti-Semitism, and wars fought in the name of the Prince of Peace might actually be rooted in the Bride's marriage vows (scripture and doctrines) need never be considered. Such possibilities are unthinkable.

If unrecognized, undiagnosed, and henceforth untreated, the disease is left to fester. While some symptoms may be repressed as drugs will dull a sharp pain, others abruptly manifest. How often, for example, has the Church been forced in recent years to apologize (and pay compensation) for sexual abuse? Naturally, the Church has plenty of excuses: the present culture, the porous self at the mercy of evil that dwells in the "enchanted world," human weakness, and so forth. Never will the Church look inside its own doctrines and psychology. How many sincere Catholics yearn to see women in the priesthood? How many, while still remaining committed members of the Church, find ideas from other religions appealing and worth incorporating into their religious practice?

There is something even darker and more sinister about this basic denial. Sin, as *Memory and Reconciliation* preaches, is always personal, and social sin is the merely accumulation of individual sins (paragraph 6). Again, during the Crusades certain enemies (Muslims to be exact) were (conveniently) declared social enemies and not personal enemies subject to Jesus' admonishment to "love your enemy." Are the sins of these enemies, then, not personal when those specific sins—say Muslim criticisms of the Trinity—define the social enemy?

John Paul, believers are told, respected the dignity of individuals and taught the freedom of religion. His criticisms were not of people but of doctrines. Should one not apply an identical standard to the Catholic Church? Its sins are social, the result of doctrines and not individuals. Perhaps certain popes were mistaken in their theological justification of torturing women suspected of witchcraft? Perhaps, after deeper theological reflection, the doctrine of just war is antithetical to the teachings of Christ? Perhaps the risen Christ is not a physical human *male* being, but the community of the baptized, which includes females as part of the definition of the risen Christ.[1] Deeper theological thinking need not remain in the shallows of doctrine.

Look at the intervening years, the vast temporal and theological distance (time is like a dimension of space in relativity after all) between John Paul and the birth of Christianity. Surely there were a few errors. Maybe even papal ones. To imply that doctrines and the men who created them were mistaken, John Paul sets himself up as a judge of the historical Church. Over the Vulgate itself, no less, and its "inspired" interpreters. Yet, this is the source of his power to make such judgments in the first place—physician heal thyself.

The children's crimes cause their Mother suffering. Given some recent financial settlements, this is a physical fact. *The Holy Church is a victim of its own crimes*. Like Christ persecuted by the Jews in the gospels, the Church is crucified by its own people. Victimization is thus co-opted. Here is another outcome of atonement theology, the obsession with the suffering and death of Jesus at the expense of his (ultimately uncertain) teachings. If his early followers spoke of his death as affirmation of his teachings, which

---
[1] Elizabeth A. Johnson, *She Who Is*, p. 162.

was how antiquity understood a noble death, the modern Church following in footsteps of St. Anselm makes a fetish of his cross. The "culture of death" critique is a textbook case of projection.

The Mother, innocent and deeply wounded by her children, makes herself "responsible in all times for the burden created by their sins" (paragraph 15). She is the Mother of Sorrows, suffering for them vicariously. And since the Church on high is Christ, the sinful children are required to apologize not to real flesh and blood victims, but to God.

This sheer arrogance in the name of humble penance is breathtaking. There is a price to be paid. Father Maximilian Kolbe, a Franciscan priest, was martyred at Auschwitz (less for religion and more for politics). He is now a Catholic saint. Edith Stein, a Jewish convert to Catholicism and martyred at Auschwitz, is also a Catholic saint, even though the Nazis murdered her for being a Jew. Descendants of the real victims of Nazi racism, Jews, protested: "Do not Christianize Auschwitz and the Shoah."[2] By explicitly declaring its own victimhood, the Church's theology of apology wounds the real victims all over again. Reconciliation becomes an empty gesture.

Matthew burdens "all the people" with the blood guilt of deicide. In the fourth gospel all the people oppose Jesus from the beginning, not just the Jewish leaders as in the Synoptics. Jews are of the devil, they represent darkness. Today the Church no longer teaches the doctrine that all Jewish children are born with the inherited defect of the blood curse. Yet, that "all the people" will someday accept the New Covenant remains an article of Catholic faith.

---

[2] The quote can be found in James Carroll, *Constantine's Sword*, (New York, 2001), p. 4.

Chapter 24

The Kingdom of God

> *Judas said to him, "I know who you are and from what place you have come."*
>
> *The Gospel of Judas,* from Nag Hammadi.

The Church communicated its call for penance and reconciliation to a world audience. The ceremony was significant merely because it was enacted. World headlines carried an initial appraisal of the enacted strategies. For instance, *The New York Times* reported in its headline "Pope asks forgiveness for the errors of the church over 2,000 years". The world press framed the mass as an unprecedented event in which the pope would ask for forgiveness for the sins committed in the name of the church. Whatever the theology, citizens of the world would understand the event in this media-constructed frame. Clearly, the global public (excepting the most conservative of Catholics) would accept such a step as a positive development. The mere existence of enacted discourse by the Pope on these issues most likely improved the image of the Catholic Church around the world as the Church had hoped.

However, the image restoration attempts enacted by Pope John Paul did not appear to influence his image in the minds of the U.S. public. When asked whom they admired the most, 6% of those polled in December 1999 and December 2000, identified Pope John Paul II (Gallup, 1999, 2000). There was no change in his admired rate from before the apology to after the *mea culpa*. Thus the strategies enacted by John Paul had little discernible impact on public opinion, at least in the United States.

Consumer culture creates a near insatiable hunger for a continual and accelerated rush of imagery. As passive spectators, consumers glide from spectacle to spectacle and never linger long enough to engage the symbol on anything more than the most shallow level. John Paul's image conveyed sincerity, saintliness, and a vague "spirituality," which can mean anything, although in general the word "spirituality" is designed to produce happy and eager consumers. But people hardly paid attention to his declarations and admonishments. Since Vatican II, American Catholics have gone their own way, behaving more like Protestants. Religion is a personal matter, and few will listen to the Pope when he intervenes in the bedroom. Moreover, consumerism encourages selfishness. Anti-materialism can be used to sell material goods. People wearing John Paul tee-shirts stood listening to his critique of materialism. In the brilliant stage light of spectacle, the most eloquent words disappear like stars in the daylight.

The apology spoke to complex historical issues. Media culture is thoroughly addicted to what is happening "now." History is re-packaged and sold in the most elementary and disconnected bites. Like an unexcavated archaeological tell, historical information comes homogenized in the form of a quick glimpse of a small rise, a series of disconnected photos, a sentence or two from some expert—usually a Church official "explaining" "Vatican procedures" or giving a tour of Vatican grounds with a select seasoning of historical references.

The deep roots of the sins committed by Catholic clergy, emissaries, and the fathers of the Church remain unexamined and untouched if not strengthened by John Paul's drive towards centralization. One solution to the dilemma may require a new narrative. Such an interpretation entails recognition that the theology of exclusion, domination, and repression is not necessarily inherent in the teachings of Jesus as close as certain schools of modern scholarship are able to approach what it was Jesus actually taught (more on this below). As far as one can tell from such uncertain source material, it is probable that Jesus never intended to establish a new religion, a new Church, nor any sort of authoritarian hierarchy.[1] This interpretation has it that Jesus proposed the Kingdom of God in place of the Roman Empire, a new kingdom free from hierarchy and patronage in which everyone was a child of God.

The gospels seem to indicate that the historical Jesus taught against patriarchy. This is a plausible interpretation. As this book shows, the Roman Empire was based upon the ancient family with the Father as the model for the God-Emperor. The so-called "hard sayings" of Jesus are clear:

> Whoever does not hate one's father and mother cannot become my disciple. And whoever does not hate one's brothers and sisters and take up the cross in my way will not be worthy of me (Matthew 10:37).

Perhaps he said something like this. Perhaps he did not. The saying does appear to contradict the commandment to honor your parents, as has been noted. Heaven and earth will pass before one jot of the Torah is changed. Perhaps Jesus the Jew said *that*. Someone in Matthew's community said the former for reasons one may only guess.

A true follower of Jesus lives as Jesus lived (taking up the cross) and possibly dies as Jesus died, a rebel. Taken literally, such an ethic would result in the end of Christianity; there would be no Christians left. Symbolically (admittedly a shaky game), it could mean that the ancient patriarchal family, both Jew and gentile, is to be replaced by the new

---

[1] Arthus J. Bellinzoni, *The Future of Christianity. Can It Survive?* (Amherst, NY, 2006), p. 25.

community of which Jesus himself is a member. He implicitly rejects the old measure of power and status. This first Jesus community was radically egalitarian—no father, no Emperor, and by implication, no priests, no bishops—*no popes*.

This is not a primitive Protestant version of the early Church. It is not a Church at all. No organization is allowed to stand in the way of social justice and quality, which is the Kingdom of God.

And this Kingdom, founded in some eschatological dream world, exists only as a myth.[2]

Over the long centuries, theologians as patrons of the "Christian Empire" built their own kingdom of ingenious solutions to the imperial contradiction that became the Catholic Church. It is always instructive to note how after a parade of erudition, their conclusions always seem to agree with traditional doctrine.[3] Stripped to its bare essentials, the *raison d'être* of the Church always comes back to Matthew 16 in which the apostle Simon is given the Keys of the Kingdom by Jesus. From this highly fictionalized legend, through a chain of rather tenuous links, Simon-renamed-Peter comes to be the first bishop of Rome and is martyred there.

It is instructive to compare this scene in Matthew with the same legend in the early gospel of Mark. After recognizing Jesus as the Messiah, *Simon is straightaway told to shut up*. Mark's redacted version of Jesus is the mystery messiah. Matthew, basing his gospel upon Mark (in theory) and the hypothetical sayings gospel Q, paints Jesus as the new Moses (Jesus gives his Torah on a mountain, the Sermon on the Mount, according to Luke it is on the plain) who builds a new temple. Here is another theological principle: the history one emphasizes and gives precedence to is selected based upon one's institutional needs. This is scripture read through the eyes of faith.

Enough volumes have been written on these issues to fill several vast libraries, or build more than one Tower of Babel. Many more are sure to be composed. *Memory and Reconciliation* pleads for a critical historical hermeneutics. Tongue in cheek, this book proposed the Heisenberg Uncertainty Principle of Biblical Hermeneutics.

Until the Encyclical *Divino Afflante Spiritu* of Pope Pius XII in 1943, the Catholic Church rejected the higher criticism, or what may be called the historical critical method in the examination of scripture. But Pope Pius XII accepted its use, once again transforming

---

[2] Myth's linguistic unit is the story. "Thus, the truth of a narrative in this sense does not arise from the 'correspondence' of its words or sentences to 'reality,' but from the coherence of the story as a whole. Just as a poem cannot be paraphrased conceptually without irreparable loss, neither can such narratives be." Robert N. Bellah, *Religion in Human Evolution: From the Paleolithic to the Axial Age* (Cambridge, MA, 2011), p. 33.
[3] G.A. Wells, *Religious Postures: Essays in Modern Christian Apologetics and Religious Problems* (La Salle, IL, 1988), p. 21.

what could become challenges to Church authority into supporting columns of the Church's teachings, much like the well-honed method of "distinct but not separate:"

> The commentators of the Sacred Letters, mindful of the fact that here there is question of divinely inspired text, the care and interpretation of which have been confided to the Church by God Himself, should no less diligently take into account the explanations and declarations of the teaching authority of the Church, as likewise the interpretation given by the Holy Fathers...With special zeal should they apply themselves, not only to expounding exclusively these matters which belong to the historical, archaeological, philological, and other auxiliary sciences—as, to Our regret, is done in certain commentaries—but, having duly referred to these, in so far as they may aid the exegesis, they should set forth in particular the theological doctrine in faith and morals of the individual books or texts so that their exposition may not only aid the professors of theology in their explanations and proofs of the dogmas of faith, but may also be of assistance to priests in their presentations of Christian doctrine to the people, and in fine may help all the faithful to lead a life that is holy and worthy of a Christian (paragraph 24).

Modern historical criticism, then, is only useful in so far as it aids dogmatic exegesis. Ignored completely is the old warning that if, after all the digging and textual criticism, you come up with a historical Jesus who snuggly fits your preconceived image, it is probably *not the historical person.*

Pope Benedict XVI's book on the historical Jesus, *Jesus of Nazareth*, 2007, is a lesson on how the Church approves the historical critical method and then proceeds to ignore it. Written, he says, as a personal expression and not an official pronouncement of the Magesterium, the former Cardinal Ratzinger graciously allows that anyone is free to contradict him (pp. xxii-xxiv). This statement follows from the principle that the pope condemned "so and so" speaking as a man and not as pope. Is one to understand that one would not be free to criticize the same book if Benedict XVI had written as Pope? One must hurry before he changes his mind. The book is a beautiful illustration of what the Church means by its acceptance of modern historical methodology.

In *Jesus of Nazareth* one discovers such statements as: "The first point is that the historical method—specifically because of the intrinsic nature of theology and faith—is and remains an indispensable dimension of exegetical work"(p. xv); "If we push history aside, Christian faith as such disappears and is recast as some other religion" (p. xv); "Canonical exegesis—reading the individual texts of the Bible in the context of the whole—is an essential dimension of exegesis. It does not contradict historical-critical interpretation..." (p. xix).

The latter statement is highly questionable to say the least. How could such a method not contradict modern critically minded scholarship when, as discussed above in the case of redaction criticism, there are significant divergences among the individual evangelists? Some favor the Church's interpretation, others do not. What if scholarly consensus establishes the priority of those others? Also, does not "the context of the whole" resurrect anti-Semitism in that it requires a Christian reading of the *Tanakh* positing it as partial or incomplete, as Benedict himself said elsewhere? And further, numerous modern historical studies generally agree that there is no *single* Bible. There are many possible Scriptures, changed and still changing over time (for popular accounts see Bart Ehrman, *Lost Christianities*, 2003, *Lost Scriptures*, 2003, and *Misquoting Jesus*, 2005; also see Hector Avalos, *The End of Biblical Studies*, 2007).

As might be expected, Benedict XVI is quick to point out the so-called limitations of the historical method. Finer and finer distinctions between layers of tradition obscure the figure of Jesus, he says, until Jesus begins to look like the historian (p. xii). Sometimes he looks like Vatican art, if the historian happens to lean in that direction. To his credit, then, Benedict does appear aware of problem of preconceived notions. Tradition guards the Church against such an abuse as long as one accepts the preconceived notion that tradition is guaranteed the Holy Spirit. Such a notion, in its metaphysical sense, is hardly open to scientific verification and is antithetical to critical history. Contradictions are explained away by new readings that start from the premise: What God *really says*... The Pope plays a game he cannot lose.

Modern scholarship is hardly able to explain the development of Christology and the amazing spread of Christianity in the early years after the crucifixion, Benedict XVI complains. Sorry, modern scholarship *does explain* the development of Christology in terms of the categories people of the times used to interpret their experience of Jesus. But the former Grand Inquisitor derisively dismisses such explanations with the sweep of a grand rhetorical flourish: "How could these unknown groups be so creative? How were they so persuasive and how did they manage to prevail?" (p. xxii). Having once belonged to the Nazi Youth, Ratzinger ought to know. His own exegesis (hardly an argument) leads him to a predetermined goal:

> Isn't it more logical, even historically speaking, to assume the
> greatness came at the beginning, and that the figure of Jesus really
> did explode all existing categories and could only be understood
> in the light of the mystery of God? (p. xxii–xxiii)

Are the faithful given a reason *why* this is a more logical assumption ("*even historically speaking*") except that Benedict XVI personally finds it difficult to swallow modern explanations? And does not his trumpeted respect for critical historical method carry with it a default explanation labeled "the mystery of God?" In actual fact, there are plenty of good historical explanations that require no question-begging assumptions of greatness at the beginning, which is essentially metaphysics disguised as hermeneutics. Ramsey MacMullen easily demonstrates how Christianity could have caught on:

> And I know, I have seen, I have heard, they have related to me, they
> have books, they have a special person, a sort of officer. It is true.
> Besides and anyway, if you don't believe, then you are doomed when
> a certain time comes, so say the prophecies; whereas if you do, then
> they can help even in great sickness. I know people who have seen

or who have spoken with others who have seen. And healing is even the least that they tell. Theirs is truly a God all-powerful. He has worked a hundred wonders.[4]

MacMullen does not even require the name of Jesus, or Christ, or Christian to make his point. If there is a mystery—and maybe it is not a mystery at all—it must be the how easily desperate people are convinced that the mystery of God is an explanation for anything. In *The Birth of Christianity*, John Dominic Crossan dissects the first 50 years of the early movement and how the "Jewish Mediterranean peasant" was interpreted by later generations using those categories that Ratzinger thinks Jesus exploded. The peasant's story, says Crossan, comes to resemble that of the Emperor Augustus, descended from Aeneas whose mother was Aphrodite, declared god after his death, nicely slipping like a perfectly round peg into a perfectly round hole the category of "divine man".[5]

Another member of the Jesus Seminar, Stephen Patterson, views Jesus as a visionary who attracted a following dedicated to his dream of a radically egalitarian Kingdom of God (or God's Imperial Rule). As it had in the cases of thousands upon thousands of other rebels, the Roman Empire killed him. Some of his followers fervently believed that his cause was just and therefore a just God would resurrect him. But only the great and mighty like Caesar returned in divine form. Jesus was a nobody. His followers were nobodies. He had convinced them that they were *somebodies* to God. He, not Augustus, was their Son of Jupiter. So they proclaimed his resurrection.[6]

There are many other explanations. Each must be weighed on the scale of probability analysis. It could turn out that the whole thing is a myth and Jesus exists only in the pages of the New Testament. Every classic encourages a plurality of possible interpretations.[7] Many of these interpretations do not require the "light of the mystery of God." Benedict XVI is not finished. The historical method, he goes on, cannot take into account the living presence of the Holy Spirit that unites the Church past, present and future. It has been forever uncertain, never coming to a definitive conclusion. Its findings remain in the past, it cannot bring Jesus to life as present today (p. xvi). Again, this assertion goes back to Augustine who made the distinction between the objective past in which "now is not" and the present past, the living present of memory, of words used to recall the past, which occurs in the present (*Confessions*, p. 242). From God's point of view, all time is the eternal "now." Again, an appeal is made to the metaphysical realm. Once this superior measure is established, the Church is able to fault the products of modern historical research. One cannot bring history back to life since for humans here on earth—the horizontal dimension—the past does not objectively exist. Well, of course not.

History is the reconstructed past. It comes to life in the mind of the historian and her readers. Every reconstruction is always open to revision. But the process is not all

---

[4]Ramsay MacMullen, *Christianizing the Roman Empire, A.D. 100–400*, (New Haven, 1984), p. 41.
[5]John Dominic Crossan, *The Birth of Christianity: Discovering What Happened in the Years Immediately After the Execution of Jesus* (New York, 1998), p. 414.
[6]Stephen Patterson, *Beyond the Passion*, p. 118.
[7]David Tracy, *The Analogical Imagination*, p. 113.

or nothing. Interpretations are refined, new data are discovered, better, more promising accounts are constructed, the changing present opens unsuspected horizons to the past—*history is a process that is very much alive*. Degrees of freedom exist in the best or most certain reconstructions, giving history a certain level of uncertainty that all historians are forced to make peace with. An unchanging dogmatic interpretation that desires a rigidly determined "objective" past in order to maintain itself is threatened by the historical uncertainty principle. Therefore, it must retreat into the heavens by proclaiming the inadequacy of history, just as evolution cannot account for the special dignity of *man*. This is no longer the critical historical method. Yet it pretends to judge other reconstructions from its throne on high. Dogma masks itself as hermeneutics and shrilly protests against historicism.

So much for the prelude. When Benedict XVI actually begins to reconstruct his "historical" Jesus, he feels free to completely ignore the rich yields of recent historical scholarship available to him. Nowhere in his book does he discuss the contemporary debate between the eschatological prophet Jesus versus the Jewish cynic wisdom teacher of Q, or the Jewish charismatic sage or the Zealot revolutionary, or the mythicist argument, or...the feminist Jesus. Nowhere does one find an analysis of the Gnostic Gospel of Thomas. One hears nothing of the manuscript issues, the problems associated with oral traditions, contributions made by sociology, literary analysis, or archaeology. Even if this is a personal book, one would think that a man so intimately bound to his subject would eagerly embrace the tiniest bit of information. Such is not the case. Benedict XVI is like a soccer player kicking the ball around in the bleachers. The real action is on the field but he is nowhere near it.

Jesus of Nazareth illustrates just what the critical historical method means to Benedict XVI. He notes with stern disapproval tendencies to recover the psychology of the savior. But then he tells the faithful that Jesus' *intention* is not to abolish the family or the Sabbath (p. 120). Not only does he ignore the so-called "hard sayings" (above) but he assumes what he just condemned. Somehow *he* is privy to Jesus' intentions. And even if Jesus explicitly stated his intentions, how can one ever know unconscious desires, repressions, or preconceptions, to name a few, lurking beneath the consciousness of the "objective" person or masquerading as conscious statements?

The former Cardinal Inquisitor shows no uncertainty. Here is a prime example of the establishment of historical fact by theological necessity. The Church, says Benedict XVI with an eye to the evils of secularism, defends the family as the core of the social order (p. 121). If Schussler Fiorenza has a point, then it is precisely the family as the core of the social order *in the Roman Empire* that Jesus attacked.

Benedict XVI, however, does prove a point he made in his Foreword. The reconstructed Jesus, the only one open to us, does indeed begin to resemble the Pope-historian. Ironically, when it serves his purposes he does accept to New Testament scholarship. For example, he happily endorses the long-refuted theory of Joachim Jeremias that Jesus's use of the word *'abba* implied his special child-like relationship to the "father," *'abba* meant "daddy" like the babbling of a child. This was refuted decades ago.[8]

---
[8] Geza Vermes, *Christian Beginnings*, p. 47.

Upon occasion, Benedict lets down his guard and revealed what he was really about. Contemplating the Temptations in the Wilderness, he wrote, "The alleged findings of scholarly exegesis have been used to put together the most dreadful books that destroy the figure of Jesus and dismantle the faith" (p. 35).

Like the Mother Church victimized by her erring children, the gospel is victimized by the critical historical method. The Church seems to be the victim at every turn, even when it is engaged in the worst crimes against human beings. The press exaggerates and sensationalizes the pedophilia of priests. Without exaggeration, one might easily say that by perpetually claiming victimhood, the Church remains faithful to its image of Jesus. Jesus is a mirror in which the Church sees a distorted image of itself. Like him, it is unfairly persecuted. Like him, it suffers martyrdom at the hands of a wicked and perverse modernity. The Church refuses to recognize the real source of its persecution in its own teachings. Like an alcoholic, a drug addict, an obsessive gambler, the Church has yet to take the first and most difficult step towards a cure: "I am not a victim."

The same mentality haunts the apologia. John Paul II seeks to lead the Church under principles of liberal social justice while reifying a fundamentally conservative catechism. He fought to maintain a highly centralized reign and has attempted to maintain the integrity and prominence of the papal office by means of charisma and image, that is, tyranny with a smile.

Most Catholics, the so-called weak and sinful children, are not and have not been guilty of the sins recognized by the Church. Rather, it is the Church hierarchy and teachings supporting an undemocratic institution, which like all institutions is dedicated to the exercise of power over the lives of its members. The burden of guilt rests here. Members must come to terms with the idea that the patriarchy that rules over the Church defends and propagates ideas seriously at odds with their personal beliefs—and, without much exaggeration, not a few serious interpretations of the teachings of Jesus.

Questions remain. Can Catholics who do not agree with the Roman Catholic patriarchy on fundamental issues of faith continue to identify themselves as Catholics? Benedict thinks not. Can women be ordained. No, thunders the Pope, it is as grave a sin as child abuse. Will the Church renounce once and for all imperial ambitions and give the purple back to Caesar? We think not. Perhaps we are mistaken.

This book has touched upon the richness and diversity of early Christianity. *There was no single primitive Church*. Ironically, those Catholics who desire alternatives may be closer to original "catholic" Christianity than the dogmatic modern Church. Doctrines such as the "atonement" and the Trinity, common to Catholics, Orthodox, and Protestants, may require drastic revision, perhaps even outright rejection. The Asian religions, which both John Paul and Benedict seem to despise and fear, could provide the inspiration for such changes. Real religious dialogue would be helpful.

John Paul's admirers praised his courage during his final years of illness and suffering. By refusing to retire and remove himself from public scrutiny, the Pope gave dignity to suffering including the suffering of others. His public death, gushes Peggy Noonan, got people thinking about dying—and living.[9] This is just plain silly as anyone who has suffered a serious illness or lost a loved one can testify. Maybe it got Peggy thinking. Like his suffering Poland, like Christ, he refused to surrender and chose rather not to conceal his suffering from the world. She quotes John Paul as saying: "Christ didn't come down from the cross".[10]

Cardinal Ratzinger nearly merged John Paul and Christ in his Funeral Homily of 2005:

> The Holy Father was a priest to the last, for he offered his life to God for his flock and for the entire human family, in a daily self-oblation for the service of the Church, especially amid the sufferings of his final months. And this way he became one with Christ, the Good Shepherd who loves his sheep (p. 2).

But *how* did he share it? Like everything else, his suffering was packaged and sold as a media spectacle. Those who found themselves thinking about suffering and dying (and living) by watching the show unfold as media imagery are consumers just as much as those who desire happiness by possession of a certain product. Valued for its emotional intensity, the spectacle of suffering becomes a parade of signifiers separated from causes and actual things.

Having caused its fair share of suffering—*and still causing it*, for example, with its opposition to contraception in the face of the AIDs devastation, its abuse of the innocent, its repression of women—the Church would make of suffering a virtue. To repeat, suffering and death trump the *teachings* of Jesus. Is it not human suffering from sin that drives the Church's plot with its drama of crucifixion, resurrection and redemption? Does not all humanity suffer from a congenital illness it cannot cure on its own? The benefactors of humanity outside the Church are like medieval physicians helpless before the great plague. Only by means of more suffering, the shedding of divine blood, is the illness cured.

Theology at last is only able to affirm by faith—the evidence points in the opposite direction—that the risen Christ signifies evil does not have the last word.[11] Thus believers have a mythical cure, the risen Christ, as empty as the incarnate one.

The Buddha taught that suffering serves a purpose. But that purpose is to lead people to enlightenment which is meant *to end suffering*, right here in this life. He taught suffering and the end of suffering. It also means compassion for the suffering

---

[9] Peggy Noonan, *John Paul the Great: Remembering a Spiritual Father*, (New York, 2005), p. 11.
[10] This reading should be compared to John Cornwell's discussion of the infinite problems created for the Church by John Paul's infirmities, *The Pontiff in Winter*, 2004. Jesus does come down from the cross in numerous fictional accounts, the latest being Dan Brown. If one is prepared to dismiss them, then one must show how the gospel accounts are not fictional, or are better interpretations of unrecoverable historical events. They probably are, but the operative word is "probability."
[11] Elizabeth A. Johnson, *She Who Is*, p. 159.

of all sentient creatures, again right here. The spiritualized media kind of suffering, the kind that got Noonan thinking, actually creates a "cult of apathy".[12] It is sanitized. It evokes pathos more than real empathy and compassion. If one becomes weary, one changes the channel.

In Buddhism, suffering—*duhkha*—describes human interaction with the world of impermanence. It is everyone's condition. It is the First Noble Truth, called by the Chinese "a wonderful truth." If human beings really could do nothing about *duhkha*, if suffering could not be changed, that is if it were some absolute unchanging truth defining the human condition, then there really would be cause for sorrow.

If human beings could do nothing about suffering except rely upon questionable historical accounts of shadowy saviors for its removal *in the vertical dimension*, then such a religion built upon these precepts could be truly labeled pessimistic. Such a faith denies one the dignity of one's own resources. It would deny the simple evidence of modern medicine to relieve suffering. This explains the Church's ambivalent attitude toward medical science. It cannot deny the obvious without looking silly. Thus, biology is unequipped to treat the whole person, the human condition characterized by sin. The ultimate suffering is promoted to a metaphysical world and declared absolute. Humans are helpless. Only Christ and his Church possess the cure. Is this not Popper's nihilism?

Once more, the Church reduces people to the status of children. The faithful return to the age of tutelage.

Here is another version of the story.

Human beings possess a vicarious dignity derived ultimately from an ancient fairy tale of two innocent children, who resemble their Father, playing in his backyard garden. The two fall prey to the sly words of a clever snake. Like a typical child, as one recalls, Eve informs the serpent that God told them not to eat of the fruit, *nor to touch it* (Genesis 3:3). But the "touchingly" innocent children disobey their Father and become the first victims of the snake-philosopher who, like all good rationalists, questions authority. From the very beginning, there is a curse upon questioning and curiosity. The court in Athens condemned Socrates for the same reasons: a curious person, who questions into things under the earth and in the heavens, Socrates is guilty of corrupting the youth and not believing in the gods of the state. Adam and Eve corrupted the world. The biblical story begins with victimization and proceeds to suffering.

Their stern father, owner of the garden, prone to blinding anger, banishes them and heaps such punishment upon them that they are helpless to do anything but suffer. Fortunately, their elder brother eventually comes to the rescue, but only after untold *millennia of human suffering*. As it turns out, this elder brother is really a rebirth of the father who sometime in the past faded away like old tyrants do—he became a still small voice in the wilds. However, the elder brother's "rescue" requires *more suffering* as its instrument of change. He must suffer like his younger siblings, only worse since he pays an infinite debt. The elder son's suffering is almost unbelievably bloody and

---

[12]Vincent Miller, *Consuming Religion*, p. 134.

bestial (see the Mel Gibson passion movie). And yet, when it is all over and the Son is reborn again—resurrected—human suffering on earth continues, and in the first half of the twentieth century reaches a quantitative level undreamt by the most vicious ancient deity. In fact, suffering in the world finally ends with the end of history *as people know it*, and this means that the entire world is destroyed in a final scene, which is the mother of all suffering (but continues forever for a vast number of poor souls confined to the "negative" vertical dimension).

How can anyone, believing such things, care enough about the world to try to end suffering here and now like the Buddha? This is not about secularist utopias or romantic visions of a better future. Nor does this book deny that many Christians hope and work for a better world. Building a fence around the Torah meant creating new habits of thought and behavior. Christ *in our tentative reconstruction* desired a person who did not have to be told not to kill, but a person who as a person could not kill at all. The Torah indeed rested in the heart.

The faithful cannot remain the children the Church wishes believers to be. His children stole their father's high powered rifle when he was otherwise preoccupied. Allow us to amend what was posited in the beginning: what people truly fear today are true believing, emotionally, and intellectually immature children armed with nuclear weapons.

Chapter 25

An Interpretation of a Dream

Jesus said, "I am not your teacher. Because you have drunk, you have become intoxicated from the bubbling spring that I have tended.

The Gospel of Thomas from Nag Hammadi, #5

In the Gospel of John, Jesus claims for himself the title "I am," belonging originally to the god who confronts Moses in Exodus. Pilate then asks his great question. *What is Truth?* The Christian reader, of course, knowing that Jesus is "I am" has no problem with the gospel's final examination question. Therefore, Jesus does not directly answer Pilate. The question is addressed to all human beings. Jesus is the Truth because in this gospel he claimed to be *I am*—Truth. Many scholars see this as a further development in Christology, one of the many elements that set John apart from the synoptic gospels. It is the foundation for what will become in 300 years identity, the *homoousios* of Nicaea.

In 1543, John Paul's countryman Nicholas Copernicus put the planet earth into motion. Since then, one by one, many universal certainties have been jettisoned from their comforting repose and spun into space. This is an old version of history, labeled by Paul O. Ingram as "rather priggish."[1] His reasoning, however, betrays a deep wish that things will ultimately turn out differently. Science, he argues, is an ongoing process; the Copernican and Darwinian revolutions stand at the beginning of the history of modern science. Ingram and so many like him anxiously scan the future scientific horizon, straining their vision to the utmost. They hope to catch a sign, a puff of smoke perhaps, a peculiarly shaped cloud, that will point the way back to the deity.

---

[1] Paul O. Ingram, *Buddhist-Christian Dialogue in An Age of Science*, (Lanham, Maryland, 2008), p. 53.

Chances are, with a strong faith and a strong draught of ingenuity, they will find it. Some are prepared to announce the discovery.

The most terrifying thing about an earthquake is the very feeling of the once-solid earth, which one has taken as an unquestioned fact of everyday experience, suddenly shifting beneath one's feet. The foundation of the earthly base, almost written into our cells, becomes frightfully uncertain. The fear can be overwhelming.

Today, astronomers report that our globe spins through space about a rather average star in a galaxy of billions of stars, on the Orion arm of an average galaxy which is one of billions. All these galaxies are flying away from one another as space-time expands. They are accelerating too. Einstein's cosmological constant (the Λ function first meant to halt the expansion) has now been transferred to the energy-momentum tensor side of his field equations. Thus, it represents an anti-gravitational dark energy, a form of dark matter, that makes up nearly 70% of the matter in our universe. We have no idea what nearly 70% of the universe is made up of. The universe is quite strange, maybe stranger than we can imagine (as has been often repeated).

The matter of which human beings are constructed, the stuff people can see from out all-too-human perspective, may be merely a small percentage of the total matter in the universe after dark matter and dark energy are factored in.

Perhaps there is some *truth* (a strange word for us, eh?) in John Paul's assertion of modern fear. Humanity has not yet come to feel at home in the universe, to steal a phrase from Stuart Kauffman. But the faithful cannot return to the old position. *There is no old position.* Aristotle's absolute rest—natural place—has departed the stage. Rest for Newton is a special case of dynamics, and in Special Relativity there is no way to distinguish rest from inertial motion.

Similarly, the old myths no longer possess the certainty they once had. The faithful cannot read them like innocent children any longer. Educated people of conscience cannot hear them without experiencing the suspicion of the modern. Deep inside, no matter how hard one tries to ignore it, one hears Pilate's great question. If they truly are classics, the faithful will have to discover other meaningful interpretations that speak to them in their language, in their age. There ought to be plenty.

Modernity's illness may not be, as John Paul believed, the result of subjectivism, nihilism, or human autonomy. Modern genocide, argues Ian Kershaw, is based upon unchangeable stamps of "ideologically defined identities."[2] Combined with technology and bureaucratic planning, fueled with the dreams of future utopias, absolute truths (the cousins of religion) became the source of violence in the first half of the twentieth century.[3]

---

[2] Ian Kershaw, *Hitler, The Germans, and the Final Solution*, p. 372.
[3] Hector Avalos, *Fighting Words: The Origins of Religious Violence*, pp. 317–318. Avalos writes: "Nazis were often more like scientific creationists of today who believe their pseudoscience supports the Bible."

The racial theory of history might give meaning to the betrayal of a seemingly victorious army, for example—the stab-in-the-back explanation of the German defeat in the First World War—where the providence of Christian historical meaning had failed. Marx's predictions of a classless society, like Christian hopes for a new Eden populated by a new Adam and a new Eve (or the communism in the Book of Acts),[4] were believed with absolute certainty. What mass movement, party, faith, or any assertion that demands faith, would deny its ability to know its truth with certainty? God is always on our side, whether he is the vengeful deity of an ancient tribe or the dialectical materialism of historical progress. There are differences, to be sure. Religious conversion is always possible. Yet, so too is ideological transformation—re-education. Converts are always suspect. Jewish converts to Catholicism were not allowed into the Society of Jesus. Racially, they were still Jews. On the other hand, Nazis were prepared to set aside strict racial theories when it served their purpose. The Japanese could be called Aryans because of their samurai culture and the warrior code of bushido.

Further, if one claims that human beings cannot live with uncertainty and without God, and if one bases the truth of this claim upon the evidence of twentieth century disasters, one has yet to show that human beings cannot *ever* find a way to adapt to a world of uncertainty. It cannot be shown for certain that these frightful events were not anomalies or that humans have not learned from them. It is simply too early to tell. It cannot be claimed that it is impossible for human beings to evolve into creatures who are able to live in the Heisenberg universe with dignity, compassion and in peace without the vertical dimension. The Church answers in the voice of Augustine: *non posse non peccare*. Without special qualifications, without primal events, theological prehistory and ontological leaps, the evidence for such a claim is rather thin. Further yet, even if these objections miss the point of the Pope's critique, or can easily be swept aside, *it has to be shown how the admission of women or married men to the priesthood leads to the culture of death? How does the post-modern suspicion of all metaphysics drive priests to rape young boys?*

If John Paul really wanted to end misogyny and sexual abuse, he might have had to reconsider his position, especially after hearing the Buddha's testimony. Unlike so many other classic religious texts, *The Dhammapada* does not begin with God or the gods (the vertical) but with mind:

If with mind polluted

One speaks or acts,

then pain follows.

If with mind pure

one speaks or acts

then ease follows (3).

---

[4] Acts 5:1-6. A certain couple, Ananias and his wife Sapphira, sold a possession but kept part of the profit as private property, not donating the whole to the Church. Peter confronts him with the lie ("Satan filled thine heart"), and he falls dead. Greedy profit-hungry capitalists are purged from the Church. Stalin would have approved.

Or with Moses Maimonides in *The Guide for the Perplexed*: "The thoughts about sin are more dangerous than the sin itself" (p. 263).

John Paul longed for the days of a central earth, with God firmly in his Empyrean Sphere and human beings occupying the middle link in the Great Chain of Being. The symbolism was there in his very language: man is not alone for "he is surrounded by the love of the Creator!" (quoted in Weigel, p. 14). He would undo the work of his countryman Copernicus. He and all those who praise him yearn for the old Aristotelian universe of natural place, the soothing cradle of the absolute.

But look here, says Jacob Bronowski. In a strip of three photographic frames one sees him bending over the pond at Auschwitz, grasping a handful of mud and grass which most certainty contains the remains of the camp's victims. An ironic but telling image for a book entitled: *The Ascent of Man*. Bronowski writes:

> I owe it as a human being to the many members of my family who died at Auschwitz, to stand here by the pond as a survivor and a witness. We have to cure ourselves of the itch for absolute knowledge and power. (p. 374)

"The itch for the absolute."

Bronowski can still entertain hope where many others have found it impossible. Despite the bleak landscape of Auschwitz, his book can still celebrate the *ascent of man*. But it is not a vertical ascent into the realms of the absolute. That is the itch humanity needs to cure. Summarizing his golden legend of the saint, Weigel makes the opposite assertion: "A yearning for the absolute, it seems, is built into the human condition" (p. 863). Nearly negating this sentence, he follows with the statement that Auschwitz and horrors like it sprang from barbarians who made fragments of the truth absolute. How could they not if this yearning is "built into" them?

Is not Church itself one of those fragments? Any absolute truth must exist outside the world of change and contingency. To be communicated it must arrive on earth through the medium limited human language. Creeds and dogmas must be necessarily fragments. The Church concedes the point when it says that the fullness of Truth will be known at the end of the world. Is this a "fully" true declaration? Deeper theological thinking which makes image restoration possible in the first place demands it. So, the Church ends with the proposition: The patriarchs alone possess the only truth which is really not *the truth*—not now, but they alone possess it.

For John Paul, Weigel, and many like them, the Enlightenment optimism that once pumped hope into modernity stands condemned by Auschwitz. The heavenly city of the eighteenth century philosophers proved just as fragile as any other city of man. In their minds, faith in progress is a historical artifact like the Age of Faith was for the Enlightenment. After civilization's roll call of disasters since the First World War, Jurgen Moltmann says:

> We have seen the killing fields of history forbid every attempt to find a meaning for them, and every theodicy, every ideology of progress, and every satisfaction in

globalization fails to suffice. In that century progress left in its wake ruins and victims, and no historical future can make this suffering good. ("Progress and Abyss," p. 16)[5]

By fiat then, like the totalitarianism he condemns, Moltmann proclaims that human beings are helpless to find meaning, to hope, and make good from suffering without the so-called spiritual dimension. The lesson many people would like to draw from such horrors is that human beings cannot find hope or the meaning of life within profane history. For them, John Paul's truth revived hope. If Marx were here to observe this development he might have rewritten his famous passage describing religion as an opium, the sigh of the oppressed creature. He might say that *religion is the sigh of relief of the pessimistic absolutist.*

In this way John Paul is a post-modernist. The ambiguity of the human project, fear, pessimism, and the uncertainty of a meaningless future have made hope almost laughable for him and his many followers. Be not afraid, he shouts. Departing post-modernism, his solution is to re-introduce the absolute under the guise of the Church's uncertain interpretation of uncertain history.

John Paul II was the physician, prescribing the only cure for the nihilism and moral wickedness of modernity. First, he had to heal the Church. Hence the apology. John Paul failed. The sufferings of the innocents stand as our witnesses. And so one should ask:

Whither the Church?

According to another interpretive legend: Two thousand years ago a young Jew taught a rebellious vision of a kingdom of love, non-violence, and social justice. He included women. The imperial power of the day, the Roman Empire, crushed him. He left a small following composed of nobodies who kept his vision alive. Upon occasion, the Empire persecuted them, but mostly it ignored them. They were nobodies and of no great consequence to some-bodies. Over time, his followers changed his teachings. His vaguely remembered sayings were altered to meet new circumstances. They evolved. But suddenly for numerous reasons, perhaps many yet to become clear, the nobodies became the Empire. They became the very power against which they rebelled.

Like all Empires, this one, founded in the name of the executed Jew, eventually lost worldly political power. The forms remained and it still commanded a vast following, but the real physical power and authority, the kind that comes from blood and iron joined to loyalty and belief, had slipped through its fingers. A gang of new gods had arrived on the

---

[5]See Orlando Figes, *A People's Tragedy: A History of the Russian Revolution,* 1996. Figes writes that if we've learned anything from communism and fascism it must be that "social engineering" cannot make people into better human beings (pp. 823–824). This method makes things worse. This is probably true. But it does not mean that people may not become better human beings at all by their own initiative and outside the tutelage of the Universal Church.

scene. The one-time followers of the Jewish visionary—although it is difficult to maintain that most of them were truly *his* followers—once again became rebels.

They then discovered that rebellion had become a fashion, an empty symbol, a sign that could be used to sell a nearly infinite number of commodities. The most clever among them realized that the adoption of empty symbols could be used to regain their lost authority. First, a symbolic apology had to be offered for the days of power. This symbol, infinitely flexible, indicated a return to innocence, a claim to victimization. They were new feminists, rebelling against the oppression of secular feminists who would rob women of their "special dignity."

The Millennial Penance seemed to indicate that the Church had renounced the methods of coercion for good. The Church stood for human dignity. John Paul was praised for his courage and his humanism. He was bold enough to admit that something was wrong, that the ages of power and authority had demonstrated the futility of the Empire. Before the Church could stand before the world in the garb of the world's physician, the physician had to "heal thyself."

Yet, an all-too-familiar, very human tendency blocked the way forward. *Denial.* Although quite self-obsessed, the Church refused to look deeply. Like the medieval physician it bled the patient instead. Members were blamed for what is an illness of the heart. The disease and its cure have yet to be fully explored. In this book we have tried to diagnose the disease. Allow us a bit of speculation on a possible cure.

Sacred Scripture becomes a commodity in the hands of theology much as modern capitalism tears products out of their natural context and advertises them as commodities without a history. Interpreted as divine activity in the world, commoditized Scripture creates a "Christian outlook," a mental framework for engagement with the world. Historical analysis challenges this Christian mentality, says Burton Mack in his book about the lost gospel Q.[6] The Christian mentality gives privilege to certain events: events that are unique, dramatic, original, miraculous, and apocalyptic. Such privileged events, Mack shows, become clichés and attitudes for negotiating the world. Compromise, humor, the give and take of dialogue, of chit-chat, the daily mundane encounters with the world and our fellow human beings, are often considered banal, frivolous, and of small consequence.

The Christian mentality exists as a habit, generally without overt reference to Scripture (many clichés, however, do arise from this source, but again they are commodities). The gospel story is applied everywhere and to everything. The Q Gospel, the Gospel of Thomas, the scholarly discovery of ancient variations of Christianity, the present version being a single member of a larger set, challenge this mentality. They provide alternatives to what it means to be a Christian. And they provide alternatives to what may be destructive tendencies in unexamined mentalities.

Today Pope (retired) Benedict XVI stamps his foot and proclaims that outside the Church is no salvation. Human progress is impossible without God. Human autonomy

---

[6] Burton Mack, *The Lost Gospel: The Book of Q and Christian Origins*, (New York, 1993), p. 250.

leads to disasters. Free speech leads to mental confusion and pornography. Despite transparent attempts to soften such exclusiveness—other religions possess Christ in fragments, "seeds" of the gospel, or God has not abandoned the Old Covenant—the Church's claim to possess the "final word" is the infection that poisons the apology. It is the beating heart of the Empire, more dangerous than armies of five million soldiers. It is the imprisonment of the human mind. It is coercion of the soul, the forced obedience of the slave.

All else is symptom. Embodying exclusive claims to the truth in an institution dedicated to power gives birth to tyranny. Ossifying such claims into dogma makes real dialogue within and without impossible. The very existence of alternatives challenges the infallibility of the Pope's claim. The very existence of women, as the jealous old god of Eden knew, challenges the institution as it stands. The logical outcome of this challenge must be that either the female is ignored (which is becoming less and less a possibility), the Church re-examines its own dogma (which is unlikely as this book has shown), or *the other is forcibly silenced.*

As Mack points out, the symbols for solving this crucial problem are already at hand. At the beginning stands a vicarious crucifixion and at the end apocalyptic destruction. Violence at the beginning and unthinkable violence at the end. And John Paul has already lectured that God will reveal the "fullness" of the truth on the other side of total devastation *of this world which is the only world we know.* When the ancient Greek philosopher Diogenes heard someone talking about heavenly things, he asked: "And when did you get back?"

The central thesis of this book is the Catholic Church can enact effective corrective action to prevent sexual abuse of children and subsequent efforts to hide these crimes through inclusion of more diverse clergy. This reform must be cut deeply into the theology and dogma on gender and sexuality. We have penetrated the obfuscated theological arguments that give rise to the problems. We challenge members and leaders of the Catholic Church to have the courage and faith to cure the infection rather than merely apologize for the rape of children and the treatment of our daughters as second class citizens in the Kingdom of God embodied in the earthly Church. At its best, the Church must bear witness to the dignity of all people: women, children, and men. Only then may its members claim to be true disciples of the Jew named Yeshua. This means a re-focusing on the teachings of that first century charismatic Jewish sage. It is time to let go of the fantastic image of a godlike being who descends *to earth* as an uncanny image of his human creators—who springs from a male-ideal of the perfect woman *on earth*, which turns out to be a delusional wish-fulfillment, a dream, that mothers never die.

Critics sometimes claim that the teachings of Jesus as presented in the New Testament are impractical. Giving away your possessions, taking no thought for tomorrow (like the wild flowers of the field), and especially the non-resistance to evil (turning the other cheek) belong to the morality of a people who believe the world is about to end.[7] They may be correct. The so-called hard sayings are eschatological and hardly livable in the present world.

But that may be the point. Hyperbole, indirect speech, over-statement, pithy sayings, paradoxes and metaphors all comprise the teachings of the Jewish charismatic.[8] This may true of all wisdom teachers. The gods love to hide. Shocking statements that required unraveling, study and contemplation, would be the easiest to remember and pass down in an oral tradition. The very impracticality of the statement may indicate its depth. So too its context. In a world of frightful social injustice (the sexual commodification of slaves, for example), and insanely unequal distributions of wealth, such as the Roman Empire (or a world mad with consumerism), an absurdly impractical morality might prove a devastating critique. What is considered absurd by an absurd world would be sane. Jesus may have been more subtle and complex than previously thought.

Perhaps it is time to recover that critique. The cause of suffering, said the Buddha, was *trsna*, craving, thirst, the Second Noble Truth. Everything points back to the self, this craving for permanence of the atman. The craving for fame, wealth, to be right, for commodities, the desire to desire, even for religion, all come back to the self. But that thirst is not in the things themselves, rather our approach, our attachment to them as if somehow they guarantee permanence—but the Kingdom is within.

Analysis sucks the life out of such wisdom teachings. So Jesus teaches in parables, promotes a crazy way of living, *rejects the patriarchal family and speaks of an impossible world called the Kingdom of God.* In a consumer-crazy world driven by advertising dedicated to the trivial, the message requires up-dating, not only in theology and dogma but in behavior. Such are the concrete steps that would constitute the real corrective action John Paul promised in his *apologia*. First, the Catholic Church should once again accept female clergy, as was the case the first three hundred years of the Church. Second, married clergy should be ordained, as was accepted in the first thousand years of Church history. These two reforms would alleviate an atmosphere that is conducive to sexual abuse of children by clergy members and the conspiratorial efforts to hide these heinous crimes. And third, perhaps the most important of all, the Church must recover, as an alternative reading (but not absolute truth), the social message *in this world*.

After a period of schoolboy atheism—which comes with the discovery of reason and ends with the realization of its limitations—the writer and United Nations undersecretary general Shashi Tharoor discovered that he was quite happy to describe himself as a believing Hindu. Among the reasons he notes:

> As a Hindu, I claim adherence to a religion without established church or priestly papacy, a religion whose rituals and customs I am free to reject, a religion that does not oblige me to demonstrate my faith by any visible sign, by subsuming my identity

---
[7] A. C. Grayling, *The God Argument: The Case Against Religion and for Humanism*, (New York, 2013), p. 238.
[8] Geza Vermes, *The Religion of Jesus the Jew*, (Minneapolis, 1993), p. 199. "Jesus' tendency to accentuate a message by means of over-statement is, as had been noted many times, an essential constituent of his popular rhetoric."

in any collectivity, not even by a specific day or time of or frequency of worship. As a Hindu, I subscribe to a creed that is free of the restrictive dogmas of holy writ, that refuses to be shackled to the limitations of a single holy book. Above all, as a Hindu I belong to the only major religion in the world that does not claim to be the only true religion. I find it immensely congenial to be able to face my fellow human beings of other faiths without being burdened by the conviction that I am embarked upon a "true path" that they have missed."[9]

The Church must discover for itself its own solutions. It cannot borrow Hinduism or any other religion, though it may learn from them. It has its own tradition to celebrate and share in terms of equality and sisterhood with the rest of the world. Only then will the Catholic Church be able to lay down the burdens of the past and bear witness to human dignity. Then will it be truly able to call itself a disciple of Jesus the Jew, a witness for the Jesus who, when a man kneeling at his feet called him "good teacher," responded: *Why do you call me good? No one is good—except God alone* (Mark 10:18).

---

[9]Sashi Tharoor, *India: From Midnight to the Millennium and Beyond,* (New York, 1997), p. 55-56.

Bibliography

Unless otherwise indicated, all papal documents and documents from the Second Vatican.
Council come from the Vatican Website: http://www.vatican.va/phome_en.htm.
Biblical citations in English are from the NIV, 1984.
Biblical citations in English for Chapters 9 and 11 are from *New American Bible*. Online at http://www.usccb.org/bible/. Commentary from *St. Joseph Edition of New American Bible*. (1986). Catholic Book Publishing Co.: New York.
Biblical citations from the Hebrew are in *Hebrew-English Tanakh*, 2nd Edition, Philadelphia: the Jewish Publication Society, 1999/5759.
Biblical citations from the Greek are in *The Interlinear Greek-English New Testament*, Grand Rapids, Michigan: Zondervan, 1958/1975.
Abelson, R. P. (1959). Modes of resolution of belief dilemmas. *Journal of Conflict Resolution*, 3, 343–352.
Accattoli, L. (1998). *When a pope asks forgiveness: The mea culpas of John Paul II.* Trans. By J. Aumann. Boston: Pauline.
Ackerman, D. (1994). *A natural history of love.* New York: Random House.
Alter, R. (2004). *The five books of moses: A translation with commentary.* New York: W. W. Norton & Company.
Altmann, S. L. (2002) *Is nature supernatural?* New York: Prometheus.
Ambrosini, M. L. with Willis, M. (1996/1969). *The secret archives of the Vatican.* New York: Barnes & Noble.
Aquinas, St. T. (1948). *Summa theologica*, ed. Anton C. Pegis. New York: The Modern Library.
Aquinas, St. T. (1947). *The Summa Theologica.* (Trans. Fathers of the English Dominican Province). Benziger Brothers Edition, London.
Aristotle, (1941). *The Basic Works of Aristotle.* R. McKeon (Ed.). New York: Random House.
Armstrong, K. (1987). *The Gospel according to women: Christianity's creation of the sex war in the west.* Garden City, NY: Anchor Press.
Armstrong, K. (1993). *A history of god: The 4000-year quest of Judaism, Christianity and Islam.* New York: Ballantine.
Armstrong, K. (1996). *In the beginning: A new understanding of genesis.* New York: Ballantine.

Atran, S. (2002). *In gods we trust: The evolutionary landscape of religion.* New York: Oxford University Press.

Associated Press. (2002, June 9). Hundreds rush to sue in church sex scandal. *Columbia Daily Tribune*, p. A12.

Augustine. (1972). *Concerning the city of god against the Pagans,* trans. Henry Bettenson. New York: Penguin Classics.

Augustine. (1982). *The confessions.* (Trans. Edward Bouverie Pusey). Pennsylvania: The Franklin Library.

Augustine, (2002), *On Genesis.* trans. Matthew O'Connell. New York: New City Press.

Austin, J. H. (1998). *Zen and the brain: Toward an understanding of meditation and consciousness.* Cambridge, MA: MIT Press.

Avalos, H. (2007). *The end of biblical studies.* Amherst, NY: Prometheus Books.

Avalos, H. (2005). *Fighting words: The origins of religious violence.* Amherst, NY: Prometheus Books.

Barbour, I. (1990). *Religion in the age of science: The gifford lectures 1989-1991,* Vol. 1. San Francisco: Harper & Row.

Barbour, I. (2002). *Nature, human nature, and god.* Minneapolis: Fortress Press.

Barstow, A. L. (1982). *Married priests and the reforming Papacy.* Lewiston, NY: Mellen.

Beaudoin, T. (1998). *Virtual faith: The irreverent spiritual quest of generation X.* San Francisco: Jossey-Bass Publishers.

Bellah, R. N. (2011). *Religion in human evolution: From the paleolithic to the axial age.* Cambridge, MA: Harvard University Press.

Bellinzoni, A. J. (2006). *The future of Christianity. Can it survive?* Amherst, NY: Prometheus Books.

Benedict XVI (Pope) (Joseph Ratzinger). (2007). *Jesus of Nazareth: From the Baptism in the Jordan to the transfiguration.* (Trans. Adrian J. Walker). New York: Doubleday.

Benedict XVI (April 8, 2005). "The Pope's Funeral Homily," *The New York Times.*

Benedict, J. & Keteyian, A. (2013). *The system: The glory and scandal of big time college football.* New York: Doubleday.

Benoit, W. L. (1995). *Accounts, excuses, and apologies: A theory of image restoration discourse.* Albany: State University of New York Press.

Berlinski, D. (2009). *The Devil's delusion: Atheism and its scientific pretensions.* New York: Basic Books.

Bernstein, C. and Politi, M. (1996). *His holiness: John Paul II and the hidden history of our time.* New York: Doubleday.

Bilaniuk, P. B. T. (1968). Celibacy and Eastern tradition. In: G. H. Frein (Ed.). *Celibacy: The necessary option* (p. 40). New York: Herder & Herder.

Blamires, A. (Ed.). (1992). *Woman defamed and woman defended: An anthology of medieval texts,* Oxford, UK: The Clarendon Press.

Blaney, J. R., & Benoit, W. L. (1997). The persuasive defense of Jesus in the Gospel according to John. *Journal of Religion and Communication*, 20, 25-30.

Brandon, S. G. F. (1968). *The trial of Jesus of Nazareth.* New York: Dorset Press.

Branscomb, B. H. (1931). *The teachings of Jesus.* Nashville, TN: Abingdom Press.

Brennan, Christine. (2006). *Best seat in the house: A father, a daughter, a journey through sports.* New York: Scribner.

Bronowski, J. (1973). *The ascent of man.* Boston: Little Brown & Company.

Brown, N. (1968). *Love's body.* New York: Vintage Books.

Brown, P. (1988). *The body and society: Men, women, and sexual renunciation in early Christianity.* New York: Columbia University Press.

Brown, R. E. (1997). *An introduction to the New Testament.* New York: Doubleday.

Brown, R. E. (1993). *The birth of the Messiah.* New York: Doubleday.

Brown, R. E. (1994). *The death of the Messiah* (2 Volumes). New York: Doubleday.

Bruce, F. F. (1951). *The acts of the apostles.* Grand Rapids: Wm. B. Eerdmans.

Bruce, F. F. (1951). *The growing day—The Progress Of Christianity from the Fall of Jerusalem to the Accession of Constantine (A.D. 70-313).* New York: The Paternoster Press.

Bruni, F. (2002, July 28). *New York Times.* Pope Tells Crowd of 'Shame' Caused by Abusive Priests. p. A1.

Bryan, C. (2005). *Render To Caesar: Jesus, The Early Church, and the Roman Superpower.* New York: Oxford University Press.

Buttiglione, R. (1997). *Karol Wojtyla: The thought of the man who became Pope John Paul II.* trans. Paolo Guietti and Francesca Murphy. Grand Rapids, Michigan: Eerdmans.

Caputo, J. D., & Vattimo, G. (2007). *After the death of god.* J. Robbins (Ed.). New York: Columbia University Press.

Carr, A. (1988). *Transforming grace: Christian tradition and women's experience.* San Francisco: Harper & Row.

Carrette, J., & King, R. (2005). *Selling spirituality: The silent takeover of religion.* New York: Routledge.

Carrol, V., & Schiflett, D. (2002). *Christianity on trial: Arguments against anti-religious bigotry.* San Francisco: Encounter Books.

Carroll, J. (2001). *Constantine's sword: The church and the jews,* New York: Houghton.

Cassirer, E. (1951). *The philosophy of the enlightenment.* (Trans. C. A. Koelln and James P. Pettergrove). Boston: Beacon Press.

Catechism of the Catholic Church. (1995). New York: Doubleday.

Catholic News Agency. (2005, July 6). Pope Benedict decries "cafeteria Catholicism".

Chilton, B. (2008). *Abraham's curse: Child sacrifice in the legacies of the West.* New York: Doubleday.

Chuvin, P. (1990). *A Chronicle of the last pagans.* trans. B. A. Archer, Cambridge, MA: Harvard University Press.

Clement of Alexandria. (2005). *Fragments from Cassiodorus, chapter IV.* translated into English by William Wilson. Obtained Online at http://christianbookshelf.org/clement/.

Communion and Stewardship: Human Persons Created in the Image of God (2000-2002). International Theological Commission. Approved by Cardinal Joseph Ratzinger.

Confessions of Sin, (Official Vatican Translation) ZE00031323, ZENIT is an International News Agency, Copyright March 12, 2000, Innovative Media, Inc.

Connor, J. A. (2004). *Kepler's Witch: An Astronomer's Discovery of Cosmic Order Amid Religious War, Political Intrigue, and the Heresy Trial of His Mother.* New York: HarperCollins.

Cornwell, J. (2004). *The pontiff in winter: Triumph and conflict in the reign of John Paul II.* New York: Doubleday.

Council of Trent. (1848). *The canons and decrees of the sacred and oecumenical Council of Trent* (pp. 192-232). J. Waterworth (Ed. and trans.). London: Dolman. Obtained online at http://history.hanover.edu/texts/trent/ct24.html.

Cozzens, D. B. (2000). *The changing face of the priesthood.* Collegeville, MN: The Liturgical Press.

Cross, F. M. (1973). *Canaanite Myth and Hebrew Epic: Essays in the History of the Religion of Israel.* Cambridge, MA: Harvard University Press.

Crossan, J. D. (1998). *The Birth of Christianity: Discovering What Happened in the Years Immediately After the Execution of Jesus.* New York: HarperCollins.

Crossan, J. D., & Reed, J. L. (2004). *In Search of Paul: How Jesus' Apostle Opposed Rome's Empire With God's Kingdom.* New York: HarperCollins.

Dawes, G. W. (2001). *The historical Jesus question: The challenge of history to religious authority.* Louisville: Westminster John Knox Press.

Dawkins, R. (2006). *The god delusion.* Boston: Houghton Mifflin Company.

De Waal, Frans. (2006). *Primates and philosophers: How morality evolved.* Princeton, NJ: Princeton University Press.

De Waal, F. (2013). *The Bonobo and the Atheist: In search of humanism among the primates.* New York: Norton.

Dever, W. G. (2003). *Who were the early Israelites and where did they come from?* Grand Rapids, MI: William B. Eerdmans.

Dever, W. G. (2005). *Did god have a wife? Archaeology and folk religion in ancient Israel.* Grand Rapids, MI: William B. Eerdmans Publishing Company.

Dennett, D. C. (2006). *Breaking the spell: Religion as a natural phenomenon.* New York: Viking.

Deutscher, I. (1966). *Stalin: A political biography.* New York: Oxford University Press.

The Dhammapada. (2004), (Trans. Glenn Wallis). New York: Random House.

Digha Nikaya: The long discourses of the Buddha. (1995). trans. Maurice Walshe, Boston: Wisdom Publications.

Dignitatis Humanae: Declaration on Religious Freedom. On the Right of the Person and of Communities to Social and Civil Freedom in Matters Religious. (7 December 1965).

Dostoevsky, F. (1990). *The brothers Karamazov.*(Trans. Richard Pevear and Larissa Volokhonsky). New York: Alfred A. Knopf.

Ehrman, B. D. (2003). *Lost Christianities: The battle for scripture and the faiths we never knew.* New York: Oxford University Press.

Ehrman, B. D. (2003). *Lost scriptures: Books that did not make it into the new testament.* New York: Oxford University Press.

Ehrman, B. D. (2005). *Misquoting Jesus: The story behind who changed the Bible and why.* New York: HarperCollins.

Ehrman, B. D., & Jacobs, A. S. (2004). *Christianity in late antiquity, 300-450 C. E.* New York: Oxford University Press.

Ehrman, B. D. (2011). *Forged: Writing in the name of god—why the Bible's authors are not who we think they are.* New York: HarperCollins.

Eisler, R. (1987). *The chalice and the blade: Our history, our future.* San Francisco: Harper & Row.

Erikson, E. H. (1969). *Gandhi's truth: On the origins of militant nonviolence.* New York: W. W. Norton.

Eusebius. (1965). *The history of the church from christ to constantine* (G. A. Williamson, Trans.). New York: Dorset Press.

Faggioli, M. (2012). *Vatican II: The battle for meaning.* New York: Paulist Press.

Feuerbach, L. (1841/1957). *The essence of Christianity.* (Trans. George Eliot). New York: Harper & Row.

Finkelstein, I., & Silberman, N. A. (2001). *The bible unearthed: Archaeology's new vision of ancient Israel and the origin of its sacred texts.* New York: The Free Press.

Fiorenza, E. Schussler. (1983). *In memory of her: A feminist theological reconstruction of christian origins.* New York: Crossroad.

Flanagan, O. (2011). *The Bodhisattva's brain: Buddhism naturalized.* Cambridge, MA: The MIT Press.

Foucault, M. (1988). *The history of sexuality: The care of the self,* Vol. 3. trans. Robert Hurley. New York: Vintage Books.

Foucault, M. (1990). *The history of sexuality: The use of pleasure.* Vol. 2, trans. Robert Hurley. New York: Vintage Books.

Fontaine, C. R. (2008). *With eyes of flesh: The bible, gender and human rights.* Sheffield, UK: Sheffield Phoenix Press.

Fox, M. W. (2011). *The Pope's war: Why Ratzinger's secret crusade had imperiled the church and how it can be saved.* New York: Sterling Ethos.

Fox, R. L. (1987). *Pagans and Christians.* New York: Alfred A. Knopf.

France, D. (2004). *Our fathers: The secret life of the Catholic Church in an age of scandal.* New York: Broadway Books.

Fredriksen, P. (1999). *Jesus of Nazareth king of the Jews: A Jewish Life and the emergence of Christianity.* New York: Alfred A. Knopf.

Frei, Hans W. (1974). *The eclipse of Biblical narrative: A study in eighteenth and nineteenth century hermeneutics.* New Haven: Yale University Press.

Frend, W. H. C. (1984). *The rise of christianity.* Philadelphia: Fortress Press.

Fromm, Erich. (1957). *The art of loving.* London: Unwin Books.

Funk, R. W., & Hoover, R. W. and the Jesus Seminar. (1993). *The five gospels: The search for the authentic words of Jesus.* New York: Macmillian.

Gay, P. (1988). *Freud: A life for our time.* New York: W. W. Norton.

Gazzaniga, M. S. (2005). *The ethical brain.* New York: Dana Press.

Gibbon, E. *The decline and fall of the Roman Empire.* 3 Volumes. New York: The Modern Library Edition.

Giles, Kevin. (1992). *Patterns of ministry among the first Christians* (2nd ed). Sydney: Collins Dove Publishers.

Gimbutas, Marija. (1989). *The language of the goddess.* New York: Harper & Row.

Ginzburg, C. (1966, trans. 1983) *The night battles: witchcraft & agrarian cults in the sixteenth and seventeenth centuries.* Baltimore, MD: Johns Hopkins University Press. (trans. by J. Tedeschi and A. Tedeschi).

Ginzburg, C. (1989 trans. 1991). *Ecstasies: Deciphering the witches sabbath.* New York: Randon House (Trans. by R. Rosenthal).

Girard, R. (1979). *Violence and the sacred*, trans. Patrick Gregory, Baltimore: The Johns Hopkins University Press.

Graham, L. & Kantor, J.-M. *Naming infinity: A true story of religious mysticism and mathematical creativity.* Cambridge, MA: Harvard University Press.

Grayling, A. C. (2013). *The god argument: The case against religion and for humanism.* New York: Bloomsbury.

Grentz, S. J., & Kjesbo, D. M. (1995). *Women in the Church: A Biblical theology of women in ministry.* Downers Grove, IL: InterVaristy Press.

Hanegraaf, W. J. (1998). *New age religion and western culture: Esotericism in the mirror of secular thought.* Albany, NY: State University of New York Press.

Harper, K. (2013). *From Shame to Sin: The Christian transformation of sexual morality in Late Antiquity.* Cambridge, MA: Harvard University Press.

Hauser, M. D. (2006). *Moral minds: How nature designed our universal sense of right and wrong.* New York: HarperCollins.

Heidel, A. (1951). *The Babylonian genesis: The story of creation* (2nd ed.). Chicago: University of Chicago Press.

Hill, R. C. (2007). *Theodoret of Cyrus: Commentary on the letters of St Paul* (2nd ed.). Brookline, MA: Holy Cross Orthodox Press.

Hogan, R. M., & LeVoir, J. M. (1985). *Covenant of love: Pope John Paul II on sexuality, marriage, and the family in the modern world.* San Francisco: Ignatius Press.

Hopkins, K. (1999). *A world full of gods: The strange triumph of Christianity.* New York: The Free Press.

Husserl, E. (1970). *Logical investigations: Volume I: Prolegomena to pure logic.* Trans. J. N. Findlay. New York: Humanities Press.

Husserl, E. (1962). *Ideas: General introduction to pure phenomenology.* Trans. W. R. Boyce Gibson. New York: Macmillan.

Ingarden, R. (1975). *On the Motives which led Husserl to transcendental idealism.* Trans. Arnor Hannibalsson. Der Haag: Martinus Nijhoff.

Ingram, P. O. (2008). *Buddhist-christian dialogue in an age of science.* Lanham, MD: Rowman & Littlefield Publishers.

James, W. (1982). *The varieties of religious experience*, New York: Penguin.

Jay, N. (1992). *Throughout your generations forever: Sacrifice, religion, and paternity.* Chicago: University of Chicago Press.

Jenkins, P. (2003). *The new anti-catholicism: The last acceptable prejudice.* New York: Oxford University Press.

John Paul II, Pope. (Karol Wojtyla). (1979). *The acting person.* trans. Andrzej Potocki. Dordrecht, Holland: D. Reidel Publishing Company.

John Paul II. (10 November 1979). Discours De Jean-Paul II En Commemoration De La II Naissance D'Albert Einstein.

John Paul II. (Karol Wojtyla). (1981). *Love and Responsibility.* Trans. H. T. Willetts. San Francisco: Ignatius Press.

John Paul II. (15 August 1988). *Mulieris Dignitatem: On the Dignity and Vocation of Women On the Occasion of the Marian Year.* (Apostolic Letter).

John Paul II. (7 December 1990). *Redemptoris missio.* (Encyclical).

John Paul II. (31 October 1992). "Discours De Jean-Paul II Aux Participants A La Session Pleniere De L' Academie Pontificale Des Sciences, 31 October 1992."

John Paul II. (1994). *Terio Millenio Adveniente* (As the Third Millenium Approaches) (Apostolic Letter).

John Paul II. (25 March 1995). *Evangelium Vitae. Encyclical Letter on the Value and Inviolability of Human Life.* www.newadvent.org/library/docs_jp02ev.htm.

John Paul II. (25 May 1995). *Utunum sint* (Encyclical).

John Paul II. (22 October 1996). *Truth Cannot Contradict Truth: Address of John Paul II to the Pontifical Academy of Sciences.* http://www.newadvent.org/docs/jp02tc.htm.

John Paul II. (1997). *The Theology of the Body: Human Love in the Divine Plan.* Boston: Pauline Books and Media (Daughters of St. Paul).

John Paul II (1998). *In my own words.* Compiled and Edited by Anthony J. Chiffolo. New York: Gramercy Books.

John Paul II. (14 September 1998) *Fides et ratio.* (Encyclical).

John Paul II (19 May 1999). *Dialogue with the Great World Religions. L'Osservatore Romano.* http://www.catholicculture.org/docs/doc_view.cfm?recnum=1071.

John Paul II. (12 March 2000). *Universal Prayer: Confessions of Sin and Asking for Forgiveness.* Obtained online at http://www.catholiclinks.org/sacramentodelperdonuniverpra.htm.

John Paul II. (17 March 2001). "Holy Thursday Letter."

John Paul II. (22 November 2001). *Eccelsia in Oceania.* (Exhortation).

John Paul II, (17 March 2002). *Letter of the Holy Father Pope John Paul II to Priests for Holy Thursday 2002.* Obtained Online at http://www.vatican.va/holy_father/john_paul_ii/letters/2002/documents/hf_jp-ii_let_20020321_priests-holy-thursday_en.html

John Paul II. (28 July 2002). *Homily.* Obtained Online at http://www.vatican.va/holy_father/john_paul_ii/homilies/2002/documents/hf_jp-ii_hom_20020728_xvii-wyd_en.html.

John Paul II. (2003). *Crossing the threshold of hope.* V. Messori (Ed.). New York: Alfred A. Knopf.

John Paul II (28 June 2003). *Ecclesia In Europa.* (Exhortation).

John Paul II. (2005). *Memory and identity: Conversations at the dawn of the millennium.* New York: Rizzoli.

Johnson, D. (2004). *The future of hope: Christian tradition amid modernity and post-modernity.* Grand Rapids, MI: William B. Eerdmans.

Johnson, Elizabeth A. (1992). *She who is: The mystery of god in feminist theological discourse.* New York: Crossroad Publishing Company.

Kass, L. R. (2003). *The beginning of wisdom: Reading genesis.* New York: The Free Press.

Kauffman, S. A. (2008). *Reinventing the sacred: A new view of science, reason, and religion.* New York: Basic Books.

Kennedy, E. (2001). *The unhealed wound: The Church and human sexuality.* New York: St. Martin's Griffin.

Kershaw, I. (2008). *Hitler, the Germans, and the final solution.* New Haven: Yale University Press.

King, K. L. (2003). *The gospel of mary of Magdala: Jesus and the first woman apostle.* Salem, OR: Polebridge Press.

Kolakowski, L. (2001). *Religion if there is no god…On god, the devil, sin and other worries of the so-called philosophy of religion.* South Bend, IN: St. Augustine's Press.

Kramer, H., & Sprenger, J. (1971). *The Malleus Maleficarum.* Trans. Montague Summers. New York: Dover.

Krauss, L. M. (2012). *A universe from nothing: Why there is something rather than nothing.* New York: Free Press.

Komarnitsky, K. D. (2009). *Doubting Jesus' resurrection: what happened in the black box?* Draper, UT: Stone Arrow Books.

Kowalski, A. P. (2005). *Married catholic priests: Their history, their journeys, their reflections.* New York: Crossroads Publishing Company.

Kugel, J. L. (2007). *How to read the Bible: A guide to scripture, then and now.* New York: Free Press.

Lawrence, D. H. (1960). *Love among the haystacks and other stories.* New York: Penguin.

Lear, J. (1998). *Open minded: Working out the logic of the soul.* Cambridge, MA: Harvard University Press.

Lemonick, M. D. (July 11, 2005). "Honor Among Beasts," *Time,* 166(2): 54-56.

Levenson, J. D. (1988). *Creation and the persistence of evil: the Jewish Drama of Divine Omnipotence.* New York: Harper & Row.

Levine, A.-J., Allison, D.C. Jr., & Crossan, J. D. (2006). *The Historical Jesus in context.* Princeton, NJ: Princeton University Press.

Lincoln, B. (2003). *Holy terrors: Thinking about religion after September 11.* Chicago: University of Chicago Press.

Lindley, D. (2007). *Uncertainty: Einstein, Heisenberg, Bohr, and the struggle for the soul of science.* New York: Doubleday.

Lumen Gentium: Dogmatic Constitution of the Church (21 November 1964).

Mack, B. L. (1993). *The Lost Gospel: The Book of Q and Christian origins.* New York: HarperCollins.

MacDonald, D. R. (2000). *The homeric epics and the gospel of mark.* New Haven: Yale University Press.

MacMullen, R. (1984). *Christianizing the Roman Empire, A. D. 100-400.* New Haven: Yale University Press.

Madison, K., & Osiek, C. (2005). (editors and translators), *Ordained Women in the Early Church.* Baltimore: The John Hopkins University Press.

MajjhimaNikaya: The Middle Length Discourses of the Buddha (2nd Ed., 2001). (Trans. Bhikkhu Nanamoli and Bhikkhu Bodhi). Somerville, MA: Wisdom Publications.

Martin, M. (2002). *Atheism, morality, and meaning.* Amherst, NY, Prometheus Books.

Marx, K. (1967). *Capital.* Vol. I. (Trans. Samuel Moore and Edward Aveling). New York: International Publishers.

Mazar, A. (1990). *Archaeology of the land of the Bible. 10,000-586 B.C.E.* New York: Doubleday.

McClory, R. (1997). *Power and the papacy: The people and politics behind the doctrine of infallibility*. Liguori, MO: Triumph.

McDannell, C., & Lang, B. (1988). *Heaven: A history*. New Haven: Yale University Press.

McGinn, B. (1991). *The foundations of mysticism, Vol. I, The presence of god: A history of western mysticism*. New York: Crossroad.

McGinn, B. (1998). *The flowering of mysticism: Men and women in the New Mysticism—1200-1350, Vol. III, The presence of god: A history of Western Mysticism*. New York: Crossroad.

Meeks, W. (1983). *The first urban Christians: The social world of the Apostle Paul*. New Haven: Yale University Press.

Meeks, W. (1993). *The origins of Christian morality: The first two centuries*. New Haven: Yale University Press.

Meier, J. P. (1991). *A marginal jew: Rethinking the historical Jesus, Volume I: the roots of the problem and the person*. New York: Doubleday.

Memory and Reconciliation: The Church and the Faults of the Past. (December, 1999). Vatican City: International Theological Commission. Mifflin. (2001).

Miles, J. (1995). *God: A biography*. New York: Random House.

Miles, J. (2001). *Christ: A crisis in the life of god*. New York: Alfred A. Knopf.

Miller, B. A. (2002). *Divine apology: The discourse of religious image restoration*. Westport, CT: Praeger.

Miller, V. J. (2004). *Consuming religion: Christian faith and practice in consumer culture*. New York: Continuum.

The Mishnah.(1988). trans. Jacob Neusner. New Haven: Yale University Press.

Mitford, N. (1957). *Voltaire in love*. New York: Carroll & Graf Publishers.

Mlodinow, L. (2008). *The Drunkard's walk: How randomness rules our lives*. New York: Random House.

Montefiore, S. S. (2007). *Young stalin*. New York: Alfred A. Knopf.

Murphy, C. (2012). *The inquisition and the making of the modern world*. Boston: Houghton Mifflin Harcourt.

Murphy, B. F. (September-October 1999). Letter to Allen Moore, President of CORPUS U.S.A., published in CORPUS Canada: The Journal 2, no. 5. Online at http//corpuscanada.org/995bishop.html.

O'Malley, J. W. (2002). Some basics about celibacy. *America*, 187(13): 9.

The Nag Hammadi Scriptures (The International Edition, 2007).(Ed. Marvin Meyer). New York: HarperCollins.

Nasr, S. H. (2002). *The heart of Islam: Enduring values for humanity*. New York: HarperCollins.

Neusner. J. (2001). *A rabbi talks with Jesus*. London: McGill-Queen's University Press.

Noble, D. F. (1992). *A world without women: The Christian clerical culture of Western Science*. New York: Oxford.

Noonan, P. (2005). *John Paul the great: Remembering a spiritual father*. New York: Viking.

O'Flaherty, W. D. (1973). *Siva: The erotic ascetic*. New York: Oxford University Press.

O'Malley, J. W. (October 28, 2002). "Some basics about celibacy," *America*. 187(13): 9.

Otranto, G. (1991). *The problem of the ordination of women in the early Christian priesthood*. Lecture delivered in the USA in 1991. Trans. by Dr. Mary Ann Rossi. Obtained online at http://www.womenpriests.org/traditio/otran_2.asp.

Otto, R. (1958). *The idea of the holy* (2nd ed.). New York: Oxford University Press.

Pagels, E. (1979). *The gnostic gospels*. New York: Random House.

Pagels, E. (1988). *Adam, eve, and the serpent*. New York: Random House.

Pagels, E. (2005). *Beyond belief: The secret gospel of Thomas*. New York: Random House.

Patterson, S. J. (1998). *The god of Jesus: The historical Jesus and the Search for meaning*. Harrisburg, PA: Trinity Press International.

Patterson. S. J. (2004). *Beyond the passion: Rethinking the death and life of Jesus*. Minneapolis: Fortress Press.

Paul VI, Pope. (25 July 1968). *Humanae Vitae*. Encyclical Letter of Pope Paul VI on the Regulation of Birth. http://www.newadvent.org/docs/pa06hv.htm.

Pelikan, J. (1971). *The emergence of the catholic tradition (100-600). The Christian tradition: A history of the development of Doctrine* (Vol. 1). Chicago: University of Chicago Press.

Pelikan, J. (1974). *The spirit of Eastern Christendom: 600-1700. The Christian tradition: A history of the development of coctrine*. Vol. 2. Chicago: The University of Chicago Press.

Pelikan, J. (1984). *Reformation of Church and Dogma (1300-1700). The Christian tradition: A history of the development of Doctrine* (Vol. 4). Chicago: The University of Chicago Press.

Pelikan, J. (1988) *The Christian tradition: A history of the development of Doctrine. The Growth of Medieval Theology (600-1300)*. (Vol. 3). Chicago: The University of Chicago Press.

Pelikan, J. (1989). *The Christian tradition: A history of the development of Doctrine. Christian Doctrine and modern culture (since 1700)* (Vol. 5). Chicago: University of Chicago Press.

Perakh, M. (2004). *Unintelligent design*. Amherst, NY: Prometheus Books.

Peters, F. E. (2007). *The voice, the word, the Books: The sacred scripture of the Jews, mitive Christianity: Its writings and teachings in their historical christians, and muslims*. New Jersey: Princeton University Press.

Pfleider, O. (1965). *Primitive Christianity: Its writings and teachings in their historical connections* (Vol. I) (Trans. W. Montgomery). New Jersey: Reference Book Publishers.

Pham, J.-P. (2004). *Heirs of the fisherman: Behind the scenes of Papal Death and succession.* New York: Oxford University Press.

Pius XII (30 September 1943) *DivinoAfflanteSpiritu. Encyclical of Pope Pius XII on Promoting Biblical Studies, Commemorating the Fiftieth Anniversary of Providentissimus Deus.*

Pomeroy, S. B. (1975). *Goddesses, whores, wives, and slaves: Women in classical antiquity.* New York: Schocken Books.

Plato. (1961). *Plato: The collected dialogues.* E. Hamilton & H Cairns (Eds.). Princeton, NJ: Bollingen Series LXXI.

Polkinghorne, J. (1997). *Quarks, Chaos and Christianity: questions to science and religion.* New York: Crossroad.

Popper, K. R. (1962). *The open society and its enemies: The spell of Plato.* Princeton, New Jersey: Princeton University Press.

Price, R. M. (2003). *The incredible shrinking son of man: How reliable is the Gospel tradition?* Amherst, NY: Prometheus Books.

Price, R. (2007). *Jesus is dead.* New Jersey: American Atheist Press.

Quinnipiac University. (2013, March 8). Obtained online at http://www.quinnipiac.edu/institutes-centers/polling-institute/national/release-detail?ReleaseID=1863.

Raab, K. A. (2000). *When women become priests: The Catholic women's ordination debate.* New York: Columbia University Press.

Rachels, J. (1991). *Created from the animals: The moral implications of Darwinism.* New York: Oxford University Press.

Ratzinger, Joseph Cardinal (Benedict XVI). (1995). *In the beginning...A Catholic understanding of the story of creation and the fall.* (Trans. Boniface Ramsey). Grnad Rapids, MI: William B. Eerdmans Publishing Company.

Ratzinger, J. (2004). *Truth and tolerance: Christian belief and world religions.* H. Taylor (Trans). San Francisco: Ignatius Press.

Reese, T. J. (1996). *Inside the Vatican: The politics and organization of the Catholic Church.* Cambridge: Harvard University Press.

Rifkin, J. (2004). *The European dream: How Europe's vision of the future is quietly eclipsing the American dream.* New York: Jeremy P. Tarcher.

Ruether, R. (1993). *Sexism and god-talk: Toward a feminist theology.* Boston: Beacon Press.

Schillebeeckx, E. (1989). *Christ: The experience of Jesus as Lord.* trans. John Bowden. New York: Crossroad.

Schmitz, K. L. (1993). *At the center of the human Drama: The philosophical anthropology of Karol Wojtyla/Pope John Paul II.* Washington, D.C: The Catholic University of America Press.

Schonborn, C. C. (July 7, 2005). "Finding Design in Nature," *New York Times.*

Schussler Fiorenza, E. (1982), Tablesharing and the oncilium. In M. Collins & D. Powers (Eds.). *Can we always celebrate the Eucharist?* (pp. 3-12) New York: Seabury.

Schwartz, R. M. (1997). *The curse of cain: The violent legacy of monotheism.* Chicago: The University of Chicago Press.

Schweitzer, A. (1968). *The quest of the historical Jesus: A critical study of its progress from Reimarus to Wrede.* New York: McMillan.

Segal, A. F. (1990). *Paul the convert: The apostolate and apostasy of Saul the Pharisee* New Haven: Yale University Press.

Service, R. (2000). *Lenin: A biography.* Cambridge, MA: Harvard University Press.

Sharpe, E. J. (1985). *The Universal Gita.* La Salle, IL: Open Court Publishing Co.

Smith, M. S.(1990). *The early history of god: Yahweh and the other deities in ancient Israel.* New York: Harper & Row.

Sobol, D. (1999). *Galileo's daughter: A historical memoir of science, faith, and love.* New York: Penguin.

Spillane, M. (2002). Law's the law in Boston. *The Nation, 274*: 7-8.

Spinoza, B. (1999). *Tractatus Theologico-Politicus.* In: G. W. Dawes, (ed). *The historical Jesus quest: A foundational anthology.* Leiden: Deo Publishing.

Spoto, D. (2002). *Reluctant saint: The life of Francis of Assisi.* New York, NY: Viking Compass.

Stark, R. (1977). The Role of Women in Christian Growth. *The rise of christianity.* San Francisco: Harper Collins.

Steiner, G. (2001). *Grammars of creation.* New Haven: Yale University Press.

Stevens, W. (2002). *Demon lovers; witchcraft, sex, and the crisis of belief.* Chicago: University of Chicago Press.

Stone, M. (1976). *When god was a woman.* New York: Harcourt.

Stoyanov, Y. (2000). *The other god: Dualist religions from antiquity to the Cathar Heresy.* New Haven: Yale University Press.

Taylor, C. (2007). *A secular age.* Cambridge, MA: Harvard University Press.

Teilhard De Chardin, P. (1959). *The phenomenon of man.* (Trans. Bernard Hall). New York: Harper & Row.

Tharoor, S. (1997). *India: From midnight to the millennium and beyond.* New York: Arcade Publishing.

The Church Teaches: Documents of the Church in English Translation. (1973). The Jesuit Fathers of St. Mary's College, St Mary's Kansas. Rockford, IL: TAN Books.

The Council of Trent. (1848). Ed. and trans. J. Waterworth. *The canons and decrees of the sacred and oecumenical Council of Trent.* London: Dolman. pp. 192-232. Obtained online at http://history.hanover.edu/texts/trent/ct24.html

The Koran, trans. N. J. Dawood, New York: Penguin Classics, 1956.

The New English Bible. (1970). Oxford and Cambridge: The Oxford and Cambridge University Presses.

The Rig Veda. (1992). trans. Ralph T. H. Griffith, New York: Motilal Banarsidass Publishers.

Thich Nhat Hanh. (1995). *Living Buddha, Living Christ.* New York: Riverhead Books.

Thomas, Keith. (1971). *Religion and the decline of magic.* New York: Charles Scribner's Sons.

Torjesen, K. J. (1993). *When women were priests.* San Francisco: HarperSanFrancisco.

Tracy, David. (1981). *The analogical imagination: Christian theology and the culture of pluralism.* New York: Crossroad.

Tyerman, C. (2006). *God's war: A new history of the crusades.* Cambridge: Harvard University Press.

The Upanishads (2 Vols.) (1879, 1884, 1962) (Trans. Max Muller). New York: Dover Publications.

Vermes, G. (Ed). (1997). *The complete dead sea scrolls in English,* New York: Penguin.

Vermes, G. (1993). *The religion of Jesus the Jew.* Minneapolis: Fortress Press.

Vermes, G. (2003). *Jesus in his Jewish context.* Minneapolis: Fortress Press.

Vermes, G. (2012). *Christian beginnings: From Nazareth to Nicaea.* New Haven: Yale University Press.

Wade, N. (2006). *Before the dawn: Recovering the lost history of our ancestors.* New York: Penguin.

Wakeman, W. (1996). Women priests: The first years. London: Darton, Longman + Todd.

Wallace, B. A. (2007). *Hidden dimensions: The unification of physics and consciousness.* New York: Columbia University Press.

Weigel, G. (2005). *Witness to hope: The biography of Pope John Paul II 1920-2005.* New York: Harper Perennial.

Wells, G. A. (1988). *Religious postures: Essays on modern Christian apologists and religious problems.* La Salle, Illinois: Open Court.

Wills, G. (2000). *Papal Sin: Structures of deceit.* New York: Doubleday.

Wilson, E. O. (1998). *Consilience: The unity of knowledge.* New York: Alfred A. Knoph.

Witherington, B. (1988). *Women in the earliest churches.* Cambridge: Cambridge University Press.

Wittgenstein, L. (1922). *Tractatus Logico-Philosophicus.* (C. K. Ogden, Trans.). Boston: Routledge and Kegan Paul.

Zimmer, C. (2001). *Evolution: The triumph of an idea.* New York: HarperCollins.

About the Authors

Anthony M. Alioto, PhD, is Professor and the Althea W. and John A. Schiffman Endowed Chair in Ethics, Philosophy and Religious Studies at Columbia College, Columbia, Missouri. He is the author of *A History of Western Science*, Prentice Hall, 1987; Second Edition published in 1993, a work of fiction entitled *Toad Familiar*, 1996, and a memoir, *The Ninefold Path*, published in 2012. His research and teaching have covered such subjects as: ancient, early-modern, and modern science, philosophy of religion, psychology, ancient and modern cosmology, the quest for the historical Jesus, as well as Asian philosophies and religions. He also teaches at the University of Missouri-Osher Foundation Institute for Lifelong Learning. He taught "The Buddha and Buddhism" at the Chautauqua Institute in New York.

John P. McHale is a member of the Secular Order of Franciscans. McHale is an Associate Professor in the School of Communication at Illinois State University where he primarily teaches media writing and documentary film production. McHale is the author of *Convergent Writing: Telling a Good Story Well.* (2nd Ed.; 2012), and *Communicating for Change: Strategies of Social and Political Advocates* (2004). McHale edited *Crafting Messages in a Multimodal Communicative Environment* (2013). McHale is the coauthor of *Lights, Camera, Conscience, and Soul: Creating documentaries that make a difference* (2013), *Bush versus Kerry: A functional analysis of campaign 2004* (2007), *Campaign 2000: A functional analysis of presidential campaign discourse* (2003), *The primary decision: A functional analysis of presidential primary debates, 1948-2000* (2001), and has published a number of book chapters and academic articles on political discourse. McHale has written, directed, produced, and executive produced over 20 films, and has received over 10 awards for his film work from a number of organizations including the 2012 Grand Prize for Short Film Writing for his television dramatic program pilot episode of *The Last Exit to Normal* from Flickers: Rhode Island International Film Festival. Also of particular note, McHale wrote, directed, produced the awarding winning *Picture This: The Fight to Save Joe*, narrated by Danny Glover, which was an important catalytic factor in Joe Amrine's release from Missouri death row in 2005. McHale was awarded the FYI Walter Cronkite Civic Engagement Leadership Award in 2005 at the United Nations in New York.